DATE DUE		

THE
GREAT BIG BOOK
OF GUYS

ALSO BY ERIKA RITTER

ESSAY COLLECTIONS
Urban Scrawl (1984)
Ritter in Residence (1987)

NOVELS
The Hidden Life of Humans (1997)

PLAYS
The Splits (1978)
Automatic Pilot (1980)

THE GREAT BIG BOOK OF GUYS

ALPHABETICAL ENCOUNTERS WITH MEN

ERIKA RITTER

M&S

National Library of Canada Cataloguing in Publication

Ritter, Erika, 1948–
    The great big book of guys : alphabetical encounters with men /
Erika Ritter.

ISBN 0-7710-7536-7 (bound)

    1. Men.   2. Ritter, Erika, 1948–   – Relations with men.
3. Man-woman relationships.   I. Title.

HQ1090.R47 2004   305.31   C2004-903478-2

We acknowledge the financial support of the Government of Canada through the Book Publishing Industry Development Program and that of the Government of Ontario through the Ontario Media Development Corporation's Ontario Book Initiative. We further acknowledge the support of the Canada Council for the Arts and the Ontario Arts Council for our publishing program.

Words on p.152 from *With a Little Bit of Luck* by Alan Lerner and Frederick Loewe © 1956 (renewed) Chappell & Co. All rights reserved. Used by permission of Warner Bros. Publications U.S. Inc., Miami, Florida 33014.

Typeset in Bembo by M&S, Toronto
Printed and bound in Canada

This book is printed on acid-free paper that is 100% recycled, ancient-forest friendly (100% post-consumer recycled)

McClelland & Stewart Ltd.
The Canadian Publishers
481 University Avenue
Toronto, Ontario
M5G 2E9
www.mcclelland.com

1 2 3 4 5   08 07 06 05 04

CONTENTS

For my father, in the hope that reading this book
might have enabled him to forgive me for writing it.

AMIGOS

IT SEEMS TO ME that when we're young, a platonic friendship between a woman and man demands an element of poignancy. You're attracted to him, but assume that he's not to you. And therefore resign yourself to sloppy seconds, as the little sister he never had.

Or, you assume he's in love with you. But since you're not that way inclined toward him, you flatter yourself you're doing him some sort of ongoing favour by deigning to allow him to act as your escort at family outings, fill up your Friday night when nobody better's on tap, or get first crack at comforting you if the one you do love has let you down.

Once we're older, a platonic friendship between a man and a woman works best when fuelled by something less fraught: the reassuring knowledge that neither one of you could ever crave the other, not even if you were the last two people on earth. You can, as a result, relax and just enjoy the straightforward pleasures that friendship provides, without either of you having to invest in new clothes, pick up the bar tab, or tell any lies about your lays, past and present.

I met my first and perhaps greatest male friend in Montreal, another Westerner eagerly adapting to the East. Initially, Bill was just one of a number of students – male and female – who hung around the apartment I shared with three other girls in the McGill

University ghetto. I can't readily recall the point at which we two made a particular connection.

From the start, it was a connection based much more on affection than attraction. I had a boyfriend on whom to lavish my love, and Bill had a hopeless crush on one of the other students allied with us – a sly and spirited girl named Jill, who liked to joke around with Bill, but preferred to sleep with brawnier, ballsier men.

Poor Bill. He struggled to swallow that pill, and presumably succeeded. But the taste of defeat seemed somehow to linger, and for the rest of his life he appeared drawn to doomed alliances.

For one brief period, and half-heartedly at that, he made an effort to convince us both that he wanted me. If my current relationship came a cropper, he assured me, he'd be there to take up the slack.

I felt flattered to be admired hopelessly and from a convenient remove. But also a little discomfited, too, by the air of prophecy with which this pledge was delivered. I didn't want any man but the one I was with, however critical Bill seemed to be of the way he treated me. Besides, I was someone from Regina who'd lucked into love with an Easterner, an American to boot. After that, it would feel unbearably anticlimactic to end up with a Lethbridge boy.

Still, I tucked away Bill's promise as a squirrel would stow a nut for future use, and took private pleasure in the prospect of having someone convenient to catch me should I happen to fall. Which made it all the more perplexing, some months later, to discover what Bill would actually prefer to fall his way.

It was on one of those silly Saturday nights – on the edge of final exams, but with enough time remaining in the term to risk another early spring weekend of waste and indolent shame. There was beer; there was dope; there was a Ouija board or a game of Risk or something similar. The next thing we all knew, the game was over, the beer and grass were gone, the sun was nearly up, and it was time to move on to a different diversion. Like a walk up Mount Royal to greet the dawn.

For some reason, Bill had not elected to be in on the action that night — which struck us as odd, but easily remedied. We'd swing by his place on our way and invite him along.

The window of his one-room apartment was on the ground floor and right out front. My boyfriend stopped the car, one of our number hopped out and tapped on the window. Then, when she got no response, Lizzie raised the sash, hoisted herself up on the sill, and slithered, headfirst, into Bill's room.

A moment or two later, she came slithering out again and rushed back to the car. Even in the gritty half-light, Liz looked flushed, and though she was laughing, her hilarity sounded forced.

"What's the matter?" we all demanded. "Was he mad that you woke him up?"

"No-o-o . . ." By now, she was back in the car, and merely giggling. "He wasn't asleep, exactly."

"Oh, God," groaned my boyfriend. "Don't tell me you burst in on old Bill while he was getting lucky."

"Yes-s-s- . . . I–I guess you could say that!" Again, Lizzie was off in a gale of nervous giggles.

In my dark corner of the back seat, I felt my face flush with some emotion I couldn't identify. Jealousy? Not quite. I was, after all, still ensconced in my relationship; it was my boyfriend at the wheel of the car. Regret? Not possible. I wished Bill well in his love life, I genuinely did. Then what? I couldn't tell. I only knew that it hurt me — however illogically — to learn I'd lost him to some other girl.

It took me a moment to register that Lizzie was also struggling with something she found difficult to communicate. "It . . . he . . . Oh, God, I just feel *awful*! He . . . he's in bed with another *guy*!"

Our appetite for hiking the Mountain abruptly abandoned us. As we drove the few blocks home, we digested the news in shock. It was, after all, the 1960s. The dawn of sexual liberation, so-called, but by twenty-first-century standards an era of staggering tameness. Especially when it came to what are now called same-sex partners. The idea that Bill – our friend Bill, so lately enamoured of Jill and as apparently wholesome as the Alberta hills from which he'd sprung – could be found in bed with some unidentified male was, in that innocent epoch, an enormity from which none of us could easily recover.

Particularly me. What no one else in that car knew – not a soul in the world but Bill – was the way he'd proffered his allegiance, should I ever become available to accept it. Not that I'd ever hoped anything like that might come to pass, but still . . . to find out now that the offer had come from someone who secretly slept with men!

It was a long time before he and I actually talked about it. And when we did, he insisted his discovery of his true sexual self did nothing to preclude an occasional enthusiasm for women – whether or not that enthusiasm expressed itself in bed.

Bullshit, I thought. Jill rejected him, and all I am is encouragingly unavailable. Either that, or I'm unthreateningly androgynous enough to have some appeal. No matter which way I looked at it, I felt insulted. For a while, the affection went out of our relationship. Until enough time had elapsed for me to smarten up and see him – gay, straight, or a blend of both – for the unswerving friend he still was.

Bill and I were of the same stuff. Prairie people, always a little off-balance in the world for which we'd rejected the West. Overly inclined to frankness in our feelings, and insufficiently protective of our flanks.

Although Bill believed in some things that I did not – such as the importance of telling people truths they did not necessarily want to hear. It was from him that I got my first suggestion that my own husband was latently gay. Impossible, I protested. This, after all, was the same man who – back when he was my boyfriend – had been almost as shocked as I was to learn from Lizzie what Bill was up to.

"I didn't say he *approves* of homosexuality," Bill countered, somewhat pedantically. "Approval and orientation are two different things."

And how. It was only after a protracted struggle that my husband managed to accept his gayness. My own struggle to come to terms with it took even longer.

The first step was to find myself somewhere else to live – on my own, for the first time in my life. Bill helped me with that, circling classifieds and driving me to view the places advertised. Even as he and I were moving my few effects into a furnished bachelor in the Annex area of Toronto, my husband's new "roommate" was moving into the west-end apartment he and I had shared.

Bill was right. My husband didn't need to endorse – or even fully acknowledge – his true orientation in order to act on it, especially once I'd obliged him by making the first move.

Suddenly single at thirty, I floundered through those awful encounters, affairettes, and all-out affairs I'd tried to spare myself by marrying early and supposedly for good. After several months in the furnished bachelor suite, I was ready to accept that my new status was – if not what I'd ever planned on – at least what I'd better start planning *for*. I moved into a larger, more permanent place in an oddball old Cabbagetown building, consisting almost entirely of apartments suited to the single tenant. Not long afterward, Bill moved into the same building, right downstairs.

It was a great arrangement. Coming home at night from one of his waitering jobs, he'd check for a light in my window, to judge whether to drop in for a nightcap or late-night toke. If he was ever out of town, I looked after his plants, and he looked in on my cats if I stayed out overnight on one of my errant quests for Mr. Right, or failing that, Mr. Goodbar.

We discussed our romantic travails on bike rides to the Islands or the Beaches. We shared friendships with neighbours in our friendly, funky apartment house; we included each other in party invitations and movie dates. We found the same things funny; we found the same things sad.

We were, in other words, the perfect couple – even in our candour with each other about what constituted true love and good sex. Apart from the fact that our separate yearnings for true love went unrequited and the little good sex we got was never with each other, you could say Bill and I had it made in the shade – even if, admittedly, we'd each have preferred more sun.

Though no luckier in love than he, I was not nearly as outright luckless when it came to awful complications. Bill was forever picking up strangers – from whom he picked up unpleasant and recurrent ailments. Either that, or some ill-considered trick he'd brought home would pick up his watch and wallet from the dresser before making a conclusive getaway. Bill is the only person I've ever met whose gifts were stolen right from under the tree – along with the tree – one Christmas Eve when he was out trolling for someone to share the season with.

Relationships, sooner or later, always failed him. Good jobs eluded him as well; even bad ones evaporated at the worst possible moment. Throughout, he maintained some sort of stubborn hope, a stony optimism bred in generations of his forebears, out West in "next year country," facing down the worst of what the current year could inflict.

It was a quality in him that stood me in good stead, too. One night – drunk, dispirited, and at the end of my romantic rope – I made a half-assed attempt to wash down some shelf-dated sleeping pills with the remains of the Scotch I'd been bottle-feeding my courage all evening.

In a vague way, I knew I'd just done something very stupid. Somehow, I got myself to the phone, managed to dial the restaurant where Bill was working, and left an incoherent message that at least included my name.

By the time he got the message, finished his shift, and stopped in at my apartment to find out what I wanted, I was – he later reported – sprawled on the living-room floor, with my two cats staring at me in transfixed alarm.

Poor Bill. It took the ambulance crew little time to determine I hadn't taken enough pills to cause much more than a giant headache when I awoke. And when I did awake, aware of nothing that had gone on the night before, it fell to Bill to read me the riot act. Which he did, scathingly and to good effect, before bundling me off to Montreal to visit a girlhood friend turned therapist.

There was nothing judgmental in any of this. Bill had suffered too many indignities of his own, and gazed too often into the gaping maw of despair to dismiss anyone else's claim to terminal unhappiness. But in my case, he knew enough to separate the staginess of the gesture from the genuine nub of misery that underlay it.

Eventually, Bill moved back to Alberta. I visited him in Edmonton at one point, to find him happier, more fulfilled, seemingly less harried by the petty pretensions of self-satisfied Toronto, where he'd never truly prospered.

Bill did return one more time, in effect to say goodbye. By then, he had AIDS, and with the illness had acquired a brand of activism that may have been the only way he could meet that final helping of bad fortune without succumbing to the incipient self-pity that was always the flip side of his optimism.

Our last encounter was devoid of the old mirth. But surprisingly, he looked healthier than some of the other men we both knew with full-blown AIDS. He'd dyed his hair, and was meticulous about his dietary supplements, his regimen of pills, and his rights as a victim of a killer disease.

Less surprisingly, there was a "Why me?" edge to his anger, a kind of generalized resentment of the many – straight and gay alike – who'd been luckier not only in love, but in opportunities to exhibit their abilities in exchange for the world's approbation.

My friend Bill was a smart guy, a nice guy, an able guy, a funny guy. Yet somehow he'd stood in the shadows, while those arguably less capable and deserving were getting the girls, or the boys, or the breaks, or the glory. Mostly, we'd stood shoulder to shoulder, he and I. And yet even in our relationship there'd been moments of "Why me?" when his luck was out, and "Why you?" when mine was in.

We were, after all, both Westerners, with similar aptitudes and aspirations. Yet I was the one who'd managed to make a career in the East, to garner some attention, and to emerge from even my darkest adventures to something brighter and better. Bill, meanwhile, was the one who'd waited for fame while waiting on tables, who embraced one initiative after another, only to watch each aspiration fade in succession, and who – whenever he dared to take a chance – seemed to get caught.

I met him when we were both nineteen, and he was barely more than forty when he died. In all its phases and over all those years, ours was a friendship that managed to cover much ground and many bases, without – for the most part – turning sour or cynical.

What we initially wanted from each other was what we ultimately got — a rare claim for any two people to be able to make, about any relationship. And somehow, having what we had with each other made it easier not to have what we wanted, in so many other ways.

BAD BOYS

IT WAS IN GRADE Ten that my best friend Ruth and I turned our backs on Confederate diehards, bodice-ripping bucks with names like Birk Random, and steely-eyed high-plains drifters in order to embrace gangsters as our primary literary passion. It was a passion we pursued in a very businesslike way – ransacking the public library for books on the Cosa Nostra and the Schultz Gang and the Volstead Act, and making notes with a zeal we would have done well to apply to legitimate school assignments.

If you'd suggested to either of us that we were somewhat in love with the underworld, we'd have denied it indignantly. Mobsters were heinous; their crimes were legion. Only through knowledge of their ways could organized criminals be overcome.

To push the point, Ruth decided to make the evils of gangland the theme of her speech for the school's annual oratorical contest. It was an audacious choice. Ours, after all, was a convent school, more accustomed to earnest addresses on "The Continuing Need for a Celibate Clergy," and "Faith, Hope, and Charity in Everyday Action."

When Ruth stood up in front of the Grade Ten class, her hands clasped demurely at her waist, there was no reason to anticipate anything out of the ordinary. Until, in her high, clear, piping voice, she began to lay out a catalogue of murder, mayhem, extortion, and torture, to everybody's astonishment.

Including mine. Even as her best friend and colleague in criminal scholarship, I couldn't help but be struck by the contrast between Ruth, the chubby cherub in her navy-blue tunic and light brown pigtails, and the vivid images of garrotting, firebombing, and Tommy-gunning she strove to evoke.

Sister Mary Angela, our hulking and somewhat slow-witted English teacher, seemed transfixed. But then – as Ruth began to describe in urgent detail how Mafiosi castrated their slain victims – the nun sprang into action, and effectively rang the curtain down. "Ruth! Thank you! That's quite enough!"

Ruth was, I think, truly mystified by the sensation she'd created. As for me, I was affronted on her behalf, but also somewhat annoyed with her for scattering the pearls of our research before such swine.

Plainly, though, she learned a lesson. When Valentine's Day rolled around, she was in complete agreement that we keep our observance of the date to ourselves. After school, we baked a cake, spread it with luridly blue-tinted icing, and inscribed in red across the top with a frosting gun: "Happy Valentine's Day, From Al."

It was, of course, a commemoration of the St. Valentine's Day Massacre in that Chicago garage where Al Capone eliminated rival Bugs Moran and seven of his men. For good measure, Ruth and I spattered our cake with drops of red food colouring, and studded it with spent shotgun shells we'd found someplace, to serve as candles.

Because February 14 fell on a weekday that year, we were obliged to hold our memorial at school. There, the day would be marked for other reasons and in other ways. All around, cutesy cards would be traded, chocolates proffered to teachers, and red paper hearts strung up in the common room in anticipation of a weekend sock hop.

In the midst of all this sugar-coated girlishness, Ruth and I huddled under the second-floor staircase, with our gore-spattered cake, toasting Big Al and poor Bugs, too, in blood-red cranberry juice.

That staircase hideout was our salvation. In fact, the entire schoolhouse had a kind of dark creepiness that easily fed our fantasies. We took to hanging around after school hours – even beyond the time we were regularly kept in detention for smudged white buck shoes or a carelessly pinned tunic hem.

By around four-thirty, the place would seem deserted. Only the creaking tread and murmuring voices of the nuns offered evidence of life going on behind the heavy doors marked "Cloister," in a secret domain off-limits to students.

Back in the 1920s, the four-storey house had been erected as a convent. Only later did it come to double in daytime as a school. By the time Ruth and I numbered among its student population, the cohabitation of nuns and pupils had become decidedly unwieldy.

It was the poor Sisters who bore the brunt of the inconvenience. During school hours, they were forced to retreat into the cloister like hibernating bats. At night, they'd emerge – flapping noiselessly, I always imagined – to reclaim their territory. Girls returning late in the day to pick up forgotten homework or misplaced shoes might enter an erstwhile classroom, only to surprise some poor postulant bathing in a big tin tub that had been dragged out once the coast was deemed clear.

Not only was the old brick house overcrowded, it was falling apart. The wind whistled through chinks in the plaster. In winter, the snow sifted in around the window frames and drifted in wisps across our desks.

From November to April, we girls studied our algebra shivering in our coats. We conjugated Latin verbs in handwriting made clumsy by winter gloves, and recited our catechism through blue and trembling lips, while the nuns paced and stamped in front of the blackboard, exhorting us to Christian fortitude in puffs of visible breath.

But on the plus side, from Ruth's and my point of view, there were the shadowed crannies and creepy corridors. Most particularly, that space we discovered under the second-floor stairs, which no one else seemed to know about. The surer we became of that, the more boldly we provisioned our lair with books, pens, paper, a store of chocolate bars, and even a candle, melted into a saucer.

Within the security of our hideout, we could keep an eye on the nuns and what went on in the house after hours. Anything, certainly, was possible – including an illegal distillery in the basement, operated, perhaps, by the dwarfish little janitor, who pretended to simple-mindedness and communicated only in Low German.

That was the kind of criminality we could almost believe in. Certainly more readily than in those more hackneyed convent yarns that circulated among the rest of the girls: the secret rooms where tiny corpses of nuns' illegitimate offspring were interred; lesbian liaisons between selected novices and overbearing Sisters; kinky rituals of self-flagellation straight out of *The Nun's Story*.

For that brand of twisted spookery, Ruth and I lacked all patience. But the idea of a bootlegging operation, or an opium den, masked by the odour of incense, or . . . a prostitution ring?

With the early, false spring a species of brash giddiness had come upon us. One afternoon we came friskily close to the pale by lettering up scraps of paper, rolling them into balls, and pitching them out the window to the street below. "Help!" read our notes. "We are innocent schoolgirls being held captive by a ring of white slavers posing as nuns."

When a thoughtful passerby found one of these messages and turned it over to the Sisters, Ruth and I were high on the list of suspects. And were even questioned, as I remember, by a wry and slightly bemused Mother Mary Roberta, our principal.

For all we could tell, she knew we were guilty as sin. But with nothing to link us directly to the crime, we managed to beat the rap. We slunk gratefully out of her office, vowing to each other that we'd never, ever push our luck like that again. Then once in the clear, promptly forgot the lesson, and set out yet again to court disaster.

By now, May was well underway, and with it came the final assignments of the year. In English class, Sister Angela announced that each of us was to write a short story of our own devising – "no copying from the classics, please" – and hand it in by the end of the month.

Groans and sighs and much rolling of eyes greeted this decree. How long does it have to be, Sister? At least eight pages! More groans, more sighs, even a few tears shed by the most severely literarily challenged.

Ruth and I, meanwhile, exchanged smiles of confident anticipation. Writing stories was, after all, old hat to us. In our historical romance phase, hadn't those tales of men named Birk Random and spirited heroines with eyes as deep and dewy as pansies virtually flowed from our pencils? Then, there'd been our short-lived mania for TV Westerns, during which we'd cranked off numerous *Rawhide* scripts, packed them off to Hollywood by post, and been startled when they came back utterly unremarked upon, and obviously unread.

On this assignment of Sister Angela's, we would collaborate as always. And naturally, our setting would be the Chicago of the 1930s. But with none of the distasteful gore of Ruth's oratorical effort – a point I sought to impress with a stern, unflinching look, to which she responded with meek agreement.

Once we had cooked up the storyline, we planned simply to

split it down the middle, each authoring a separate half, and then conjoin them before we handed it all in. It was an exciting prospect; we could hardly wait to map the outline and get down to the savoury business of writing.

Our lengthy plotting sessions under the stairs made me chronically late for meetings with Sister Mary Philip, the adviser to the school paper. It was Sister Phil (as she liked the girls to call her) who had made me editor – a dubious honour generally reserved for a Grade Twelve girl with no social life, but offered to me early in my student career in hopes of mending my anti-social ways.

Fat chance. I hated working on the paper, mostly because it took after-school time away from Ruth – precious hours already sorely curtailed by the frequency and severity of our detentions. Sister Philip knew, of course, that I worked with her and the rest of the newspaper staff strictly under duress, while I knew that weaning me away from my friend was the real strategy behind my appointment.

All that mutual knowledge made for a tense relationship. As I skidded into the newspaper office, panting and very late, Sister Philip would smile her brightest, stagiest smile and shake her head in mock disapproval. "You know, my pet, they don't call it a deadline for nothing. On a real newspaper, you'd be out of a job."

"I know that, Sister," I'd reply, trying not to let my face show how devoutly I wished it *were* a real newspaper for just that reason.

On one of these encounters, smack in the midst of my most intense involvement with Ruth on our story, I remember Sister Philip's smile fading as she surveyed me with moist grey eyes. "You shouldn't spend so much time just with Ruth. You need other people to hang around with."

Hang around. It was chummy phrases like that which made her so popular with the other students. That and her full-bodied laugh – totally unlike the discreet little titter of most of the nuns –

and the running shoes she donned so sportily when she came out
to play softball, in vintage Father-Flanagan-of-Boys-Town style.

"I'll think about it, Sister."

"Oh, bull. You will not."

I was startled that she'd dropped the cajolery and come out
swinging.

"Stop humouring me, my pet, and just listen to what I'm
telling you. Don't make the mistake of discarding everything and
everyone in favour of your games with Ruth. Because one day,
you're going to need the very people you think you're too good
for now."

She couldn't know, of course. She couldn't possibly know anything of aspirations on the grand scale. Couldn't know that I casti-
gated myself not because I wasn't one of the popular girls with
glossy hair and an attentive boyfriend, but because I wasn't Scarlett
O'Hara, Catherine the Great, and Ma Barker, all rolled into one.
To be personable, desirable, or even attractive in Sister Phil's terms
would, I knew, be the finish of me. Small portals would open into
boyfriends' cars and suburban bungalows, but the wide door of
destiny would clang shut forever if I yielded one inch.

But these were not the kinds of sentiments that could be
expressed aloud, not even to someone as shrewdly intelligent as
Sister Philip. I contented myself with a wan smile that was meant
to reflect gratitude, and the nun relented sufficiently to smile back.

She was likeable, genuinely likeable, and I could see that she
wanted some indication from me that I, as much as the others, was
susceptible to her charms. Yet, perversely, I needed to leave something lacking in her abundant, good-natured life.

Besides, work on what Ruth and I now termed The Story had
become all-absorbing. The villain of the piece was, of course, a
gangster, and I especially looked forward to writing the parts that
featured him.

"Clemenza di Tito came into the dressing room of torch singer Brandy Alexander without knocking. There was an expensive Havana cigar between his fleshy lips, and the outline of a holster evident under his flashy pinstriped suit." It was with becoming pride that I pushed back from my bedroom desk to survey sentences like those.

My bedroom was painted Dusty Rose; the bedspread and curtains were sprigged with small, delicate flowers, and the lamps on my matching night tables were pretty pink ladies shaded by fringed parasols. Hardly the habitat of a hard-hitting crime writer. Nevertheless, a 1912 Underwood typewriter that my father had recently unearthed from the basement of the store he managed added some backbone to the operation, and gave me the illusion, as I tapped away two-fingered at the keyboard, of adult enterprise.

Much discussion had gone into the naming of the characters who enlivened our little drama. At first Infesta Populatione – an idiom from our Latin book that meant "spreading dire destruction" – had been our choice for the name of our mobster. But after consideration, we dismissed it in favour of the far more subtly ironic "Clemenza di Tito" – a name Ruth had spied on the spine of an album on her mother's record shelf.

"Brandy Alexander" was a natural for the streetwise but oddly saintly chanteuse in a nightclub run by racketeers. Then there was the rookie cop named Lewis, to whom Brandy spilled mob secrets in order to redeem herself, but he didn't interest us as much. It was Clemenza di Tito we cared about, and his odious exploits we gloried in committing to paper.

" 'Somebody's been tippin' off da cops to my operation,' di Tito growled, chewing thoughtfully on his cigar and running his eyes, like patent-leather buttons, up and down Brandy's svelte yet innocent form." The patent-leather simile was something of which I was particularly proud, and when I pulled out the piece of paper and replaced the cracked old leatherette cover on the Underwood that night, I felt calmly certain of an A from Sister Mary Angela. Why, on length alone, Ruth and I had high marks coming. Already we were calculating the finished product at forty pages, easy.

Once both parts of The Story were finally completed, combined, and submitted, Ruth and I sat back smugly to await our reward. It wasn't long in coming. Two days after we'd turned The Story in, Sister Angela told me to stay after class.

She was, as I've said, a large woman, rather mannish, nick-named Sister Mary St. Sonny Liston behind her back. But such a gentle soul, with her sad brown eyes set in a large leathern face, and her soft, pleading voice, that I was surprised when she rounded on me, the moment the classroom door was closed.

"I am astonished," she said, spitting out her words. "Astonished and horrified that you could be party to such immoral highjinks. Your friend Ruth — to whom I will speak separately — is not of our faith. And while that by no means excuses what she did, it helps explain it a little. But you, from a good Catholic family, to be party to such, such . . . filth! Well, I hardly know what to say to you."

Shocked as I was, it took me some moments to realize that the "filth" she referred to was The Story. Our underworld morality tale of crime and retribution reduced to "filth" by this ignorant, uncomprehending woman!

"But, Sister, I don't understand. There's nothing bad about what we wrote. I mean, Brandy Alexander — that's the heroine — she redeems herself by ratting the gangster out. I mean, she even dies and everything —"

"'Everything' is right." Sister Mary Angela's eyes were blazing with righteous wrath. "It will be some time, my girl, before I am able to rid my mind of the image of that . . . woman, expiring in a pool of blood, with her bosom hanging out!"

What story had Sister been reading? Certainly not anything penned by Ruth and me. We hadn't even thought of giving Brandy Alexander a bosom, much less having her expose it on the final page.

"Oh, no!" I exclaimed. The words were out of my mouth before I could think better of them. "You made that up, Sister."

Mottled blotches of colour stood out on the nun's cheeks, in contrast to the starched white serenity of her wimple and stiff black veil. "That will be enough from you. I know what I read."

It was too late to try for tact. "Show me," I persisted. "Show me the part in our story that says . . . well, what you said."

"That so-called story of yours is where it belongs, in the furnace."

"You *burnt* it? You burned our story up?"

I hardly knew which was the greater outrage – the destruction of our masterpiece or the ugly distortions the nun had imposed upon its memory.

"You're lucky I didn't turn it over to Mother Roberta instead. Or to Sister Mary Philip, who has such faith in your future. Myself, I can only imagine you ending up writing for the *Police Gazette*, or something worse. But I'll light a candle in the chapel and pray that I'm wrong."

For a moment, I stopped being outraged and felt suddenly, oddly, flattered. What associations Sister Mary Angela might have to the *Police Gazette*, I had no idea. But I was pleased she would think I could aspire so high. And a candle lit for me in the chapel! Clemenza di Tito himself might be honoured to be rated so mad, bad, and dangerous to know.

My sense of accomplishment was, however, short-lived. The Story was gone, Ruth and I had each been awarded an F on the assignment, and – worst of all – our secret hideout under the stairs had apparently been discovered. It was that revelation that prompted Mother Mary Roberta to split us up, at least while on school property. And it was that decree, in turn, that prompted Ruth's father – who, being Jewish, was inclined to suspect the nuns of prejudice – to remove his daughter from the Sisters' influence and enrol her at the public collegiate.

The words of Sister Philip came back to haunt me. "One day, you're going to need the very people you think you're too good for now."

She was right. After several weeks of unbearable loneliness, I began prowling like a circumspect dog around the edges of the social sphere that encompassed the other Grade Tens. Eventually, advisedly, I was allowed in. And ultimately wound up as part of the "circle" of girls who called her "Sister Phil."

I always did wonder, though, what role she might have played behind the scenes. Once, I even went so far as to ask her how Mother Roberta had found out about the place under the stairs.

The nun's smile did not fade, but it dimmed a little, and I can't recall receiving any kind of direct answer. In the end, none of it really mattered, anyway. Ruth and I would have abandoned gangsters – and each other – in due course, without the nuns' intervention.

I miss those days, even so. In a world now rife with Godfathers and Goodfellas and Tony Sopranos, I miss the innocent menace of Clemenza di Tito, with his patent-leather button eyes and ominously bulging holster. Had she known this, Sister Mary Angela would have been well-advised to keep on lighting candles for me, even long after my apparent conversion to wholesome, girlish normality.

CODGERS

IT WAS A FEMALE friend of mine who best summed up the problem of being with an older man: "You have to go through aging and decrepitude twice – first with him, and then by yourself. Because by the time it's *your* turn, he's either dead or has moved on to someone younger."

Okay, so in spite of that obvious drawback, why is it that older guys appeal to so many women? The flip answer is that they remind us either of the fathers we had, or the fathers we wish we'd had – or, the fathers we're glad we didn't have.

But if that's the case, why don't younger men lust equally often after women of their mother's generation? In *The Graduate*, we cheer young Benjamin when he manages to slip free of the clutches of Mrs. Robinson to go after her far more suitable daughter, Elaine. Conversely, in *The Misfits*, it's a mark of new maturity in Marilyn Monroe that she ends up in the cab of the elderly Clark Gable's pickup truck and lets him take her home by following "that big star straight on."

That these films date from the Sixties ought to disqualify them, but it doesn't. It's one respect – perhaps the only one – that's remained unchanged at the movies in the last half-century. In a society increasingly obsessed with youth, it seems men still hold on to theirs by embracing younger and younger women, while women try to remain youthful by seeking out the company of men who still perceive them to be so.

And why not? Isn't it a pleasure to be seen as girlish, lithe, and limber – even if by a septuagenarian who doesn't, in fact, see all that well any more? And whose tendency to paternal indulgence where you're concerned generally inclines him to err on the side of positive assessment.

As very young women, we regard it as a testament to our sophistication if we attract the attention of older, wiser men. It's only as we ourselves age that we begin to notice the drawbacks inherent in spending a lot of our time with someone whose personal allotment of the stuff was pretty close to spent before we met him.

If men in general seem preoccupied with mortality, older men are utterly absorbed. In part, it's understandable. Men do, on average, die younger than we do. But not *that* much younger, and it's not as if constantly watching the pot with an anxious eye is going to prevent it from boiling.

Why is it that women, for all their fear of aging, worry so much less about actually dying? Possibly because we're too involved in worrying about more momentous things – like why Weight Watchers appears to work only for other people. And how it is that platform shoes could manage to make a comeback from the rightful oblivion to which they'd been consigned.

To be fair, not all older men are obsessed with death. Some are merely obsessed with illness – a long, lingering illness to which death would be infinitely preferable. Especially as the last thing on earth they want to be is a burden. And if constantly hearing about the burden of fearing becoming a burden becomes a fearful burden to you? Well, you have only yourself to blame for being involved in the first place with an older man.

To be even fairer, it's not as if older men just sit back and wait for death to claim them. Many rush headlong to meet it – if unintentionally – by exercising with an almost religious ferocity, or by adhering to a diet so reduced in fats and sugars that intermittent emergency antidotes of Double Stuf Oreo ice cream, deep-fried pork rinds, chips with gravy, and Mile High Coconut Pie must be administered – usually while walking home from the gym or while idling in front of an open fridge, in the naïve belief that food consumed in a standing position doesn't actually count.

Older men have habits they had time to cultivate during all those years they were forced to fill while waiting for you to be born. Habits like crumbling bits of bran muffin into their yogurt, trimming their nose hairs over the sink, turning on the bedside lamp without warning in the middle of the night, forgetting to shoulder-check before changing lanes, and falling asleep during sex. And not only do they recall vividly – and often – where they were when they heard President Kennedy had been shot, they also remember what they were up to when the bad news came about President McKinley.

Rolling her eyes behind your father's back was sufficient for your mother to relieve her irritation with Dad's time-worn crotchets. But your mother *knew* those crotchets; she pre-dated those crotchets, had all the time in the world to observe her man evolve from an unformed young buck into an uninformed old codger whose preferences and peculiarities could not only be predicted as reliably as the chime on the courthouse clock, but also adopted as her own.

Your father has always heaped his salad right onto his dinner plate; so now does your mother, you notice. And these days Mom puts the bottle of dressing directly on the table, though she used to complain if your father did that. Neither of your parents thinks much of the current crop of movie stars. Both keep the temperature in their house cranked up so high that the fireplace periodically ignites by spontaneous combustion. And nowadays, the one who falls asleep first in front of the TV with a luxuriant snore is just as likely to be your mother.

You, on the other hand, lack the advantage of such long-term habituation. And so, in fact, does the older man you're with. You find him stuck in his fidgety little ways. He finds you arbitrary, vacillating, inconsistent.

While he's soothed by the hum of an air conditioner, you're outraged to find the window closed against the evening breeze and the urban roar. While you pounce on him for audibly sucking his teeth, he's revolted by the rasp of your emery board. His friends are self-involved, right-wing, petty, and deaf. Yours, mean-while, are unintellectual, superficial, and dull.

For all of that, the age-old allure of the aging older man per-sists. At least for those of us in whom the seed – or need – was sown early, and went on to blossom, season after season.

My own first encounter with an Older Man occurred the very first summer I had a job. I was seventeen; he was around twenty-five. Oh, I know, hardly in the league of aging Humbert Humbert preying on little Dolores Haze. But I was a very *young* seventeen – fresh from four years in a convent school, bookish, brittle, and shy, but free for the first time in memory to wear thick makeup and short short skirts. He, meanwhile, was a rather tired twenty-five, who may or may not have made his Grade Twelve. Certainly, he appeared to prefer boozing to books, and on my first day in the office, he met my timid glance with a hard yet indifferent gaze. The perfect match, in other words, just waiting for some friction to help it catch fire.

That first summer job was, in many ways, the best job I've ever had. I wrote TV commercials for a local station in Regina. And while I was also required to spell the steno-receptionist by answering phones and doing the filing and minding the teletype, I actually did get to work on the occasional piece of ad copy.

Not only was it a dream job, I had a dream of a boss. Her name was Virginia, and she was tall and humorous and groovy – somewhat in the same mould as my high-school nemesis turned mentor, Sister Phil – with a relaxed self-confidence and enormous zest. There were just the two of us cranking out those TV spots in a cramped little office, and while it was only downtown Regina as opposed to Madison Avenue, we had tremendous fun together.

Some of the fun was shared by the cameraman, whose name was Danny, and whose job it was to go out with Virginia to shoot the live-action commercials she devised. Danny adored Virginia – who wouldn't? For me, he had faint regard. The skinny, flat-chested, over-earnest convent schoolkid who'd barely been out with a boy . . . ? As well, I was rumoured to be a brainiac, with a scholarship awaiting me in September at some big university down East there.

At first, I thought as little of Danny as he did of me. Sure, the fact that he was much older appealed. Far beyond the unsophisticated league of Catholic boys who represented the closest thing to "eligible men" in the high-school world I'd just left. Danny lived in an actual apartment building; he owned a car. And just by the way he walked and talked, he made it clear he'd had some history with women.

Even so, he seemed crass to me, unoriginal. "Hey, check your charts," he'd chide when he caught your attention wandering. "We got 'er built" was his way of signalling that all was proceeding according to plan. He had a fund of stock phrases like that, all of which I felt sure were borrowed from someone on television he'd deemed cool.

Virginia was a whole lot sharper – and a lot older – than Danny. Still, they got along famously. Much riotous laughter always accompanied them out the door on their way to location filming. On their way back in, hours later, they'd still be laughing together, and firing droll remarks laced with sexual innuendo back and forth.

That was their bond, this joint appetite for sex talk. Towering Virginia was married to an elfin little man named Alan, and made it obvious that what he lacked in stature, he more than made up for in bed. I'd never met an adult woman so frankly lustful in her conversation, and I wasn't entirely sure I liked it. Especially when Danny got in on the act, matching her verbal outrage for verbal outrage.

Still, I always felt abandoned when he and Virginia went off together, leaving me to mislay the files, gum up the Xerox machine, and try out different accents on the ad agency men who phoned to chat. The ten-second spots I was allowed to work on never entailed live-action shoots. Which meant that while Virginia and Danny were yukking it up in some auto showroom or at the bandshell in Wascana Park, I was stuck trundling my ad copy over to some great, silent, floury baker or a tense little furniture-store owner for grudging approval – or, more likely – outright rejection.

So when the chance came to involve myself in one of Virginia's commercials, I took it, hook, line, and sinker – along with the bait she artfully dangled. It seemed she'd had a brilliant inspiration to write a series of funny little spots for my dad's clothing store, patterned after silent-movie one-reelers, featuring a little Chaplinesque figure who'd get caught in one classic dilemma after another – trapped on a railroad track with an onrushing train, hanging by his fingernails from a window ledge, and so on. Virginia suffered no shortage of bright ideas; she lacked only a man diminutive enough, and foolhardy enough, to play the part.

With furrowed brow, she solicited my help. I'd been active in high-school plays. Didn't I know someone small and sufficiently hammy to don a suit, a bowler hat, a fake moustache, and mug for the camera with a walking stick?

Flattered to be consulted, I thought and thought. But there was nobody I could come up with.

Too bad, Virginia lamented, especially since my father was so hot on the concept that he'd already dug up a very small old black suit jacket and pinstriped pants from the store basement, perfect for a would-be Charlie Chaplin. All that was lacking was the talent to put in the togs.

Such very small togs, she added, still frowning. More a woman's size, really, and not a large woman at that. Meant for someone . . . well, someone of my dimensions, actually, now that she came to think of it. Someone slender and theatrically gifted like myself, who, with her hair hidden up under a bowler hat . . .

It didn't take me long to stumble upon the idea that I might make a good Charlie Chaplin. When I proposed the idea to Virginia, her face lit up. Why, of course! She only marvelled that she hadn't thought of it herself.

The day we drove out to shoot the drowning-in-Niagara-Falls episode was hot – hinge-of-hell hot, as is typical of a southern Saskatchewan summer. Mercifully, I was not required to wear the jacket and wool trousers in the car. I changed into them behind a towel Virginia held up to shield me from the view of Danny and a lumbering friend of his who'd been brought along to pull me out of the lake as needed.

The idea was I would be filmed flailing my arms as I leapt from the end of a dock, and then superimposed against Niagara Falls. I never have been a strong or willing swimmer and was terrified at the prospect of jumping into water of an unknown depth and thereupon plunging to the bottom in my sodden dress suit. Despite Danny's assurances that his friend – whose nickname was Turk – would quickly pluck me from the drink, I took my first running jump into the lake with a sense of doom.

But no. Turk pulled me up by the scruff as easily as if I were a kitten. Much hilarity ensued at my soggy expense – followed by

Danny's announcement that, for some technical reason I no longer remember, we'd have to do it all over again.

"We"? What he meant was that I would have to repeat the stunt, after rewrapping my hair up under the bowler, and having Virginia redraw my grease-pencil moustache. Socks squishing inside my swollen Oxfords, I hurtled myself down the dock once more, and once more into the lake.

This time, somehow, no Turk appeared to drag me to the surface. For what seemed like the longest interlude, I sat bubbling at the bottom – like one of those little deep-sea divers you find in fish tanks – awaiting rescue. None came. Panicking, I tried to fight my way to the surface, but each swollen Oxford felt like an anvil, and I couldn't seem to kick either off.

Panicking even more, I attempted to wriggle free of my water-logged suit jacket, but my fingers fumbled in vain with the buttons. I was drowning. Exactly as I'd feared all along, but had been too full of ambition to broach as a concern. Now, I would pay the price for my hubris, and my overwhelming desire to please Virginia.

Just as the blackness seemed about to engulf me, I felt a firm hand grip my collar and pull me up toward the light. I broke the surface gasping and coughing, with a strong brown arm support-ing my chin. Wet blond hairs lay along that arm, and I knew it did not belong to Turk. It was Danny to my rescue.

Turk had found himself caught in weeds some yards from where I hit the water. And so Danny – in Virginia's words, "all in a lather" about my welfare – had thrown aside his camera, stripped to his shorts, and gone in after me.

I could barely conjure with the glorious sensation of being borne out of the water by attentive arms. Despite Danny's off-hand disclaimer about only fearing the loss of my father's account if I were permitted to drown, I was sure an act of heroism had been performed. As shy, shutdown, and solemn as I'd always felt in his presence, I now believed I'd somehow inspired him to save my life.

Even a distressed damsel more self-assured than I would be susceptible to the allure of chivalrous rescue. Add to that the thrill of rescue at the hands of someone whose weary condescension had seemingly turned into an impulse to offer protection . . . and who can blame me if, for the first time in my life, I felt the flutter of ultra-femininity that only a mature man prepared to take command of one's destiny can inspire?

It was a weeknight, with work looming for all of us the next morning. But Virginia was not one to let such a mundane detail stand in the way of an impromptu outing. Especially when there was something to celebrate, like the successful completion of a commercial shoot with no loss of life.

Out came the vodka and the 7-UP and the Cameo cigarettes. All four of us sat on the empty beach in the moonlight, drinking and smoking and joking like comrades-in-arms. I knew I'd passed some important test, especially where Danny was concerned. My long hair hung in wet, wiggly clumps; my kohl-rimmed Charlie Chaplin eyes were now smudged like a raccoon's, an unattractive dinge of black pencil line lingered on my upper lip. Nevertheless, through my near escape, I felt feminine, dauntless, desirable.

Danny and Virginia, meanwhile, had changed into their bathing suits and were horsing around in the dark water. Danny attempted to pull down the front of her suit, and Virginia attempted to pretend to mind. Later, when he emerged from the water, I could see an eager bulge in his trunks that, even in my innocence, I knew was not prompted by the shock of the cold water, but rather was there in spite of it.

Nothing further passed between him and me that night. Even so, what with the vodka and the moonlight and the lake, I felt the dawn of an intense, if inexplicable, crush. Suddenly, Danny's dull little catchphrases seemed droll, distinctive, almost hip. While we filmed the rest of our ads, I sought secret significance in each raised eyebrow, every proffered cigarette, any absent-minded smile. Standing around at whatever site in my shaming ensemble of bowler hat, suit jacket, and drawn-on moustache, waiting for the camera to roll, I'd look in vain to Virginia for some signal that she knew, understood, wished me well.

All the time, I dreaded the completion of our silent-movie series of perils. As I was, in turn, pied in the face in a crowded hotel lobby, tied to a railroad track, and otherwise humiliated, I bore my sufferings with the exaltation of a Christian martyr. Soon enough, I'd be stuck back in the office, gazing wistfully after Danny as he and Virginia bustled off with their equipment to carry out new projects in which I would play no part.

As the summer days began to dwindle, my hopes started to wane as well. Until I got invited along to an out-of-town wedding with Virginia, her husband – and Danny.

I have no recollection whose wedding it was. Presumably, I knew at the time. All I really remember is that it was one of those rowdy, rural southern Saskatchewan affairs accorded an unqualified success only if and when somebody finally got drunk enough to fall into the cesspool.

For a large portion of the evening, Danny, Alan, Virginia, and I remained in the car in a far corner of the farmyard, drinking from a Thermosful of daiquiris Virginia had thought to pack for our sequestered consumption, just in case the party proved too riotous even for us. Danny and I sat together in the back, his arm resting casually across the top of the seat.

I was acutely conscious of that arm, and felt I had reason to be. In choosing my outfit for the occasion, I'd made the decision to cast aside all my standard Mod-style low-belted dresses that hung from my frame like flour-sacks, in favour of something with more obvious allure.

After all, it was by now almost the last weekend of the summer. Either I stirred Danny into action tonight, or my chances were lost. Precisely what I expected in the way of "action," I wasn't sure. Didn't, in fact, really want to speculate. With grim determination, I laid out my clothes, like a matador soberly preparing to don the Suit of Lights, mentally set on victory, but heart palpitating from time to time with the prospect of a deadly defeat.

It was a lacy shirtwaist-style dress I chose, with a tight-fitting bodice and a big full skirt. Not at all the kind of thing I usually wore but, I suspected, more the kind of thing I *should* have been wearing all summer long around the office. Beneath the dress I wore – again, uncharacteristically – a brassiere. Which, to my everlasting shame, I had stuffed with a pair of tennis socks.

In the mirror, I thought I looked great. Like someone else entirely – one of the lovely Lennon Sisters, perhaps. Chaste yet ripe, fluffy yet full-bodied, lacy yet cheesy, and – most important of all – not strange, nor sober, nor remotely scholarly.

That I'd got the look right was made clear as soon as Danny laid eyes on me. It was, quite literally, as if he'd never seen me before. And certainly he hadn't – not in this particular body, anyway, so tightly sheathed and so carefully shaped.

At some point or other, Virginia and Alan must have got out of the car – in search of more liquor, perhaps, or a chance to dance with the bride and groom in the farmyard full of swirling couples and polka music. There were Danny and I, quite suddenly alone in the back seat. Just as suddenly, his arm dropped to my shoulder, and as he pulled me toward him, we began to kiss.

The return of the others broke us up in a hurry. But all the way back to town, we murmured affectionate nothings, *sotto voce*, and plotted how to ditch our ride and reconnect for the remainder of the night.

By the time Alan and Virginia dropped me at my door, a plan had been hatched: Danny would be driven home, then would pick me up in his own car and take me back to his place for . . . well, whatever came up. If I knew what he meant. Did I? Ulp. Yes, I thought I did.

My parents happened to be out of town. Which was the only reason I could be a party to any of this. There was my brother to consider, although not very seriously. With our parents gone, the two of us were more or less ignoring each other, and I didn't even expect to find him home as I tottered up the walk on white spiked heels that matched my dress.

But he *was* home, by some mischance. And turned every bit as irritatingly parental as my father would have been, once he gathered what was afoot.

"I'm going!" I insisted angrily. "Why shouldn't I?"

With quiet disgust, my brother, a reasonably experienced nineteen-year-old, outlined what exactly was likely to befall me. I knew he was right – in some wicked way, I even hoped he was.

With an indignation I intended to sound mature, I pointed out how different it was for him: he'd been dating easily and confidently from his early teens. I, on the other hand, had been for the longest time the ugliest of ducklings, only now beginning to aspire to swanhood. Why shouldn't I enjoy the fruits of my new-found charms?

"How old is this guy?" my brother wanted to know.

I told him, and his disgust only deepened. "Twenty-*five*? And he's coming over in the middle of the night to pick up a teenager and take her back to his place? And you somehow take this as a compliment?"

Just as I opened my mouth to reply, a small car drew up in front of our house. Without another word to me, my brother was out the door and striding authoritatively down the walk. As Danny got out of his car, I noted through the window how short he suddenly seemed – and how unsteady on his feet.

I continued to look on from the house as my brother confronted the guy who'd come calling at three a.m. on his younger sister. It was a brief conversation, but it didn't appear uncivil. Within a moment or two, Danny was back in his car and off into the night. As my brother walked back into the house he looked more bemused than angry, dusting off his hands as if to say "That's that."

I continued to rage a little, if only for form's sake. But I actually felt relieved. Danny *had* seemed weaselly and drunk; the hour *was* dangerously late, and those *were* tennis socks stuffed into my bra. Had I wound up at his place, and in his embrace, the truth – and the tennis socks – would have been bound to come out.

No more older men, I vowed. Though, in fact, it had been my brother who'd come across as the more mature, the more manly, that night. And, in fact, my vow was one that I – like many other women I know – have honoured as much in the breach as in the observance. Because, whether we understand it or not, there is something undeniably appealing about older men.

Which is all I really started out to say.

DADS

I HAVE ONLY ONE memory of my mother's father, on the sole occasion he came to visit from the Coast, when I was seven. I recall a big, balding, bespectacled man, too large for our subdivision bungalow, looming over my brother and me with the bluff formality of someone uncomfortable with offspring, even his own daughter's.

In fact, he didn't seem all that comfortable with his daughter. He called our mother Margaret, instead of Marg, the way everybody else did. And took a polite but somewhat distant interest in what she tried to tell him about us, her house, her life, herself.

For her part, my mother appeared uncomfortable, too. Deferential and anxious to please in a self-justifying way uncharacteristic of her. Certainly, the day her father departed our house, there was a collective sigh of relief he may well have seconded.

Before his visit, our mother's father had already figured large in her stories about her childhood "back East" – Southwestern Ontario, actually. Her own mother had been something of a flapper, with a booze belt and a beaded cloche hat, and a restless, incandescent manner utterly at odds with the formal, bookish man she married.

When my mother was only four, her mother ran off with another man. Dismayed at the prospect of solo parenthood, her father enlisted relatives to raise his little girl. For the next decade or so, she shuttled between her two sets of grandparents, in London and Stratford.

It was not, she told us, such a bad arrangement. Both sets of grandparents were doting in their different ways, and, in addition, one of the households – I forget which – boasted my mother's Great-Aunt Mary, a warm, tender-hearted maiden lady who called my mother "little lover" and petted her, coddled her, and spoiled her – just as our mother would my brother and me.

Sadly, this idyllic interlude in her life came to an abrupt end in early adolescence with the reappearance of her father, suddenly determined to reclaim her.

It was always at this point in the narrative that our mother would begin to cry, as she described to us the parting from her grand-parents – and Aunt Mary! – in the company of the stranger her father had become. My brother and I would wail along as she reached the part where she clung to Aunt Mary at the curbside, until she was physically pried from the old lady's arms and forced into her father's car for the long, long trek west.

It also always seemed to be at this point in the story that the sound of the metal garage door could be heard to clang shut, heralding our own father's return from work.

"He's home!" Abruptly, our mother would remove me or my brother from her lap, in order to reach into her skirt pocket for a Kleenex. "Don't tell your father," she'd beg, wiping her eyes. "Don't tell your father."

Don't tell him *what*? I was never quite sure whether it was her crying in front of us that our dad would condemn, or the mere act of discussing her tragic past. Whatever she intended by it, my mother's injunction had the effect on me of intermingling events: her father's unannounced arrival from the West became forever confused with my father's return home to shut down her story. Dads, it seemed, had this way of showing up to spoil things.

As I got older, I began to appreciate more and more some of the awful complexity inherent in my mother's relationship with my Grandpa Cody. That trip across the country, for instance, must have been hellish. A shy, sheltered young girl, confined for days on end in a hot car on a hot journey over the mostly gravel Trans-Canada Highway of the time, with her sweating, fat, and forbidding father.

What on earth did they talk about over those hundreds and hundreds of miles? Where did they stay along the way, and in what proximity? Was my grandfather on hand to hear my mother crying in the night – as she must have cried – at the memory of her Great-Aunt Mary holding her close at the curb? And if he did overhear, how must he have reacted, in order to prompt her, years down the line, to keep her old sorrows secret from her husband, and to petition her children to do the same?

It had been dry and dusty and infernally hot, I do know, during that dust-bowl summer so many years ago, when my grandfather took my mother away from everything she knew, from all the love she'd ever experienced. On one of those afternoons cooped in his car, she'd been lying on the back seat, delirious with heat and half-asleep, dreaming that a kitten lay in her lap as she patted its fur. Only to jerk awake in horror at the realization that there was a huge June bug upside down in her lap, kicking its furry legs helplessly as she stroked them.

Her scream nearly sent her father's car off the road. He screeched to a stop, then turned to berate her. My mother, by this time hysterical, continued to scream until the June bug was out of the car. The episode was the low point of an already downheartening odyssey.

Their miserable trek led to an even more miserable destination. Compared to the leafy, chestnut-lined streets and genteel red brick of Stratford and London, Regina was raw, ragged, almost physically painful to her in its wood-and-stucco ugliness. Worst of all was the discovery of a lady friend in her father's adopted world.

It wasn't until the final years of her life that my mother confessed to me the sense of rage and usurpation she had felt about Florence. She was earthy, unlettered – "common," to use my mother's most damning term. What could a diffident and almost pathologically unsociable man like Max Cody see in such a creature?

Sex. As a shy teenager, it must have shaken my mother to the core to face the fact of her father's sexual side. She barely knew the man, after all. Had made no perceptible progress in gaining his understanding or approval. And now she was faced with a rival who'd clearly already won. It was bad enough that her father had made an initial unsuitable match – later resulting in her own rejection and abandonment. Here he was, poised once more on the brink of choosing for a wife a woman whose ways were all wrong for him.

Once, late in her life and after a bit too much to drink, my mother recounted to me how she'd dared to dress down her father for the mistake he was about to make. Her anger, as she described it so many decades after the fact, was shockingly out of character. Whether she actually had shown that side to her father on the subject of Florence I can't be certain. But the marriage most assuredly went ahead. Children followed. My mother, barely anybody's daughter at any point in her life, was now relegated permanently to stepchild.

Yet something warmer must have rippled beneath the surface of what lay between her father and her. As the managing editor of the Regina *Leader-Post*, he made way for the writing and artwork of teenagers – including my mother's – in the pages of the paper. And on his frequent, impulsive solo travels by coach around North America, he'd send her postcards with brief but enthusiastic news of the people he'd met and the presents he planned to bring home.

I wonder if those gifts ever did appear, or were merely part of his mythology of himself as *paterfamilias*. An image perhaps more easily cultivated out on the open road, far from his second wife and uneasily assembled family. My mother would describe him returning refreshed from one of those bus trips, full of stories of strange passengers and stranger interludes, and animated by a raw curiosity about the human condition. Utterly unlike that large, looming, unfriendly grandfather I dimly recall from my own childhood, who more closely resembled my dad and all the other dark, forbidding dads in the neighbourhood.

Fathers of the 1950s were famously remote from their families. They acted as emissaries from the outside world of Work, showing up at the end of the day to hear how things had gone on the home front. Or – in my father's case – to hear nothing revealing from any of us, in accordance with the "don't tell your father" ethic my mother impressed upon her children from an early age.

Yet, there was the occasional dad who did things differently. I remember my friend Judy's father as a sweet, sunny man with a tidy little moustache, who teased us girls with good-natured warmth, and – in the fall – pressed us into service to help him put up pickles.

I couldn't get over the novelty of a father who would laugh and joke as he directed his daughter and her friends to stuff sprigs of dill into the jars before sealing the lids. It felt unreal somehow, like watching *Father Knows Best*, where Robert Young addressed his girls as "Kitten" and "Princess," and never came storming into the house like an honest-to-God father to demand whose toys those were left out on the lawn.

An even earlier friend named Paula had a wistful, somewhat whimsical father, badly crippled by polio, who could recite to us entire Sherlock Holmes stories by heart, even "A Study in Scarlet," which was long and complicated and wholly unnerving. It was

Paula's father, rather than her mother, who presided over what he called "dunging out" Paula and her sister's bedroom, overrun, like mine, with a menagerie of stuffed animals.

Astonishingly, Paula's father knew the names of all the individual bears and camels and cats who made up his daughters' collections. He remembered which coats and hats and blankets pertained to each particular bear or dog, especially those that belonged to Paula's oldest teddy, "Tiggy," whose garments were all in a shade described by every member of the family – including her father – as "Tiggy Blue."

Imagine having a father like Paula's or Judy's, I thought. But I couldn't. Fathers like mine weren't on-site to tease or entertain or enter into the realm of our imaginations. Fathers like mine were there to criticize, to judge, to hold their approval in abeyance.

The price that fathers like mine paid for their authority, however, was high. In a good mood, my dad would banter with my friends, but badly. In a dark mood, he ignored them, or upbraided me for my failings as if they weren't there. In none of that was he different from most of the other dads I knew: autocratic strangers in their own homes.

Occasionally, our dad seemed to sense his exclusion, and would react to my mother and brother and me with irritated bafflement, like a bear rousted unceremoniously from a campsite and sent shuffling back into the woods, bewildered and still hungry. At those times, he'd retreat behind the barrier of his evening paper, or into contemplation of his tired salesman's feet.

"Oh, my aching dogs," he'd groan, Willy Loman-like, in an unintended reproach to those of us whose day consisted of far less unremitting toil.

Yet he took a peculiar pride in his work. It was evident whenever we children got the chance to stop in with our mother at the men's store where he worked for a ride home at closing time.

Ware's Limited was serious clothes only – suits, slacks, sports jackets, and coats. No shirts, no socks, nothing in the line dismissed by my father as "haberdashery." The store was a long, old-fashioned, heavily panelled place with big round wooden racks of suits and an endless linoleum floor, kept swept and shone by the caretaker, Mr. Murdoch.

Mr. Murdoch had a little smooth fox terrier named Sporty, who lived for the moments when her master would shy his ring of keys the entire length of that floor. Skidding and clattering along the linoleum, she would take off after the keys, pounce on them, ˌhake them like a rat, and return them triumphantly to Mr. Murdoch's hand – or to mine, whenever I was lucky enough to be allowed to throw them.

Apart from Sporty, the store was a man's world entirely. A sober world of dull-coloured, apparently identical suits, rack upon rack, and a silent tailor kneeling with a mouthful of pins to mark an alteration to a pantcuff or seam. As well as the small band of salesmen – Mr. Lipsett, Mr. Hoskins, and my father – hovering attendance on the customer with an air of quiet purpose appropriate to the gravity of such an important purchase.

With particularly favoured clients, my father would exhibit a heartiness and a joviality in marked contrast to the weary self he dragged home each night. Smoothing a shoulder line, or pinching a lapel between his fingers, he seemed another man, utterly in his mercantile element.

It was, in some ways, a lie. A kind of fiction of professional status that my dad felt forced to invent for himself after all his youthful ambitions had collapsed. A bright student – brilliant, perhaps – he'd graduated from the local college with a B.A. at age eighteen. Then dreamed of taking up a scholarship offered by Fordham University in New York – New York! – to study law.

The Drought, however, reigned over the West, and the Great

Depression had the entire Western world in its grip. There simply was no money to cover his expenses. Therefore, at what must have been roughly the same moment that my mother was arriving by car to face the dust-blown Prairies, my father was facing the hard truth that he'd likely never leave them behind.

Shelving the dream of a career in the law, he found a job — when jobs were few — driving a paint truck for five dollars a week. His meagre salary was doled out among his out-of-work father, a raft of younger siblings, and a mother whose reason had snapped under the weight of financial woe. Not for nothing, it seemed to me as a child listening to this oft-told story, was that period recalled as The Great Depression.

Unlike my mother, my father told the tale of his early life openly at the dinner table. A cautionary tale, designed to warn us from a tender age about the tricks that Life could play, even on — especially on — the clever and the deserving. No point in expecting things to turn out for the best, our father seemed to be saying. Not when Life had such a knack for putting you in your place, cutting off your aspirations at the knees, arranging for a fall to follow your pride, however justifiable.

I'd squirm in anxiety to hear the dire predictions of another Depression in the offing, worse even than the Dirty Thirties. Grasshoppers would come again in their millions, my dad suggested, blown in on roiling brown clouds of dust. Any day now, our family would find ourselves with only bread and homemade jam for dinner, just like my dad and his family, back in the Drought, through no fault of their own.

It was impossible to calculate the depth of my father's losses. Ambition, optimism, any genuine capacity for joy — losses that only deepened with the passage of years. In my childhood, he feigned success in his role as a menswear store manager, and bragged about the status of the customers he waited on. But as I got older, the bitterness of his lot became more obvious. The more his "dogs" ached, the more frequently he referred to the once-revered customers as "pigs," and railed against their boorishness, their stupidity, their lack of class. By the time I was well into high school, he had begun drinking rye with his morning orange juice to ease the pain of his job's servility, as well as his agonized discovery that my mother had been having an affair.

Later, once I'd reached the end of Grade Twelve, and had won a scholarship to McGill, my father's reaction was more petulant than pleased. He mused aloud that I'd be better off living at home, perhaps forgoing university altogether, and parlaying my summer job writing TV ad copy into a full-time career. At first, I couldn't believe I'd heard him correctly. Only that September, on the train heading east, did it occur to me I was embarking upon the very journey once denied to him.

If my father realized it too, he did not acknowledge the parallel. If he had, we'd both have been better off. But facing the fact that, at some level, he secretly begrudged me admission to a wider world might have been too hurtful for him. Certainly, after his initial discouragement of my university career, he did what he could to support it – in the form of a five-dollar postal order, filled out in his own rigidly upright printing, and mailed to me in residence once a week. Not much money in the mid-1960s, five dollars a week, but it was all he could spare, and I knew it. And counted myself lucky not to have to support a large family on it, as he had once done.

In the months that I was away for the school term, some of the rawness between us got a chance to heal. Our letters and occasional phone calls were cordial, even warm. But from the moment I arrived home for Christmas, or to search for a summer job, some collision would inevitably occur, and set the tone for the rest of my stay.

On the Christmas break especially it got to a point where, from the instant I came through the door, my father would turn suddenly ill and betake himself to bed for the duration of my visit. Emerging only for meals, unshaven, in his pajamas and sullenly silent. Then, on the morning of my departure, he would stumble still pajama-clad and stubbly into his overcoat to drive me to the airport, despite my mother's insistence that she could take me herself.

"Now, don't you go and make me feel worse than I do," my dad would snap at her as he shuffled queasily down the walk, car keys in hand. "It's the flu and I can't help it if I've gone and spoiled her stay, can I? Least I can do is see her off."

Angry at being discussed in the third person, affronted by his behaviour over the course of my visit, and embarrassed by his unkempt, rheumy-eyed appearance out in public, I'd snap in return. "Dad, the point is, I make you sick. Literally. Don't you see that? The very sight of me turns your stomach, and an hour after I leave you'll start feeling better. Now, why can't you just come out and admit that?"

"Bullshit!" Looking sicker than ever, my dad would set his jaw, hunch behind the steering wheel and ignore me and my mother studiously the rest of the way to the airport.

But I wasn't wrong in my diagnosis. After arriving back in Montreal, I'd phone home to let my mother know the plane hadn't crashed. "How's Dad feeling?"

"Oh, much better. Started to perk up right after we dropped you off, naturally. Sweetheart, please don't take it personally. The man's cracked, that's all. Simply cracked."

Well, maybe. Still, throughout the course of my college career, either he or I would sporadically make some attempt at *rapprochement*. Inevitably, however, something would intervene to screw it up. At first, when I told him I was studying *Death of a Salesman* in my Modern Drama class, he waxed enthusiastic. "Terrific play. That Arthur Miller, he really understood how even a top-notch salesman can fall apart, once the world of retail turns to crap the way it has."

"No, no, Dad," I informed him loftily. "Willy Loman has the wrong dreams. He's never been cut out for that work. It's always been crap. It's just that he was seduced by the fantasy of noble salesmanship that never actually existed. That's Miller's point."

My father's lips hardened into a narrow, Teutonic line and his face closed against me. "Aw, what the hell would you know about selling and about dreams? What the hell would *you* know?"

Being in the know in a world of know-nothings was profoundly important to him. So much so that it was a constitutional requirement for him to be the person with the information, the person who dispensed opinions, pointed out landmarks, and took charge of explaining the fine print. It didn't matter whether someone else in the room might have more up-to-date information, or an equally legitimate yet opposing opinion, or closer knowledge of the locality in question, or greater claim to expertise in any particular area. My dad was the one who knew, even when the only source he could cite with authority was *Time* magazine. Questions answered by anyone else diminished him. Points of view out of sync with his were abhorrent, and any admission of ignorance or confusion was utterly out of the question.

Bursting with the callow pride of the recently educated, I was, in my way, no less insufferable. Somewhere inside, I understood that my father was filled with frustration at his lost opportunities. Yet I couldn't bring myself to cut him any slack. For his part, he must have understood it was not competition I was after, but commendation. And yet, he was congenitally incapable of offering me anything but argument. As incapable as I was of proffering him compassion.

And so we were rivals, my father and I. It was only toward the end of his life that I truly understood that, and it was only gradually that I came to appreciate why. Each of us believed that the other was bent on obtaining exclusive rights to my mother.

This competition over my mother had begun back in my midteens. Because my brother was away at university when my mother's infidelity came to light, it was I who was compelled to protect her from my father's jealous wrath. Later on, after I'd moved away from home, I made clear it was only my mother I wanted to come and visit me. On the rare occasions I flew home to see my parents, I would conspicuously contrive to get time in her company, away from my father.

Eventually, after my mother had become old and ill and increasingly addled, the struggle over her only intensified. Ailing himself, my father strove to hide the nature of her illness from my brother and me, for fear of losing her to our care. Whenever I'd turn up to visit, he'd treat me with hostility, like some intrusive stranger sent from an aid agency to perform an unwelcome intervention.

"What's that woman want?" he'd demand of my mother, indicating me with an impatient gesture. Physically unable to speak, my mother would shrug, big-eyed and childlike, as if suddenly unsure herself of my identity and purpose.

Before the true extent of her affliction became known to me, I would routinely beg my father, by phone or in person, to let me take my mother on a holiday, in New York or even Toronto – any place in her beloved "back East" that would allow her the pleasure of galleries and city streets denied to her in the small town they'd retired to. Anything to give us some time together, the two girls on the go that we'd always gloried in being together.

"Don't you worry," my dad would assure me bitterly. "I'll be dead soon. After that, you and your mother can have all the time you like with each other."

By that point, any vestige of civility that had ever existed between us was long since evaporated. "Oh, but you aren't going to die first," I'd tell him, with equal bitterness. "She will. And God, will I ever make you sorry for being such a bastard!"

My mother did die first. As I left my parents' condo after the funeral, I knew that I'd never see my father again. Not because I intended to make good my threat to make him sorry, but because I knew there was no way, for what was left of his life, my presence could ever be a comfort to him – or his to me.

The last recollections I have of him are vile, scorching messages left on my answering machine at odd hours. Curses against me for not being there when he called, angry accusations that I wanted nothing from him but his money.

Truth to tell, I didn't much want his money, either. What I'd wanted from him – back when I might arguably have wanted anything – was absolution from the guilt of having been born, evidently, to occupy the space he'd longed to occupy himself, the ability to pursue the dreams he'd been denied, and the opportunity to share with my mother the confidences she'd kept closed off from him.

Only once can I recall an unencumbered adventure shared with my father. We travelled together by train, just the two of us, from Regina to Edmonton to pick up a second-hand sports car my uncle had found for him in a classified ad. I was just sixteen; I'd never been on a train before, much less behind the wheel of a sports car.

On the way home from Edmonton, my dad let me drive. Not for long and not too fast, but long and fast enough to make me giddy with delight. Then – seeming genuinely happy for once – my dad drove the rest of the way. Very fast, and with the top down, so that the wind tore our hair, dried our smiling lips against our teeth, and ripped from our mouths whatever words we might have traded, back over our shoulders, to join the plume of exhaust trailing behind.

It was, as I think back on it, more the sort of experience a father might be expected to share with a son. But then, the rivalrous enmity between my dad and me always was more Oedipal than anything else.

Besides, a teenage girl on a road trip across a prairie landscape with her father . . . ? Given my legacy from my mother, no other single memory could be more fitting.

That we never, thereafter, managed to replicate the simple pleasure of that interlude goes to show how bred in the bone was our mutual mistrust. Yet the fact that we found any measure of happiness, however brief, out there together on the open road at least hints at something that might have been. I wonder whether – looking back on her own life with her own father – my mother could have claimed even that much.

EUSTACE TILLEY

MY FIRST FANTASIES about New York were devoid of men. Unless I count the scrappy stray male dog of indeterminate breed I expected to adopt as my sole companion, in that lonely but defiant future I'd begun predicting for myself while still in my early teens.

The dog's name would be Johnny Reb, and I could picture him and me observing a Christmas of sorts as I struggled to establish my life as a writer in a low-rent brownstone on the Lower East Side. A shaky sense of Manhattan geography and real estate permitted me to imagine overlooking Central Park from my single grimy tenement window, in order to note glumly the throngs of last-minute shoppers hurrying home with their treasures.

Not for Johnny Reb and me the glowing hearths to which those shoppers were undoubtedly headed; no present-laden festivities for us in the cheery company of family and friends. A bedraggled houseplant trimmed with balled-up scraps of aluminum foil was all I could envision in the way of a Christmas tree. Beans eaten cold from the can would have to serve as my seasonal feast. And if I allowed the possibility of a gift to enter my forlorn fantasy, it was in the form of a publisher's acceptance that might or might not arrive in my mailbox in time to inject a scintilla of celebration into my first Christmas spent scratching out a literary existence on the cold cobbles of a majestic but uncaring metropolis.

At least my grasp of the harshness of the writer's lot was somewhat realistic. Everything else I imagined about New York was borrowed in bits and pieces from the myriad of usual sources, ranging from O. Henry short stories, *Bells Are Ringing* and *West Side Story*, to the snooty profile of Eustace Tilley (whoever *he* might be) staring down his aristocratic monocle from the cover of *The New Yorker*, which I could never muster the nerve even to riffle on the newsstand, much less purchase.

Ironically, by the time I actually got the opportunity to visit New York, I no longer actively craved to. I was in my early twenties by then; I'd spent my university years in Montreal; I'd already had my little-lady-alone-in-the-big-city experience with Swinging London. And everything I'd heard about the Manhattan of the late 1960s smacked of dirt and violence and . . . well, smack.

After graduation, one of my best friends from McGill had found herself a job at the UN and an apartment in a four-storey walk-up in the West Village. When I went to visit her there, I was appalled at the grubbiness of the neighbourhood, the suffocating heat of the streets, and the astronomical rent she was paying for a dark, cramped studio space that could have fit with ease into one corner of the rambling, sunny apartment four of us had shared in Montreal for a fraction of the price.

There was, however, a kind of raffish charm abounding in the Village that even I, a snobbish anglophile, had to admit seemed unique. Downstairs, in a much more appealing apartment, lived a bona fide Big Apple character: a good-looking, darkly bearded hippie type called Paco, with a large, panting sheepdog and a cordial, if somewhat guarded, attitude toward his upstairs neighbour and her visiting friends from Canada.

Paco – who appeared disinclined to supply a surname – went so far as to invite us down for a beer and some conversation one sticky afternoon. While the beer was readily forthcoming, the personal information seemed stinting, vague, and deliberately doled out in small, unspecific portions. Even the sheepdog struck me as less forthright than others of his breed I'd met.

For all that, the dog acted friendly enough. As did the master – frankly curious, and bluntly knowing in a way I found myself thinking of as particularly American. Except, of course, for that air of deep internal mystery, which, I decided, must be characteristically New York.

Some months later – I forget how many – when crime writer Peter Maas brought out *Serpico*, I suddenly understood that my friend's neighbour in New York had been characteristically nothing, except, perhaps, undercover cop. For Paco, from his hippie beard to his Perry St. apartment, to his big shaggy dog, was a careful construct. Even the element of friendly, if wary, neighbourliness must have been part of the persona NYPD detective Frank Serpico had assembled for civilian purposes.

Some months after *that*, watching Al Pacino in the film version of *Serpico* was another curious experience. An actor, playing a real-life character, who had played at various roles for a living? While not, perhaps, characteristically New York, I thought, there was nonetheless something *exclusively* New York about that particular Byzantine interplay of life, art, and imitation all borrowing from one another.

Manhattan men, it seemed to me, were even more markedly adept than the women at coming on strong, like extras in some ongoing movie, determined to stand out from the background throng by impersonating Average Citizens with more gusto, verve, and irony than anybody else in the shot.

In the late Sixties, that meant tie-dyed street characters right out of *Hair*, T-shirted junkies with the shakes, and gap-toothed panhandlers grinning as they pedalled their life stories in exchange for a smoke. Despite the climate of peace-loving, free-form brotherhood that all of us desperately wanted to prevail, I recall a dark edge even to midtown Manhattan in those days. It put us visitors on alert, even as we high-fived fellow members of the Youth Culture wherever we encountered them.

My boyfriend – who, as an upstate New Yorker, fancied himself at least somewhat more savvy to the city than a born bumpkin like myself – exercised particular vigilance when out on those potentially mean Gotham streets. Once, during a bitterly cold interlude over Christmas, he set off without me on an expedition for new jeans. He returned several hours later, with not only jeans but a look of deep chagrin.

He'd purchased the pants, and shortly after leaving the store had been stopped on the street by a man asking for directions. After giving them, my boyfriend walked on. Then halted, instinctively, to pat his pocket. His wallet was missing.

On an impulse that was pure New York, he tore after the man he'd helped, collared him, and demanded his wallet back. In the face of hot denials, my boyfriend shook the man by the lapels. Still no wallet, but the angry stranger managed to wrench himself free and hurry off.

On a long shot, my boyfriend returned to the store where he'd bought the jeans. Sure enough. There, on the fitting-room bench, lay his wallet – right where he'd set it down while trying on various pants. No one had touched it in the fifteen or so minutes since. So much for Big Apple preparedness, and playing tougher in a world of tough men.

During the early 1970s – after my boyfriend became my husband and my husband became a draft dodger – I didn't get to New York as much. Not to the city, at any rate. My excursions south were mostly confined to appearances at my in-laws' in eastern New York State. My husband held stock in the family firm, but his decision on the draft precluded his personal attendance at their meetings, so it fell to me, as his wife, to transact what business there might be to transact.

Since my husband's parents both were dead, he was spared their likely views on his escape to Canada. But among his relatives remaining, there was no shortage of strong opinion on the subject of draft-dodging American men and the Canadian women who encouraged them.

His mother's side of the family particularly – working-class Italian Americans – boasted a brigade of battle-ready male cousins, who hadn't even waited to be drafted to do their bit in Nam. The American men I'd met before had been boys at a Canadian college in radical times. I was unprepared for the love-it-or-leave-it belligerence of Cousin Joey, a proud Marine who glared at me meaningfully when inquiring after the man I'd married, now seemingly cowering out of harm's way on the other side of that long undefended border.

Upstate New York was not, of course, New York at all. But it wasn't for another decade or so that I had occasion to spend time again in what true New Yorkers call "the city" – as though referring to the only organized human habitation for thousands of miles.

Manhattan of the 1980s seemed an entirely other place from the grubby, scruffy borough of the Age of Aquarius. The city streets formerly populated by Paco lookalikes in beads and gauzy Indian shirts now thronged with the real-life inspiration for Michael Douglas in *Wall Street* – sporting slick-backed hair, pastel-pale shirts, chalk-striped three-piece suits, and gleaming power-hungry faces. Young meaty men of the Me decade, holding up their corner of a dozen trendy, noisy midtown bars, and staring hard at each woman who entered, before passing their quick and definitive judgment.

Not the only sort of men in town, of course, but very much the men of the moment, just as the tie-dyed types of earlier times had defined the masculine personality of this island-state of Manhattan, whose very name conveys the essential maleness of its image and style. Even into the eighties, New York men, much more than the women, seemed to bear the burden of playing the part of Big Apple-ites, each one determined to take the biggest bite.

Americans, in general, have always struck me as members of a society more masculine than ours. With their emphasis on muscular domination, on individual rights, yet with that oddly contradictory insistence on adherence to accepted conventions, they make us Canadians by contrast appear conciliatory, communal, waffling – and downright female. In fact, you could say all Canucks are honorary women, while all Yanks are honorary men.

Male Manhattanites, with their overbearing ways and extravagant style, should be the most archetypally macho of all. And perhaps they would be, were there not that ameliorating influence of Jewishness at the Big Apple's core. All New York men – regardless of their hue, their religion, their sexual orientation – seem somehow Jewish to me. Bluff, yet self-mocking. Bristling with entitlement, but at the same time hoping to be cut some slack. Driven to succeed, and also hilarious in recounting their moments of failure.

That wonderful high humour of Manhattan men was much in evidence back in the eighties. During those days, a friend of mine striving to make it as an actress in New York gave me a good excuse to visit, and a better-than-average billet when I got there. As two aging girls-about-town, we found a sort of unhurried sociability in the Sheep Meadow in Central Park, where the overtanned and the under-attached came in droves to recline in the bright June sunshine and observe each other in the act of acting the part.

Amongst our blankets threaded the wisecracking regulars of the Park – those sprightly, sinewy, seemingly ageless men, both black and white, who trolled for discarded pop bottles to drop into bulging, giant transparent plastic sacks that bobbled behind them like half-collapsed hot-air balloons. As these men harvested bottles and cans for deposit, they kept up a running comic riff. Mocking us yuppies for our sybaritic suntanning ways, sparring with each other over coveted localities where the discards lay thick and rich, and altogether carrying on a kind of unending performance piece on the theme of summer in the City That Never Sleeps.

Similarly, employees in the huge Broadway houses seemed to see themselves as elements of the onstage action. "Come on, you people," I heard one exasperated young usher chide the patrons at the back of the Winter Garden theatre, where he was selling over-priced soft and hard drinks at the intermission. "Come on! You paid sixty bucks apiece for the tickets, forty bucks to the sitter, another thirty in parking and tolls, and a good eighty for dinner – and you're kvetching about four-fifty for a cup of Coke? Get real, people, get real!"

The people, it occurred to me, were real enough. It was the young man serving them who'd set out to be larger than life – and largely succeeded.

In the 1990s, I got another perspective on New Yorkers when I lived for a time in Westchester (nobody ever added "County"), a half hour on the train north of Manhattan. These affluent out-skirts were not New York, any more than the environs of Albany, where my in-laws had lived. But there was a *nearly* New York-quality to those commutation-conscious suburbs that occasionally convinced me I was standing just offstage of the main event.

For one thing, the men who rode the railcars of the Metro-North into the city every morning, and came back to the burbs every night, retained a kind of citified sheen, even as they hurried the family dog along treelined streets or briskly piloted a child's stroller toward the playground in the local park.

For me, confined to the suburbs by circumstance, it was impossible to imagine why anyone – especially a male Manhattanite – would voluntarily elect exile from the steaming pavement and close-knit buildings of the urban core, in favour of the paved parking lots and endless malls and kitschy ye olde storefronts of the 914.

After all, it wasn't that the pace of life in Westchester seemed so much slower. Suburbanites in New York still drove fast and aggressively down the leafy avenues; their hard, clattering accents assaulted the ear as vigorously out there in the open as they did back in the city. No one bothered to smile or greet a stranger on the main street of the quaint "village"-style town core.

Instead, there appeared to be a determined need to re-create the energy of Manhattan at every turn. Unhappy-looking newspaper delivery men gunned the motors of muffler-deprived cars and screeched around corners at four a.m. to get the *New York Times* to the doorsteps in plenty of time for the early commute back to the city from which the newspapers had originally come. The few decent dining places had lineups out the door, just like in midtown; the many undecent ones offered a level of inhospitality equal to anything available in the urban area, at equally appalling prices.

It was as if the suburbanites I encountered in the supermarket were simply city folk with some life sucked out. Among the many retirees, the women looked as hatchet-faced as Lillian Hellman in her desiccated later days. And their husbands resembled Alexander Haig, as he might have appeared when attired for golf – tanned and taut with tartan slacks and fringe-fronted white loafers.

In Westchester, I felt approximately as close to the real pulsing heart of New York as I'd felt back in Saskatchewan as a teenager, fantasizing about life as a writer in a four-floor walk-up, with no man in my life other than the stray dog I planned to adopt.

Yet, despite all that enticing male energy abroad in Manhattan, I have never quite got around to living there. Haven't, in fact, got any closer than a subscription to *The New Yorker*, guaranteeing a welcome weekly visit from that most Manhattan of men, Eustace Tilley – confidently aware of himself as the utter archetype of everything energetically, egotistically New York.

FORNICATORS

"I THINK MY MOTHER'S having an affair."

I uttered this sentence out of the blue and in the dark to my best friend, Ruth. We were fourteen, and Ruth was sleeping over in our family rumpus room, on our family fold-out couch.

Very little sleeping went on when Ruthie slept over. Side by side, by the hour, in the pitch blackness of my parents' basement, we would lie staring up into the darkness, sharing some of the less savoury aspects of our separate existences, with a candour denied to us in daylight.

It had been on a previous sleepover that I'd learned Ruth's father possessed a handgun – an item unheard of in Regina in those days. He had even menaced her mother with it one night when he came home drunk and particularly fed up with the way she spent her days smoking and staring into space on the living-room couch, instead of getting his supper on the table and keeping the refrigerator stocked with his indispensable Cokes.

Shocking as Ruth's revelations about her father had been, I'd made it a point to evince no surprise. It was not in the nature of our friendship to exclaim, to commiserate, to reach out in the dark and offer a sympathetic squeeze of the hand.

In fact, in all the time we knew each other, I can't recall a single instance of physical contact between us. Intense as it was, the relationship was all about being brisk, businesslike, cynical, creative, and sly, with nothing girlish or giggly allowed. Consequently, when I confided my suppositions about my mother, Ruth's reaction was exactly as cool as I knew it would be.

"Well, she's certainly attractive enough."

It was true. My mother was a very attractive woman. Beautiful, I'd venture to say, with her vivacious smile, trim but abundant little figure, and vividly snapping navy-blue eyes. The kind of woman, as Ruth implied, who *should* be having affairs.

I had no actual evidence that anything was going on. Nor any candidate to nominate as my mother's secret lover. All I had was the vague suspicion that those weekly trips to her sketch club provided the perfect cover for illicit encounters. I also had a fairly firm conviction that even someone as emphatic and engaged as my mother was capable of a complete counter life.

As it turned out, I was right. Though it was months after my revelation to Ruth that my mother's relationship came to light. And when it did, I was just as surprised as I would have been without any inkling in advance.

Like most couples of their time and in that place, my parents pursued a social life built around golf and bridge. The other couples with whom they shared these pursuits inevitably became their friends. In my parents' world – or so it seemed to me – real kinship did not seem to matter much, either in forging friendships or finding a partner for life. Similarity in material aspiration, in occupation, in recreation'. . . those were the building blocks upon which all adult relationships were constructed. My assumption – and my deep-seated fear – was that by their age, I'd become that way, too.

For the most part, my parents' golfing and bridge-playing partners formed an undifferentiated mass. The men were bluff and ruddy with thick fingers and thinning hair; the women were prosaic, often adenoidal, with a bulge of midriff below the belts of their straight-cut golf skirts. As a shy child, an unattractive child, I was mostly paid no attention, once I'd bobbed my head in embarrassed deference and scuttled quickly out of the room.

The exception to this rule was Cal Fyfe. Unlike the rest of my parents' friends, Cal was quiet and shy – like me. He was a small, slight man, but with muscular forearms like Gene Kelly, a deeply sun-creased face, and a kind of steady squint that made me think of a Man of the West, softly speaking his piece while holding his ground against all comers.

For some reason or other, Cal knew how to talk to me, and I found myself able to talk to him. In fact, I teased him, corrected his grade-school grammar – much to his apparent enjoyment – and put him into what he called "conniption fits" with my propensity for dispensing five-dollar words when nickel ones would do.

I liked just about everything about him. The way he included me in conversations with my mother and father; the way he'd drive me over to the Fyfe house, just to give me a chance to pat their ancient Dalmatian; the way he hired me – instead of some boy – to caddy for him. And the way he'd admonish the other men at the tee for using curse words in front of a little girl.

In fact, the only thing I didn't like about Cal was his wife, Betty. Betty was small and stubby, like a sharp-eyed hen, and as flatly practical as my mother was fanciful and fey. Plainly, Betty believed my mother put on airs. Nor did she care much for me, with my shy, hangdog manner that appeared to melt away by magic only when her husband came on the scene.

On Sunday mornings, my father and Cal were often in the same men's foursome. Then, on Sunday afternoons, the Fyfes and my parents all golfed together. On Tuesdays, which was Ladies' Day, Betty Fyfe and my mother frequently found themselves drawn to play together. And in the long off-season, the two couples played a round of Sunday-night bridge, alternating between the Fyfes' house and ours.

Whatever the season, in whatever context I encountered him, Cal always lit up when he saw me. Shy at school, belittled by boys, the despair of my father, utterly unappreciated by anybody but my mother and Ruth, I began to entertain ideas that Cal Fyfe saw past my external ungainliness to some inner beauty all my own.

One hot summer day, when I was out on the golf course, pulling his cart across the dried-up fairway, as cracked and hard as an old dinner-plate, Cal referred to me, offhandedly, as his "best girl." Best girl. I stopped dead in my tracks and felt suddenly light-headed, as if I would faint. Like the time I actually *had* fainted, on a blazingly hot last day of school when, in spite of the heat, they'd made us clean our desks with Lysol before letting us loose.

Best girl. The Fyfes had no daughters, only a son already out of school. In my mother's opinion, I was the little girl Cal had never had. Personally, I preferred the idea of myself as an alluring adolescent, to whom he was drawn by a love too daring to speak its name – especially in a town where *Lolita* was rumoured to be kept on a shelf in the library accessible only to borrowers over the age of eighteen.

More and more – or so it seemed to me – Cal craved our family's company, with an increasingly diffident Betty in tow. Like the summer Sunday afternoon my mother's birthday was celebrated out in our backyard. My mother had attempted a Tomato Soup Cake, from a recipe she'd been given by Betty, at golf.

It was one of those awful ersatz concoctions of those times: a confection that was supposed to taste like a spice cake, though it was actually made with soup. Much like the Mock Apple Pie described on the side of the Ritz Cracker box, created from crackers soaked in lemon juice, and not a single shred of apple. To my mind, the world I'd been born into was entirely too rife with such deceptions: piggy banks made from old Javex bottles and scraps of pink felt; dolls with crocheted skirts that covered up the telephone or a toilet-paper roll. Spice cakes made with Campbell's Cream of Tomato soup.

Not only did I disapprove of the cake itself, I was appalled by my mother's temerity in attempting one of Betty's recipes – with the intention of feeding it back to her. Betty was an extremely competent cook; meanwhile, in my mother's uncertain hands, the Tomato Soup Cake had emerged from the oven a puckered and shrunken thing, burnt at the rim and depressed in the middle. With anxious embarrassment, I sought to pave over its deficiencies with icing, and by decorating it with a legend breezy enough to be worthy of its subject.

"Life Begins at Forty-Four." Cal delightedly repeated the slogan I'd swoozled over the uneven surface of the cake with a frosting gun. He gave me one of his shy, conspiratorial smiles. "I bet you thought that up all by yourself. You're one smart girl."

"She is that," my mother agreed. "Far smarter than her poor benighted mother, at any rate." Unselfconsciously, my mother cut a sagging slice of cake for Betty, and handed it to her on a plate. "Betty, I'm afraid I've made a dismal fiasco of your recipe. By whatever alchemy the soup is supposed to transform itself into something spicy and spongy and substantial . . . well, let's just say I lack that magic touch."

But she didn't sound the least bit humble in confessing such a shortcoming. Nor did Betty look to be taken in. Not when my mother was saying, plainer than words, that any person who could turn out exemplary Tomato Soup Cake merely lacked the creativity to make it fail.

"Well, now," Betty replied. "You're artistic, that's all. Me, I couldn't draw a straight line with a ruler."

Funny, I thought, how non-artistic people always used that criterion to distinguish the Picassos from the paint-by-numbers crowd. Not that Betty sounded exactly envious of my mother's drafting skills. On the contrary, there was a tone of indictment in the word "artistic."

With a sudden, unerring instinct, I grasped not only the depth of Betty's dislike, but also the cause: Disapproval. In a world enamoured of my mother's beauty, her vivacity, her flirtatious charm, Betty Fyfe apparently prided herself on standing alone in quiet, unenvious condemnation of a woman she regarded as showy, as silly, as downright absurd.

My mother, I suspected, knew nothing of this. Nobody did – not even Cal, I was willing to bet. After all, could he really afford to plumb his wife's profounder feelings, and run the risk of finding out what she truly thought of the wife of the couple with whom they so frequently socialized? Especially when his ulterior motive in keeping company with my parents was so obviously connected to me.

It must have been several months later – in the fall, as I remember it – that I received the confirmation I'd been seeking of my secret, special status.

At my mother's insistence, I had come downtown to try on a dress she'd put aside for me at Simpson's, where she worked. In her unrealistic, overly optimistic way, she was forever picking out too-fashionably cut, adult-looking clothes that she felt would transform me into the stately beauty only she saw in her ugly, gangling daughter.

For me, these sessions in the dress department at Simpson's were a hideous ordeal, under the gimlet-eyed scrutiny of the other sales staff, who were plain and dumpy to a woman, and in awe of my mother's superior chic. Into the fitting room I'd go, clutching whatever unlikely dress my mother had chosen to effect the miracle cure. Only to re-emerge dismally unimproved, my white school bucks peeking out incongruously from beneath the too-long hem, and my blotched, blushing face protruding above the too-classic collar.

Invariably, my mother would clap her hands to her heart, in a transport of delight at the sight of newly transformed me. "Oh, it's wonderful, sweetheart!"

Behind her, the stolid row of salesladies evinced no such enthusiasm. Their collective expression remained dubious, skepticism tinged with sorrow at the hopeless depth of my pretty mother's delusion about her unlovely child.

The sight of those faces was enough to send me shrinking back into the fitting room to remove the dress as rapidly as I could. No amount of coaxing through the curtain would persuade me to let my mother wrap it up and bring it home for my father's inspection. My father was worse even than the Simpson's saleswomen when it came to letting his negative assessment show in his face.

On this occasion, I'd arrived at the Dress department quite late, so that by the time I reappeared from the fitting room dressed once more in my school tunic, my mother was already cashing up her till. As she counted out the bills and sorted the various denominations into separate flannelette bags, she smiled at me.

That was the essence of my mother; however disappointed she might be in me for refusing to grasp the lifeline she'd thrown in my direction, I knew the subject would not be mentioned again. That is, not until the next overly sophisticated, unlikely-looking dress arrived in a shipment to Simpson's, and I was again summoned downtown.

While my mother wrote up her day's receipts, I helped hurry our departure by burrowing beneath the counter for her purse and "street" shoes, which afforded relief after a long day in high heels. For some reason I can't now account for, I pulled open the drawstring mouth of the plastic bag that contained her shoes, and looked inside.

There, in with the shoes, I saw a little vial of perfume with a card attached. On the card, written in ballpoint in an unfamiliar hand, was the simple phrase: "To My Best Girl. XX Cal."

I felt a shock pass through me, and then the same sensation of dizziness I'd experienced that day out on the golf course when Cal had called me his best girl.

"Oh, drat you." It was my mother behind me, her tone light and bantering. I turned to her, still holding the perfume, card, and shoebag. She had her coat on, and the expression on her face was studiously unconcerned. "I wish you wouldn't snoop, Toad."

"Toad" had been my mother's most endearing nickname for me since infancy. Yet at this moment, the warmth that usually went with it was oddly absent. It wasn't that my mother had gone cold on me. It was more that she seemed like her detached saleslady self, courteously telling a customer not to handle the merchandise.

I didn't know what to say, and merely proffered the perfume and card to her.

"No, those are for *you*, sweetheart. Cal dropped them off, and asked me to leave them under your pillow."

I stood gaping at the casual way in which she'd delivered this life-altering news. Perfume? Real perfume, and a written declaration of Cal's ardour? Yet, here was my mother, treating this marvel as no extraordinary thing. Or simply so biased in my favour that she had merely taken this tribute as befitting her lovely Toad.

"I . . . I guess I better thank him," I managed at last. "When he and Betty come over."

"Well, maybe not," my mother said quickly. "You know how shy Cal is. He just wanted to drop something off for you, unobtrusively. Why don't you write him a note, and I'll see that he gets it?"

Looking back, I can't begin to fathom the depths of my adolescent credulity. Nor can I recall if Cal and I ever spoke directly about his gift. But I do remember that, for as long as he was in my life, I kept that little vial of scent and the card in my dresser drawer, buried among the tangled woolly caterpillars of school tights and balled-up socks. Periodically, I'd unscrew the tiny cap and take a whiff as I thought worshipfully of the man who regarded me as his best girl.

What form I might have expected any involvement with Cal to take, I have no idea. Sex was something I read about avidly but was too shy to talk about, even with Ruth. The movies she and I shared – costume dramas, Westerns, gangster films, and other assorted epics – tended to be long on romantic rivalry, but otherwise mercifully unspecific. When I'd told Ruth of my suspicions about my mother, I had included no details about what an "affair" might involve.

The perfume and accompanying card I kept secret from my best friend. When – more and more – the time I spent with my mother began to include Cal, I kept that secret too. Not just from Ruth, from everyone.

Certainly, that was the way my mother seemed to want it. For my fifteenth birthday, once I finally succeeded in wheedling her into letting me buy the puppy I'd longed for all my life, it was Cal who drove my mother and me out to the country, to answer an ad in the *Leader-Post* offering "farm collie pups" for sale.

Unlike my father, Cal was firmly in favour of the idea of a dog for me. I picked out one pansy-faced little puppy of dubious lineage from the litter, and all the way back home Cal kept turning his gaze from the highway to beam on us with quiet benevolence.

Despite my father's objections, Cal, I knew, would make it right, by laying out arguments in defence of a dog in that gentle-but-firm Man of the West way he had, which my father would find himself powerless to protest. Once we reached our house, however, Cal surprised me by letting us off at the curb, then abruptly driving off.

It was a Saturday afternoon; my father wouldn't be closing the store until six at the earliest. There were hours left to get the new dog installed, and plot the way to break the news to my dad. Somehow, I'd assumed Cal would be part of it.

"No," said my mother. "I'm afraid we're on our own. Incidentally, you won't mention to your father, will you, that Cal drove us out to the farm? I wouldn't want him blamed, somehow, for my decision to let you go ahead and get a dog."

Her tone was elaborately casual – just as it had been that day at Simpson's when she'd suggested we keep from Cal the fact that I'd stumbled on his surprise. This time, however, I must have registered a moment's suspiciousness, because she came back quickly – too quickly – with a further explanation. "Besides, you know what that Betty's like, sweetheart. If she finds out Cal spent his Saturday with us, instead of running her errands . . . well, you know as well as I do what she's like."

Yes, I knew. Once again, I found myself onside with my mother, a co-conspirator in concealment. A concealment of which I – once again – would be the main beneficiary. Without further hesitation, I agreed that Cal must be protected, at all costs, from the combined wrath of my father and his wife.

That wrath, however, did descend at last. When it did, it had nothing to do with perfume or puppies or me. The affair I'd suspected my mother of having was, of course, with Cal Fyfe. Something that I had perhaps known all the time, but simply could not afford to acknowledge.

"I don't understand," I told my mother, once our house had turned into a war zone, with my father alternately drinking, raging, sulking, and drinking some more. "Why is Dad so mad at everyone?"

"Not everyone, sweetheart. He's mad at me, and at Cal Fyfe. We . . . well, we've fallen in love with each other."

"How could he? How could he?" I pleaded.

"Oh, please don't blame Cal. It's just something that's happened . . ."

She had misunderstood the source of my consternation. It was what Cal had done to *me* that mattered, and what my mother had done by abetting my illusions.

"But . . . the perfume," I insisted. "And the way he always wanted me to caddy for him . . ."

The sudden pain in her indigo eyes made it clear she finally had some grasp of what she'd done. "Oh, Toad . . . Cal cares for you very much. I told you, he always wanted to have a little girl just like you."

For a moment, I couldn't decide which of them I was angrier with. Cal, for failing to prefer an ugly adolescent to her beautiful mother. Or my mother, for using my feelings for Cal as a way of hiding her own.

But then, all of a sudden, I wasn't angry at all. Only sorry for my mother, in her endless quest to convince me that I was attractive. Surely that had also been a motive, in passing off the perfume as meant for me – the need to assure me that I, not she, was Cal's "best girl." Even now, caught in an illicit adventure that clearly had brought her joy and flattered her vanity, here she was, attempting to give me some space in the picture, some acknowledgement in the credits that accompanied this tawdry family drama.

Tawdry was indeed the word for what befell over the next few months. My father's drunken raging in the night would waken me, gasping in fright, my heart pounding as I listened to him, down the hall, berating my mother hour after hour. He called her every name in the book, and some names that weren't in any book I'd ever read. He speculated, loudly and lewdly, on what it was she and Cal Fyfe had been up to on those stolen afternoons. He cursed her bitterly, along with Cal, for destroying his life, and wrecking his home, and forcing his children to see their mother for the whore she was.

My brother was not around to hear, through our parents' bedroom door, those nightly bulletins on the subject of our mother's whorishness. It was I alone who got to overhear the tortured accusations, the angry imprecations, the bitter sobs. With my covers pulled over my head despite the early summer heat, I struggled vainly not to hear, and endeavoured vainly to fall back asleep. It was departmental exam time, I whispered to myself fiercely in the dark; I had Algebra to write next morning; I needed my rest; I was too young to be subjected to such vile obscenities, and from my own father.

One night, the level of my father's fury escalated to the point where I could hear the sound of someone being slapped. Then, for the first time, the sound of my mother's voice, crying out my name. Without even thinking, I bounded out of bed and down the hall, and flung open my parents' bedroom door. The room was in total darkness, which perhaps gave me the courage to say what I had to say: "You touch her again, and I'll kill you! I swear I will!"

It was a line right out of the movies, but I felt that I meant every word. Silence succeeded, and suddenly appalled at my own audacity, I hurried back down the hall to my own room. A moment later, my pajama-clad parents came in to sit gravely on my bed. My mother's face was streaked with tears, and my father, ill-shaven, hung his head, bleary and ashamed.

"If you're mad," I sobbed at him, "why not go and call out Cal Fyfe, like a man? Instead of beating up on my mother?"

I don't remember what my father said to that. Nor how many more such nights there were over the next several months, when my sleep was punctuated by the sounds of battle, or by the sensation of being shaken awake by one hysterical parent or the other, demanding to know of me which of them I'd prefer to go with when they split up.

What I do remember is how much I regretted that they didn't split up.

Once the overt hostilities had died down, a long, grudging Cold War began, occasionally heated up by sudden outbursts from my father, who continued to drink heavily for years. More than once, I recall coming home from the Public Library of a winter's night to find my parents framed in the front window of our bungalow – the drapes, for some reason, were never drawn – in a tableau of Misery and Persecution, my mother cowering in the armchair, my father leaning over her, gesticulating angrily.

I can also recall how I stopped short of the front walk on those occasions, then turned back down the street, to wander the neighbourhood, despite the cold, while I worked up sufficient indifference to enter that sad, stricken house.

From my adult perspective, it's amazing to me how utterly and effectively the Fyfes disappeared from my parents' world. Never was another round of golf or hand of bridge played among those four formerly close friends. Nor did Betty and my mother ever seem to get drawn to make up part of the same foursome on Ladies' Day.

At the time, I couldn't imagine what Cal must have come up with to explain to his wife this sudden, startling shift in their social calendar. All I knew was that – apart from my father's nocturnal denunciations of his name – Cal Fyfe was gone from my mother's life, and from mine.

"Why didn't you and Cal just run off together?" I remember asking my mother bluntly, a few weeks after her affair had come to light.

"We talked about it," she sighed. "But neither of us could bear the idea of leaving our children."

The laws being what they were at the time, I have no doubt she would have lost custody of my brother and me. Still, I suspected my mother would have been more than ready to abandon her old life, had Cal been willing to abandon his. It was he, I think, who got cold feet.

Certainly, my mother, in the aftermath of her affair, seemed poised for flight – sitting on her suitcase, figuratively speaking, yet increasingly aware that she was waiting in vain. What went on in her head over the months – then years – that followed, I can only conjecture. Once the real furor died down, the subject of Cal Fyfe was never again raised between her and me for the rest of her life.

My father was a slightly different story. Cal's name never came into my conversations with him, either. Yet there were oblique references over the years to a like-mother-like-daughter pattern he feared would repeat itself.

When I begged to take my Grade Twelve at a public collegiate that offered better academic opportunities and more ambitious drama productions than my convent school could provide, my father forbade the switch, on the grounds that the bad blood I'd likely inherited from my formerly Protestant mother might bubble up in that secular environment.

For years to come, even after I'd been away to university, married, and divorced, my father would still draw his lips tight at any suspected taint of bad blood. A short story of mine that made mention of unsanctified sex. Trips undertaken with men to whom I wasn't married. An overall conviction on his part that my pastimes were perverse and my alliances unholy.

Bad blood or no bad blood, it does occur to me that there have been echoes at least of my mother's affair in my own adult self. And as cheated as I'd felt by the discovery of her secret, sexual life, there's no doubt I felt titillated by it too: the clandestine encounters; the platonic pose she and Cal were forced to adopt in the company of their spouses and other interested onlookers. The sheer, spiteful pleasure of fooling all of the people all of the time – at least for a while.

The fact that I'd been fooled too may have influenced the *modus operandi* of my own later career in connivance. I made a point not to know the wives of any of the men I occasionally borrowed; I truly wished them well in their marriages. Even so, in hoodwinking the world with the stealth of my adulterous encounters, I must have felt admitted at long last into that forbidden circle that had excluded me so long ago.

Of course, nobody sets out to get involved with married men – not even those of us with some inexplicable allegiance to the lover we think we lost to our mother in adolescence. In my case, it was a failing marriage of my own that prompted the need to take out what I told myself was merely "fuck insurance" – some kind of guarantee that, should I become unavoidably single again, I would have some reasonable expectation of my romantic marketability.

Accordingly, with teeth clenched but otherwise open to experience, I embarked on my first adulterous affair – with a friend of my husband's. "Like mother, like daughter," my father would no doubt have observed, had he been on hand to witness it.

Unlike mother, however, I encountered nothing real nor lasting nor even particularly pleasurable in my first illicit dalliance. The man I'd chosen for this mission, I'd assumed to be ideal, as crudely suggestive as I was shy and sexually sheltered. No need with a man like that to set my cap, or plot seduction with practised feminine wiles, or even worry whether he found me attractive. Not when he was forever rubbing himself up against my butt, and inviting me outright to sit on his face.

But the encounter produced little elation on either side. I arrived at our assignation scared stiff, drenched in flop-sweat and too much Muguet des Bois, with the aura of abandon I'd previously given off having absolutely abandoned me. We did perform the act, but grimly, and I must have been about as much fun to make love to as a tightly furled flag.

My next adventure in adultery was, by contrast, far more successful. As well, my motivation was sharper this time: a confession by my husband that he'd cheated on me while out of town. Now, I was no longer so much in search of fuck insurance as simple revenge for infidelities actually admitted.

When circumstances next took *me* out of town – to a playwriting colony in the Rockies – I went with every assurance to my husband of planning to honour our marriage vows better than he had, but with every undeclared intention of running amok. Only problem being, in a residence where we playwrights were separated by gender and housed three to a room, running amok required some cunning.

I'm sure those laid to rest in the town's graveyard must have already witnessed a fair number of nocturnal couplings by the time my partner in sepulchral sex and I came along that summer night. Even so, the enterprise had an air of unusual intrigue, something oddly romantic, about it. The kind of thing Tom Sawyer and Becky Thatcher might have got up to, had they been older and somewhat sleazier at the point that Mark Twain chose to commit them to paper.

With every expectation of imminent arrest for performing lewd acts on hallowed ground, we got as comfortable as we could under an enveloping tree, and proceeded as quietly as we could to contravene the laws of God and Man. If it's possible to feel simultaneously juvenile and jaded, that's how I remember feeling that night. A mature married woman of twenty-six, taking a teenage holiday from all common decency and common sense.

A one-night stand in the graveyard blossomed into a full-blown affair. Soon my new lover and I were begging and borrowing bedding-down time in quarters we knew might be available for an hour or two.

Needless to say, none of this unfolding adventure made its way into my telephone calls to my husband, back in Toronto. Marvelling at my own sang-froid, I listened to my voice telling him how much I missed him, and offering up highly edited accounts of all the new friends I'd made. It wasn't that I didn't think he could handle the truth; it was that I didn't believe he deserved to hear it. Not after the way he'd abused *my* trust for so many months.

But there was more to the oddly satisfying sensation of lying than mere righteous revenge. I relished the feeling in its own right – that sense of cool disparity between what I falsely said was so, and what I actually experienced in that private realm of perfidious, unsanctioned sex.

That must have been why they called it "adult-ery," I reasoned to myself as I cradled the phone. It was so damn adult, this business of saying one thing and meaning another.

Eventually, my husband got wind of my affair, and the terminal patient that was our union took another turn for the worse. Yet somehow, miraculously, clung to life, as the very ill are wont to do, and kept him and me at the bedside a while longer, misdiagnosing the death rattle of our marriage as a last gasp of hope.

Still, a new cynicism had entered our dealings with each other. Now, it was possible for him to come home late at night without bothering to offer any explanation, serene in the knowledge that I wouldn't bother to ask where he'd been. For me, it was possible to announce I was going out to Edmonton to the opening of a play of mine in the company of another man I'd only recently met, who could arrange a cheap triangle fare that would fly both of us on to San Francisco for next to nothing.

"Oh yes?" my husband demanded with a knowing smile. "You're going on a holiday with some guy just because he gets insider deals on the airlines, and I'm not supposed to mind?"

"There's nothing to mind," I said. "It's perfectly platonic. He's married, for God's sake."

"That's reassuring. Your boyfriend in the Rockies was married, wasn't he?"

"This is completely different. I mean this guy's *wife* booked the hotel for us in San Francisco. That's how above-board this is."

"Sure it is," my husband said, still smiling. "A perfectly above-board tryst with the husband of a couple who obviously believe in open marriage. Why can't you just admit it?"

"There's nothing to admit," I insisted. "And if his wife trusts us, why can't you?"

Once in Edmonton, my travelling companion escorted me to the opening of my play, a perfect gentleman. Still the perfect gentleman, he dropped me back at the friend's place where I was staying and promised to stop by the next morning in a cab to take us out to the airport.

During the flight to San Francisco, he continued to be a perfect gentleman, and a boon companion, busily poring over maps and brochures of the sights we wouldn't want to miss. We smiled, we talked, we toasted our trip with airline wine in cheap plastic tumblers. We were the epitome of platonically travelling pals.

At the hotel – the one booked by his wife – the bellhop took us and our bags up to the room. Only one room. He unlocked the door, and set down the luggage next to the bed. Only one bed.

As my platonic travelling pal paid him off, I stood by wordlessly, determined to believe that there'd been some mistake.

"Where's my room?" I asked inanely, once the bellhop was gone.

"Your room? What's the matter?"

I couldn't imagine he didn't know. "There's only one bed."

Something like realization had begun to dawn. My formerly boon companion looked embarrassed, even a little insulted. "I . . . well, that's the idea, isn't it? I mean, when you agreed to come on a trip with me –"

"Your wife booked the hotel, for God's sake! What was I supposed to assume?"

"That we have an open marriage. Jesus, don't *you*?"

I tried not to picture my husband observing me from the corner of the room, arms folded, smiling that knowing smile.

In the end, it seemed unappreciative not to go to bed with the guy, given the cheap plane tickets and the trouble his wife had taken to get us the room. But without the savour of forbidden fruit, the undertaking felt empty, almost mechanical. Besides, whatever ardour we might have mustered was quickly cooled by my partner's discovery of a small pebble-like lump in one of my breasts.

Oh God, I thought in a panic. This is what I get for committing adultery to be obliging.

With the lump between us, so to speak, even casual sex no longer felt like much of an option. Instead, we somewhat dutifully did all the touristy things we'd so joyously planned on the flight down.

As we strolled along Fisherman's Wharf, my companion tried to leaven the mood by pointing to some crates of shellfish on a dock. "Oh look – shall we bring home a case of crabs from our trip?"

Preoccupied with my lump and imminent death, I barely bothered to smile.

On our return to Toronto, we exchanged air kisses in the cab and promises to keep in touch. Frankly, I doubted he'd even bother calling to learn the fate of my breast. Which is why I was so startled only a few days later to hear his voice at the other end of the phone.

"How are you?" he said.

"Fine. It was just a cyst. Nice of you to call and –"

"Well, I'm afraid you're not going to stay fine."

"Pardon?"

"You remember that joke I made at Fisherman's Wharf?"

"Barely. Something about . . . clams?"

"Close. A case of crabs."

"Sorry, I still don't get it."

"You *will*. That's what I'm telling you."

It turned out that my travelling companion's marriage was even more open than I'd thought. The night he and I had stayed at our separate billets in Edmonton, he'd gone to bed with an old girl-friend, who'd since called him in a panic to say she'd developed pubic lice.

Now my erstwhile travelling companion had symptoms, and it seemed that any minute, so would I. Even worse, so would my husband – that is, assuming I'd slept with him upon my return.

Ulp. Well, of course I had. Why wouldn't I, in my jubilation at the news from the doctor's office that my deadly lump was only a cyst?

"Well, in that case, he's going to have to take the treatment, too."

"Treatment?" Sitting numbly on the arm of the couch, I listened to the voice of my one-time partner in uninspired adultery reel off a list of the things my husband and I would have to do. Including applying insecticidal lotion to our nether parts and laundering every single article of clothing and all towels and bed linen I'd sullied since arriving back home. A ticklish proposition, given the necessity of first admitting to my husband what I'd been concealing since my return: the fact that he'd been right from the outset.

The good news proved to be that – thanks to the timely warning – neither my husband nor I hatched out in crabs. The bad news was the sense of tawdry despair that, from that point forward, seemed to envelop the little that was left of our relationship.

It was not too long afterward that we gave up on ourselves as a couple, and embarked upon the long, tentative process of becoming friends.

With the end of married life came the technical cessation of my brief and largely unsuccessful career as an adulteress. But if the habit of having a husband of my own deserted me, the habit of having other women's husbands did not. On came the adulterers – out-of-towners, mostly, who showed up at scheduled intervals, like a fleet of aging buses pulling off the highway for a quick fill-up and a change of oil before carrying on down the line – to indulge my appetite for stolen moments, brief encounters, and heartfelt but non-heartbreaking departures.

To the extent that nobody fell in love, nobody left disappointed, and nobody let on to any innocent third party, I and my adulterers always managed to avoid the fate that befell my mother and Cal Fyfe so many years before. At the same time, the adulterers enabled me – as has no available man before or since – to embrace each encounter with abandon, knowing that there would be no upshot, no consequences, no second act.

And no second thoughts, either. On that, I like to think I and all my adulterers would agree with my mother and Cal: if we had it all to do over again, the fact that we *shouldn't* do it virtually guarantees that we would.

GOOD GUYS

I GUESS EVERY WOMAN has grown up knowing somebody like Annabelle – the self-styled "guy's gal" who has spent a lifetime building up old-fashioned macho men at the expense of their more progressive brethren and the sort of women who prefer them. To describe Annabelle as a "lifelong friend" of mine would be to err on the side of euphemism. Annabelle is more accurately identified as a fact of my life, inescapable as earache, and she has been since we were both about ten years old.

Even at that age, Annabelle was firmly set in her guy-glorifying ways, and already an avowed enemy of anything resembling sensitive New-Age values. "I *hate* good guys," Annabelle would scowl. "They're nothing but wimps."

"Wimp" was not a word in common currency back then. It may indeed have been Annabelle who coined it. Or, if not, she certainly went on to spend subsequent decades making it her own, with frequent and repeated use. Boys who liked art were wimps. Boys who treated girls with a modicum of regard were wimpier wimps. Boys who preferred practising the piccolo to playing with their Tonka trucks were worse than wimps; they were "girly."

And what kind of guys did Annabelle *not* dismiss as girly wimps, way back when? Why, bad boys, of course. The kind who gave each other wedgies in gym, grabbed girls in the playground to frisk them for bra straps, and got kicked out of Chemistry class for lighting their farts.

While the rest of us girls were anxiously paging ahead in *Anne of Green Gables*, hoping against hope that the red-headed heroine and Gilbert Blythe would fall in love, Annabelle was pointedly reading and rereading the passage in which Gilbert calls Anne "Carrots" and gets her into Dutch for breaking a slate over his head. When our Grade Eight class was taken to see *Ben-Hur*, Annabelle rooted for Messala to win the big chariot race. Then, during the term that *A Tale of Two Cities* was required reading, she made a deliberate sensation with her book report decrying Sydney Carton as a "loser" for taking the fall in place of "ultra-wimp" Charles Darnay.

It's not that Annabelle was a tomboy. Far from it. As far back as age ten, she was treating her long, lush hair with peroxide to make it even blonder, stuffing her mother's shoulder pads into her training bra to fill out her figure, and tracing her lipline with Chap Stick, in anticipation of the day that she'd be allowed into school wearing honest-to-God cosmetics. By the point at which the sort of bad boys she fancied would start to discover girls, Annabelle expected to be ready for them, in a sweater set that called attention to her artificially amplified curves, and with a come-hither smile firmly painted on her full, pink lips.

Even at that age, Annabelle strove to be as brainy as she was beauteous. But that did not mean that she strove to find her mental match in a man. By the time she and I got to junior high, Annabelle was already dating boys about to graduate from Grade Twelve – the kind of boys poised to take up athletic scholarships from second-rate American colleges that guaranteed passing grades to academic underachievers capable of passing little but a football or a hockey puck.

Annabelle was charmed by these dumb but physically formidable guys, the way other girls her age (like me) were charmed by big, brainless dogs, or beautiful, brawny horses. She expected nothing in the way of intelligence, sensitivity, or even acceptable table manners. All she wanted was to acknowledge men as the master race, and take pleasure in subjugating her superior intellect to their social and sexual dominance.

It might seem surprising that a woman such as the one I've described should bother to make the effort to carve out an independent career for herself – particularly a career as demanding as the one Annabelle eventually chose, in the field of archaeological anthropology. It was perhaps less surprising a choice if one considers both her prodigious intellect and the fact that her graduate studies were undertaken at a time when the first of the *Indiana Jones* movies had begun to lend archaeologists – particularly male archaeologists – a species of sexy cachet.

"Sensitive New-Age men? Spare me!" was the way Annabelle herself explained it, with an eloquent shudder. "But insensitive *Stone*-Age men? Now you're talking – or better yet, letting *him* do the talking, with a mastodon-bone club and a menacing snarl!"

The way Annabelle so obviously saw it, archaeological anthropology would be a vocation made in Heaven for someone of her inclinations. Not only would she be hobnobbing out in the field with the kind of take-no-prisoners men of action she had always preferred, she'd be ideally situated to advance her own lifelong convictions about the innate superiority of the male of the human species, by tracing him back to the very dawn of Time.

So, while I toiled quietly and unspectacularly in the Department of Women's Studies, Annabelle was making tsunami-size waves for herself over in Archaeology, thanks to a seemingly endless series of high-profile publications on the results of her research at various digs around the world. "Wearing the Pants in the Family of Man – It's in His Genes!" was the eye-grabbing title of an early abstract of hers, reprinted, not surprisingly, in the arch-conservative *National Review*. "Everything Neanderthal Is New Again," Annabelle averred, in a piece picked up by *Esquire* that advised modern men how to get in touch with their Inner Anthropoid by hunting for bargain outerwear on-line, and learning how to sear various kinds of roadkill over an open grill.

For some reason, the fact that Annabelle was beautiful, blond, curvaceous, and reflexively reactionary gave a kind of *gravitas* to what I and other feminists regarded as blatantly preposterous pronouncements on the primitive predilections of the human male. Next thing I knew, she was turning up on TV talk shows in a kicky khaki safari skirt to spar with the likes of Gloria Steinem and Barbara Ehrenreich on issues of manifest masculine destiny and female inferiority, brought into bold relief by Annabelle's antediluvian assertions.

Perhaps inevitably, as time went on, Annabelle's name became less and less associated with academic expeditions, and more and more identified with media-driven causes on the political Right, such as the rise of muscleman Arnold Schwarzenegger to gubernatorial greatness in California, as well as various crusades of moral-majority militants to turn back the tide of advances in women's rights. I became accustomed to tuning in my TV set to find Annabelle in black leather and biker boots outraging the women on *The View*, or cracking up the more conservative members of "The Capital Gang" on CNN, or bringing down the house on *The Late Show*, by innocently asking Homeland Security Secretary Tom Ridge whether his official duties included making the coffee and picking up the boss's dry cleaning.

It's entirely possible that Annabelle might have gone on like that indefinitely – expounding her way around the TV dial when she wasn't peddling her retrograde ravings in print form, with such syndicated offerings as "Caving In to the Caveman in Your Life," and "Farewell, the Rights of Woman" – had not an extraordinary opportunity presented itself to beckon her back into the academic realm. Whether you happen to be up on your archaeological anthropology or not, you no doubt recall the universal excitement not long ago that surrounded the sudden and controversial discovery of the remains of so-called Kennewimp Man – an approximately nine-thousand-year-old skeleton discovered in a dried-up West Coast river, along with assorted artifacts – which then went on to invert every assumption ever made about the original inhabitants of the North American continent.

The minute the word about Kennewimp Man was out, Annabelle was on the case, winging her way from New York, presumably to challenge the profile that was rapidly emerging of a species of prehistoric masculinity as unlike the popular stereotype of her beloved Stone Age Man as could readily be imagined. Perhaps most striking, in those initial reports about this unprecedented archaeological find, was the lack of evidence, offered by the remains of Kennewimp Man and his ossified accessories, of predation as a way of life in the American Northwest, ninety or so centuries back.

In fact, according to reports in the popular press, his bony form was discovered sporting not animal skins, but rather remnants of a T-shirt-like garment adorned with a faded stencil of a basket of nuts and berries, along with the slogan "I'd Rather Be Gathering." Even more significant, nothing resembling a spear or knife or any other sharp object was recovered in the vicinity, thus lending further support to the image of Kennewimp Man as gentle agrarian rather than mighty hunter. Indeed, the only implements found anywhere near the skeleton were a set of wire kitchen whisks, in surprisingly good condition, a lawn-bowling game missing only a few of its original pieces, and a small, scissor-like tool that scientists at the site speculated may well have served as a pair of primitive nose-hair clippers.

On someone like Annabelle, the effect of such revelations was cataclysmic. She arrived on the scene swinging, and immediately entered into the debate on the side of those skeptical of the authenticity of the extraordinary relics and the astounding level of cultural refinement they evidenced about our earliest ancestors.

"Where did this creature come from?" Annabelle demanded to know, in the first of a series of articles she sent back from the site. "How did he get here? How remotely likely could it be that such a seemingly amiable anthropoid could make his way across the hostile face of an unpopulated New World – and from what conceivable direction?"

The Bering Land Bridge, her introductory piece went on to point out, had been far too competently engineered for any prehistoric figure as frankly flaky as Kennewimp man to have played a part in its design or construction.

"As for any other means of arrival on our shores," Annabelle continued in her next paragraph, "I think we can effectively eliminate any postulations of an outrigger sailed here from Asia or Africa or the South Pacific.

"Can you imagine an early man who was as much of a *girly* man as this guy – had he even existed – setting out to sea in an open boat without sunblock? Much less having any notion of celestial navigation? Seriously. All studying the stars might have inspired in this neolithic no-hoper would be the idea of pasting Brad Pitt and Britney Spears into a sequined scrapbook."

Other elements of the scientific community were more willing to grapple with the implications, should Kennewimp Man's arrival pre-date all others. "If Kennewimp's culinary utensils are an indication," a team from the University of Ohio began their monograph, "making fire may have been less a benchmark in human development than the discovery of the first really top-notch vinaigrette."

Anthropologists from England went even farther in support of the idea of Kennewimp Man as something of a Stone-Age sophisticate. "Forget the wheel," the British team advised. "Here's one primitive male who clearly would not have cared one way or the other about leaving his rivals behind in the dust, in order to impress some cute cavegirl with his forward locomotion. Far more likely, he'd have poured his ingenuity into coming up with some passable dinner conversation, or the creation of the first Thank You note."

Gradually, the debate moved into the public realm and began to polarize, and finally to coalesce, into two opposing camps. In one corner, there were the proponents of the authenticity of Kennewimp Man – stay-at-home dads, members of various a cappella male choirs, fans of racquet sports and window-box gardening, and a support group called "Guys Who Cry," all demanding further research on the remains by New-Age-man-sensitive institutions, in order to establish unequivocally that Kennewimp Man was their kind of homo-habilic ancestor.

In the other corner, there were the traditional tough guys, including the U.S. Marine Corps, the Society of Stevedores, and numerous biker gangs, making common cause with monster-truck-rally organizers and wet-T-shirt contest promoters, all pressing for rapid reinterment of Kennewimp Man's remains, in order to preserve the image of the caveman as the kind of knuckle-dragging, beetle-browed carnivore from whom today's real men could continue to be proud to claim descent.

That, needless to say, was the faction Annabelle chose to champion. Unfortunately for her, not a single man in those retrograde ranks would tolerate a mere woman on their side of the debate. Her support was discredited almost as soon as it was proffered.

Poor Annabelle. Hostilely opposed by the pro-Kennewimp camp, arrogantly ignored by the sort of macho men she'd always supported. What was a girl to do? What *could* she do, once matters had been taken entirely out of her manicured hands?

As the chattering classes continued to be consumed by Kennewimp, Annabelle found it increasingly impossible to find a forum for herself, on any subject. One by one, her contracts with the various newspapers and magazines that had carried her columns were cancelled, or merely allowed to lapse. Bit by bit, her talk-show appearances, her panel performances, her invitations to serve up pancakes at prayer breakfasts and adjudicate beautiful-baby contests, all dried up. Little by little, and quite inexorably, Annabelle began to fade from the public arena. Until, at last, she quietly disappeared.

By now, most people, I would imagine, have forgotten Annabelle so effectively that they failed even to clock her passing. I, however, did notice her departure, and, I'm afraid, took a furtive sort of satisfaction in the demise of a once-formidable ideological foe. Such is the fleeting nature of celebrity, however, that I too eventually forgot all about the woman who had previously reigned so supreme.

Thus it was with something like a shock of recognition that I spotted Annabelle, not too long ago, emerging from a bookstore in my own neighbourhood. At least, I thought it must be Annabelle, though she had changed completely from the last time I'd glimpsed her, while channel surfing past one of her inevitable appearances on *Crossfire*. Now, her once lush, blond hair had gone entirely grey; she'd given up her brightly tinted contact lenses in favour of horn-rims; she'd traded in her trademark Jimmy Choo mile-high stilettos for a pair of scuffed sandals worn with bunchy work socks.

"Annabelle? It *is* you, isn't it?"

"Of course it is! How wonderful to see you! Really, what a treat, after all these years."

Amazingly, she actually did act as if it were a treat to see me. Even more amazingly, she didn't seem the slightest bit self-conscious to be caught dressed like an environmental activist on her way to picket a toxic swamp, instead of the glamorous guy's gal I'd always identified with pale-pink angora sweaters, tight leather skirts, and mascara-edged eyes glittering with male-worshipping zeal.

"What . . . are you doing with yourself nowadays, Annabelle?" I gestured to the bag of books hanging from her arm. "Some reading, I see."

"Reading. Yes, indeed." Annabelle continued to smile, wearing an expression of gentle contentment that seemed as foreign to the woman I'd once known as her grizzled grey ponytail and sensible shoes. "Rereading, actually. Catching up on some of the classics I must have missed, the first time around."

Still smiling, she opened up her bookbag, to show me the titles she'd acquired. *Ben-Hur. A Tale of Two Cities. Anne of Green Gables . . . .*

"My God," I said, as neutrally as I could. "Catching up is right. I can't remember when I last looked through any of these old chestnuts."

"Oh, you should," Annabelle urged me. "You really should. They have so much to tell us, even today. Especially this one – *Anne of Green Gables*. That Gilbert Blythe . . . well, I don't want to spoil the surprise, but he turns out to be such a good guy, in the end!"

Heroes

THE PREQUEL TO THE fascination my best friend Ruth and I had for gangsters was an equal and equally unshakeable attraction to good guys. A commodity in short supply, however, in our young lives, where the male realm seemed populated solely by jeering schoolboys, irascible fathers, and sententious clerics. When in search of heroes, we were obliged to go where women have headed since time immemorial: to the world of fantasy. Which, in our case, meant the movies.

It was a journey each of us had made independently, long before we met. To our budding friendship, Ruth brought her already well-developed allegiance to Gregory Peck, while my contribution was an enduring crush on Roger Moore – pre-007, I hasten to say, and known to me only as the co-star of a completely forgotten film of the late fifties called *The Miracle*.

Gregory Peck, on the other hand, was a bona fide leading man, with an endless string of worthwhile hits to his credit, and an air of unflappable decency that contrasted oddly with the raffish and somewhat immature charms of the young Mr. Moore. In fact, discussing the very different attributes of these individual idols was an early aspect of my alliance with Ruth, and an activity that kept us up all night whispering during our sleepovers, or passing impassioned notes in Algebra class.

Gregory Peck – or "Gug," as Ruth liked to refer to him, in wry parody of Hollywood's gushy mock-intimacy – served as the admirable father figure neither of us felt we had in our own lives. Brave, yet self-effacing. Solid, without being stolid. And good-looking in a manly, rough-hewn way that missed, mercifully, the woodenness that characterized many other similarly sculpted male movie stars of the period. Meanwhile, Roger Moore – suffering stagily as a Napoleonic-era soldier in *The Miracle* – was pretty and British and sweetly self-satisfied, like some swoonily handsome exchange student sent over to spruce up the rowing team.

Much of my devotion to Roger Moore resided in the fact that I believed I'd discovered him. Even at the time, *The Miracle* was nothing anybody might regard as special – just a run-of-the-mill costume drama with mawkishly religious overtones. The kind of movie, in other words, tailor-made for a twelve-year-old girl to fall in love with, especially when Roger Moore in a red uniform got nursed back to health from his battlefield wound by a novice nun in a Spanish convent.

Forget that the novice was hilariously portrayed by Carroll Baker, of *Baby Doll* fame, in a wig of blue-black hair, her exceedingly modern American twang wildly out of place in Spain, and her pouting sweater-girl style in puzzling contrast to her immaculate Sister's habit. Forget, too, that the plot lurched uncertainly around the idea of some celestial curse visited upon any luckless male who dared to fall in love with her.

And further forget that the reason so many luckless men even got to meet this cloistered character sprang from some divine deal struck between the nun and a statue of the Virgin Mary. A statue that agreed to take the novice's place in the convent so that the novice could wander all over war-torn Spain – in the guise of a castanet-clattering street singer called La Miraflores – pursued by the memory of that handsome British officer she'd lost her heart to, while nursing him back to health.

Apart from these best-forgotten elements, *The Miracle* was – at least in my estimation – one hell of a motion picture.

For one thing, it was great to see men dying of love. Boy, did they die. Like the brawny gypsy who taught the novice everything she needed to know about street-singing, and who wound up smitten with her. Then shortly afterward wound up more literally smitten, by a jealous gypsy brother who wanted the nun too.

Then, when La Miraflores sought to shift her luck in love by falling for a matador (now *there's* a nice, statistically safe occupation!), the matador was felled in the ring, just before he could go shopping for one to slip on her finger. Small wonder that by the time she managed to team up once more with the British soldier – right smack on the eve of Waterloo – she concluded that his, and history's, odds of a British victory would be improved *without* her support.

What could be better, when you're a disaffected twelve-year-old girl, than the idea of a beautiful woman who's desirable yet deadly? I particularly loved the scene in which, on the afternoon of the eve of Waterloo, La Miraflores and the soldier were sprawled under a tree, with sunshine dappled all around, as they planned their lives together now that she was no longer stuck with her religious vows.

Just then – as the dappled light reflected the red of his uniform on the nun-turned-zarzuela-singer's crinolined lap – she sat up, staring at her hands in horrified recollection of the blood of luckless lovers that had so recently been splattered there.

"Oh, Michael," she sobbed, struggling to her feet and away from the ruddy reflection of his uniform on her hands. "I can't marry you! I can't!"

Wow. There was cinematic self-sacrifice on a scale generally reserved, in those days at least, for male characters alone. More than four decades have passed since I've seen *The Miracle*, but the effect of that moment is still etched in my mind. Less of a tribute to the enduring power of Carroll Baker's acting, perhaps, than to my insistence on returning to see the film over and over again.

This was no small feat, given *The Miracle*'s comparative obscurity, even in its own day. Only once in a while, over the next couple of years, would it wander back into Regina, to play on some double bill at the Roxy, where most second-run – often second-rate – movies eventually wound up.

Whenever *The Miracle* came back to town, I'd sneak off after school – either on my own or with whatever best friend of the moment – to sit through it and whichever second feature I was forced to endure, until the theatre shut down for the night. Then I'd come home and lie to my mother about what I'd seen, substituting the name – and, if called-upon, the plot line – of some other film playing in the city. I could be quite inventive if required, confident that my mother was unlikely to catch me in a lie by heading off on her own to check out *Surprise Package* or *Operation Petticoat* for herself.

Interesting, that compulsion to conceal my mania for *The Miracle*. My mother was not the sort of parent who failed to sympathize with an adolescent crush. She, after all, had raised me on stories of her own early infatuation with Ramon Novarro, star of the silent version of *Ben-Hur* back in the twenties. My mother knew what it was to savour the cinematic moment, to fall in love with a film idol for no other reason than that his eyes snapped fire, or his smile gleamed, or his devil-may-care demeanour contrasted so compellingly with the colourless men the real world had to offer her.

Why, then, did my mother not extend that sympathy to my obsession with Roger Moore and *The Miracle*? Possibly because I'd neglected to make clear to her the extremely secular nature of my enthusiasm, despite the pointedly Catholic quality of the film's title. Raised Presbyterian but press-ganged into "converting" when she married my father, my mother was not likely to look with favour on any movie that extolled the virtues of the Church of Rome.

In fact, the hokey statue-swaps-places-with-footloose-novice theme was for me the least of *The Miracle*'s attributes. What I loved it for was the sheer physical beauty of Roger Moore – first found wincing in pain and delirious from his bullet wound, then bantering cheerfully from his sickbed with the ministering angel I only wished could have been *me* rather than classless Carroll Baker, and eventually glimpsed galloping across the rolling green of a Belgian battlefield, resplendent in red tunic, horsehair-crested helmet, and gold epaulettes.

Yet somehow I couldn't manage to convey all that, not even to my accepting and accessible mother. And so I ended up adding the thrill of subterfuge to the delicious pleasures afforded by the film itself.

By the time Ruth came into my life, toward the end of Grade Nine, I already had at least a half-dozen viewings of *The Miracle* under my belt. I'd even begun to keep track of my attendance by saving the little torn ticket stubs issued by movie theatres back then. A clear plastic barrette box served to house my modest collection, each stub inked with the date on which I'd seen the film, just in case I ever ran into Roger Moore and felt compelled to offer proof of my material contribution to his career.

Ruth was entirely respectful of my enthusiasm, when her turn came to accompany me on another devotional visit to the Roxy to see my favourite film. Tactfully, she refrained from making too many comparisons to the superior magnitude of Gregory Peck's cinematic *oeuvre*. Instead, she subtly opened my eyes to another movie that turned into a far more enduring addiction of mine: *The Big Country*, starring Gregory Peck and – of all people – that same Carroll Baker.

Only this time, it was okay to be contemptuous of Carroll Baker, who played a spoiled rancher's daughter, too obtuse to appreciate the depth of the man who'd come from the East to meet her father and learn her way of life. Oh, God, but she was shallow, and oh, God, but Gregory Peck was substantial as the estimable Jim McKay, sea captain, man of quiet humour – and even quieter honour.

The Big Country was made in 1958, but the character of Jim McKay anticipated the sensitive-yet-masculine New-Age male, slated to be hawked – and sometimes mocked – decades later. Here was a man who sought to satisfy his own standards, and no one else's.

In the brash, blustering world of the West, such self-effacement was immediately mistaken for wimpishness, and Gregory Peck spent a lot of the picture embarrassing his fiancée and her father by declining to conform publicly to their specifications for a real man. At the same time, he went about quietly behind the scenes, fighting the battles he chose for himself, taking only the audience along, in order to prove to us, time and again, that true manhood required no advertisement – and, in fact, demanded modesty as proof of its authenticity.

McKay refused to ride the resident bad-tempered bronco when the ranch hands pushed it as a test of his tenderfoot mettle. But later, witnessed only by us and by an incredulous old Mexican named Ramon, he grimly endured a dozen dusty ousters from the saddle by Old Thunder, before successfully keeping his seat on the horse – and then insisted that Ramon keep silent about the entire episode.

Taunted tirelessly by the ranch foreman – Charlton Heston at his surly, creepy best – Gregory Peck refused to rise to any bait. But at last, when there was nothing left to win or lose, he called the foreman out of his bunk late at night, and the two men slugged it out in a classic fist fight that lasted til dawn, and bettered them both. Again, the Easterner took care to let nobody else in on the challenge he'd faced and faced down.

Of all the other characters in the film, only Jean Simmons, as Miss Maragon, the oddly liberated single schoolmarm, was shrewd enough – and similarly maverick enough – to see through McKay's modesty to the courageous core within. Likewise, only McKay assayed the real feminine worth of Miss Maragon, who donned dungarees to paint an old ranch building, and who gleefully competed with the former sea captain to come up with tall tales of torture and atrocity awful enough to overwhelm his own.

All in all, *The Big Country* offered such a startlingly offbeat study of men and women in the Old West, that even now I find it hard to believe it could have come from the fusty 1950s. Unlike *The Miracle* – which has apparently, and perhaps mercifully, evaporated from the cinematic archives – *The Big Country* is still alive and well in video. Along with *Gone With the Wind* – another early and enduring obsession of mine – it still operates as an efficient way for me to assess the long-haul potential of any new man who comes into my life. Does he like animals? Is he amenable to opera? How favourably does he react to *The Big Country*?

Of course, for me and Ruth in the early Sixties, it took more than *The Big Country* or *The Miracle* or even *Gone With the Wind* to satisfy our constant craving for a world richer and more various than the pallid domain we were forced to inhabit on a day-to-day basis. To undertake the job of rescuing us from the square suburban yards, low-rise malls, and dowdy downtown streets that comprised Regina, Saskatchewan, in those days, a non-stop supply of heroes was required – costumed as cowboys or Civil War soldiers, or sailors on the HMS *Bounty*, depending on our predilection of the moment.

We subjected these heroes to the most rigorously critical analysis before allowing them to invade our dreams. And even after we'd let them in, we remained somewhat aloof from our infatuations, almost mocking of our own susceptibility to girlish emotion. Hence, Ruth's patronizing references to Gug, and my continual disparagement of the post-*Miracle* career path trod by Roger Moore.

But perhaps the harshest example of the skeptical scrutiny to which we subjected our chosen heroes was the treatment we accorded Robert Stack. Unlike Gregory Peck or Roger Moore, Mr. Stack was someone Ruth and I first warmed to together – in his most famous role, as Eliot Ness on TV's *The Untouchables*.

Neither of us could quite comprehend initially the source of this powerful new attraction. Robert Stack himself had never been anything special: a wooden, second-rank actor of the time, whose previous work we were aware of but did not admire. But there was something about the puritanical understatement of his Eliot Ness that we found appealing – a drab, incorruptible, married civil servant in a cheap suit, utterly at odds with the eligible Doctor Kildare, the charismatic cowboys, and the flashy Hawaiian private eyes who made up the male roster on most television series of the time.

Almost overnight, Ruth and I abandoned wide-screen costume dramas in favour of our obsession with Eliot Ness and the entire gangster era of the 1920s and 30s. With the utmost vigilance, we watched each and every episode of *The Untouchables*, and followed up our viewing with research sessions on the period at the local library. We were shocked by some of the liberties the series took with gangland history, but remained determined to believe in its overall integrity. We drafted episodes of our own and acted them out, alternating in the roles of Eliot Ness and the bad-bargirl-with-the-heart-of-gold who would try and inevitably fail to tempt the virtuous Mr. Ness from strict adherence to his marriage vows.

Somehow, even throughout this prolonged period of idealized devotion to law enforcement, we also managed to continue to exercise our critical faculties in endless analyses of what we termed "The Show." And we never relinquished our right to look askance at Robert Stack, the mere mortal privileged to portray the hallowed hero.

Only after Warner Brothers chose to cancel *The Untouchables* did we deign to reach out directly to Robert Stack – and even then just to offer him our formal condolences as fellow devotees of the federal agent we only half-humorously referred to as "the Great Man." The letter we wrote to Robert Stack was, in our view, a masterpiece of understatement and quiet decorum, in no way to be confused with gushy fan mail from two typical teens.

To make our intentions all the clearer, we elected not to mail it to him care of the studio address found in any fan magazine, but to his Bel Air home. We knew where Robert Stack lived, of course. Showing an investigative initiative we believed worthy of the Great Man himself, we'd looked him up in *Who's Who* at the public library, having learned from the movie magazines we so derided that he sprang from a family of the sort of socialites very likely to list themselves in that type of publication.

So professionally did we conduct our correspondence that you can imagine our angry embarrassment when, some months after mailing our courteous missive, we received a big envelope straight from the studio, containing two grinning autographed glossies of

Robert Stack, and a form letter with his signature, thanking us for being fans. Oh, the ignominy! Not a word of acknowledgement of the content of our note, not an inkling of understanding that it was out of allegiance to Eliot Ness and for no other reason that we'd felt motivated to get in touch.

Suffused in shame, we chucked the photos in the bottom of my closet, and tried to move on from the pain of losing the show we'd loved. But after Eliot Ness, there were no more idols of similar magnitude for Ruth and me.

Not long after, Ruth's father moved her to a new school, and next thing I knew, word began drifting over to mine that she was being spotted in the company of boys. I understood it was the end of an era. No matter how much women yearn for heroes to whom to offer their hearts, there eventually must come a time when the unfettered world of fantasy is no match for a match made on earth.

IMAGINARY MEN

A WONDERFUL MOMENT occurs in Oscar Wilde's *The Importance of Being Earnest*, when Cecily, one of two rival ingenues, reveals the diary she's kept of her burgeoning involvement with her imaginary fiancé, Ernest. Everything about their relationship is recorded therein, from the inevitable lovers' tiffs to the day that Ernest proposed.

The fact that Ernest's ethereal nature has required Cecily to buy her own engagement ring and install it on her finger herself in no way dampens her ardour. Indeed, his insubstantiality almost enhances him.

Since nothing about the man is solidly grounded, she is obliged to be extra definite on his behalf – about the strength of his convictions, the depth of his devotion, the breadth of his passion. And most of all, the incontrovertible importance of his name.

What's so wonderful about that element of the play is that Wilde has hit upon something central to the nature of fictional fixations: They *are* fixed, as opposed to flexible. No compromises allowed, none of the negotiations that are the necessary hallmarks of relationships undertaken in the real world. An imaginary lover is a very strictly defined lover, obliged to toe the mark, answer all expectations, and perform exactly as advertised. If not, he can be easily replaced by some other invented idol, in as little time as it takes to make the wish.

Women, of course, aren't the only ones who dream up dream lovers, and draw up stringent lists of their attributes. In fact, it's men who are more often accused of hopelessly unrealistic fantasies about what their partners ought to be like – sometimes to the detriment of forming actual attachments in the domain of flesh and blood.

Personally, I suspect there's little real difference between the sexes in the incidence of idealization. It's only that men and women indulge in their inventions for different reasons. For females, there is often an element of social necessity: Cecily needs a fiancé in her marriage-minded milieu. For a man, the need to concoct an imaginary mate may be more internally motivated, arising from personal loneliness and feelings of defeat.

Years ago, I worked briefly in London at a bookstore. One of my regular customers was a tweedy, sallow-looking man of about forty, very much the English archetype familiar from espionage novels about the lost, faceless sort of fellow who becomes a cipher clerk – or simply a cipher.

I can't remember this customer's name, though the name I gave myself at the time is clearly etched in my memory. I was at that age – and at that stage of my sojourn in Britain – where I had come to enjoy the idea of my anonymity so far from home, and longed to play with the possibility of passing myself off as whoever and whatever I felt like being at any given moment in time.

So that when the tweedy-looking man became a regular enough customer to dare to ask me my name, I told him it was Heather. And when my accent prompted him to ask me where in the States I was from, I said Chicago – a city to which I'd never been.

"Chi-caggo!" His sallow face lit up somewhat as he gave the "a" that puzzlingly flat inflection English people always seem to give it, apparently unaware that North Americans pronounce the name "Chi-cawgo."

"You've been there?" I inquired uncomfortably.

"Never. Never ventured outside the British Isles, in fact. Though I'm mad keen on all things American. Especially American women." He gave the slightest suggestion of a leer.

Ah. So that's why he kept coming into the shop on invented errands, and directing his requests to me rather than any of the other clerks: the ineffable allure of an American woman. I smiled my most grain-fed Midwest smile, and barely refrained from snapping my gum. "You ought to go there sometime, then."

"Yes?" His smile was tightly compressed, as though someone had passed over it with a steam iron. "Now, is that what you-all Yankees call an *in*-vite?"

It was as horrible a stab at an American accent as I'd heard, and by that point I'd been in England long enough to have heard plenty.

"Sure," I said with a shrug. "Go right ahead and drop over. It's a free country as they – as *we* – like to say."

This was, I could tell, as close to bantering as this rather colourless man had come in a while. He was eating it up, and very soon he'd feel emboldened to make his move. Sure enough. "Look, uh, Heather, if you're not otherwise occupied after work, perhaps you'd care to take in the picture show."

The picture show? Another misbegotten attempt at Americanism, I supposed. "Sorry, I'm busy." What self-respecting young woman, after all, would admit to being available on same-day notice on a Saturday night?

"Ah, busy." He nodded, as if the concept of being busy was something with which he had a definite, if distant, acquaintance-ship. "Well, some other time, p'raps."

Again I shrugged, unwilling to commit myself even so far as "perhaps." Although, I didn't feel entirely opposed to passing an hour or so with him. As Heather from Chicago, I believed myself to be oddly immune from awkward entanglements or time-wasting encounters. Everything was grist for my investigative mill. Looked at that way – Heather's way – there was no such thing as a boring man or a bad date.

Besides, in the case of this tweedy man with his tight little smile, I wasn't absolutely positive he was angling for a date in any conventional sense. Maybe all he really wanted was to spend some time in the company of a bona fide American – or, in my case, a bogus American confident of her ability to pose as a bona fide one, at least in the dusk with the light behind her.

It was some weeks, however, before I agreed to go out with him. And it was not really "out" he was inviting me, but "round for a meal." Curious, I thought, how the English insisted on referring to dinner as a "meal." Making it sound like something flavourless and rather granular in texture, consumed for no other purpose than grim sustenance. Which, given the consistency and quality of most British cooking back then, was truthful if not entirely enticing.

"Round for a meal" meant, of course, venturing onto his home turf. I wasn't too worried about that, though – at least, Heather wasn't. Because in extending his invitation, the tweedy little man had alluded to a woman friend from next door who was a "bang-up" cook and also apparently eager to spend an evening with a shop clerk who hailed from faraway Chi-caggo.

Accordingly, the following Saturday evening after work found me walking with the tweedy man what seemed a considerable distance from the bookshop to his flat, located in an area of central London utterly unfamiliar to me. "Down-at-heel" described the neighbourhood, and downright "ramshackle" would be the word for his shabby little flat in a sad-eyed house that boasted, believe it or not, no indoor plumbing.

Heather, for one, certainly couldn't believe it. An actual out-house in the back garden, right there in the middle of a huge metropolis. It was wintertime into the bargain – far too cold to be scuttling down a drafty back passage, away from the stifling heat of the lounge and its coal fireplace and out into the yard, to pick my way in the dark across frosted foliage to a dilapidated biffy, as primitive as anything I'd ever encountered in the back-woods of Canada.

But even the overly cozy little warren of an apartment and the indignity of its outdoor privy paled into insignificance beside my realization of the vast importance attached to my arrival by the flat's sole occupant. This was no casual supper I'd stopped round for, to share with him and his culinarily gifted neighbour. This was a major affair catered by the bang-up chef, who ferried a suc-cession of dishes she'd prepared from her own flat to his, like someone engaged for the night to cook, serve, and then wash up and leave the lovebirds to their dinner *à deux.*

I had never felt so discomfited in my life. I quite liked the neigh-bour – a shy, smiling woman in early middle age – and would infinitely have preferred to spend the evening with her rather than my nervously proprietary host, who hovered over each hot dish as it arrived, and waited pointedly for his friend to make each tactful exit. And the hopeful way the shy female neighbour beamed upon me only underscored my embarrassment at being taken for someone desperate enough to be interested in a man she clearly wasn't desperate enough to be interested in herself.

I can barely recall the meal, bang-up though it may well have been. All I could think of, as I struggled through each newly pre-sented course, was what on earth I could expect to happen once we'd eventually reached the "sweet." To bolt immediately after dinner seemed unthinkably rude, even for an American – not to mention humiliating to the host. On the other hand, repairing to the cramped little lounge, with its stiff and shabby-looking furni-ture, loomed as an even less attractive prospect.

In the end, I settled on the plan of staying for a minimally courteous hour, before pleading a headache, an early-morning church commitment, a sudden attack of allergies, or whatever else might strike me on the spur of the moment as a plausible preface to a speedy exit. With the consolation of a course of action to buoy me, I headed grimly for the most severe-looking and least inviting chair, as far away as I could get from the soporific heat of the fire.

But it didn't really matter what plan I'd concocted; my host was clearly beside himself with the excitement of having a real live woman in his home. A woman other than his obliging neighbour, that is, and an American woman to boot. Before I could properly protest, I found myself steered toward a distinctly undersized couch – and then crowded up against the arm as he sank down beside me, flushed either with the heat of the moment or the radiant warmth of the fire.

But instead of unwelcome advances, what he seemed intent on bombarding me with were maps. City maps of New York, Los Angeles, New Orleans, Miami, Houston – and, of course, Chicago.

"Michigan Avenue, you see?" he demanded, as he indicated it with an eager finger. "And there's the lakeshore, and the famous Loop area, and the approximate site, I believe, of the Great Chicago Fire . . ." As his finger stabbed at each locality, he glanced from the map to me, seeking corroboration of his enthusiasm. "Oh, I've combed these streets, let me tell you, til I feel as though I'd walked them myself. Until, I dare say, I feel I know them as well as you do."

I dare say. "But why?" I asked. "What's so wonderful about Chicago? I mean, you live in *London*, for God's sake – one of the great cities of the world!"

"Oh, t'isn't only Chi-caggo I know like a book . . ." He gestured toward the stack of city maps, neatly folded on a nearby table. "Manhattan, the Hollywood Hills, the Mile High City, as they call it . . . I've studied them all."

For a terrified moment, I felt sure he intended to run through a detailed examination of each American city in succession. "But why not just go to those places?" I persisted, before he could pull the next map from the pile and begin to unfold it.

"Go?" He appeared impatient with the question. "I told you, I doubt I'll ever manage to do that in a literal sense." He glanced around the meagre confines of the room, as if to suggest it was indicative of his limited options.

At that moment, it occurred to me I had no idea what he did for a living. Something clerical, and therefore none too remunerative, was a safe supposition. After all, there was that loo out in back. "Yeah, the airfares are pretty onerous," I sympathized. "And then, there's accommodation to consider."

"Ah, yes." That wry, weary little smile again. "I couldn't very well come barging in on you in Chi-caggo, could I? Free country or not."

"I'm not *in* Chicago," I pointed out. "I'm in England. And so are you. With all these maps of cities you don't ever expect to visit. It's . . ."

"It's what?"

"Well, uh, original."

"Original!" He seemed to like that. "I'm glad you think so. It's an avocation, after all. Like learning about fighting ships, or collecting stamps, or making lists of birds one has spotted. You see, I'm a great reader of American novels – the hard-boiled kind, mostly. Chandler, Hammett, even a soupçon of Spillane *de temps en temps* . . . Then I immerse myself in the world they evoke. By reading guidebooks and poring over maps, and taking in American films at the picture show."

I wondered again if he genuinely believed Americans referred to the movies as the picture show, or if he was subtly sending up his own predilection for all things Yank.

"And, of course," he continued, moving ever closer to me on the couch, "by making a point of acquainting myself with the best American export of them all – the womenfolk."

This time, I knew he'd chosen "womenfolk" for its deliberate provocation. I saw my chance, and leapt up with an air of instantly acquired aggrievement. "Now, look, I'm not some . . . anthropological artifact you can examine, just because I'm American." In my annoyance, both feigned and authentic, I'd come to believe I *was* American.

"Oh, now look here, Heather, please don't misunderstand." He was on his feet as well, anxious not to cause offence. "I find you an extremely attractive young lady, regardless of nationality. All I'm trying to express –"

"I know what you're trying to express, and I'm afraid it's just 'not on,' as you people put it."

"But why not?" he asked ingenuously. "I mean, I merely want to get to know something about you, listen to you talk, find out more about your country, what it's like to wake up every morning as an American . . . that sort of thing."

"Yes? Well, if that's all, why not search out some American *guys*, invite them round for a meal, show them your maps, and listen to the funny way they talk?"

He sighed as he considered the prospect, then shook his head. "But you see, it's as I told you right at the outset: it's you American *women* I'm so keen on. It's you."

By "you," I understood, he did not mean me specifically, though I would certainly do. And as I snatched up my coat and purse, I couldn't tell which struck me as creepier – the idea of being the object of this shy little man's sexual desire, or being some platonic representation of American womanhood, to be approached, but strictly reverentially, as a pilgrim approaches the relics of a martyr? Creepy, though, however I looked at it. Hurrying down the stairs, I sensed rather than saw the neighbour's door open up a crack as she peeked out, presumably in some dismay, to note the early and hasty departure of the dinner guest for whom so much preparation had been undertaken.

I stifled the impulse to stop on my way out to explain myself to her. It was only once I was safely on the street that it occurred to me to wonder where in London I was. As I struck off in search of a tube station or a taxicab – whichever came first – I tried and failed not to picture the sad, shabby man in his sad, shabby flat, staring at his pile of neatly folded American maps, and puzzling at the great gap between the warm amiability of American women in imagination, and the cold asperity of American women in the flesh.

I believe it is, as I've said, more of a male thing to fantasize in that compensatory way, in order to overcome isolation and assuage loneliness. For women, an imaginary man fulfills more of a practical function – like someone's cousin enlisted as an escort for the prom. Only easier to dump, should something better happen along.

But it was some years after my misadventure with that man in London that it occurred to me I too might make up a mate, as required. The occasion was a package trip to Mexico. It was the first time I'd ever taken an all-inclusive sort of holiday, but I'd been working hard, nobody else I knew was free to travel, and I had neither time nor inclination to plan a full-fledged vacation. So I slammed down my money – including the much-reviled Single Supplement – and took my chances that the phrase "all-inclusive" might include one or other like-minded souls on arrival.

Instead, what I encountered was a bus entirely occupied by vacationing couples – honeymooners, many of them – jouncing along the miles of rutted roads that ran from the airport to the resort. Even the female holidaymakers who weren't with men appeared to be with other women.

As for the men travelling single, there wasn't one. Not unless I counted Victor, the Mexican tour representative who'd met our plane. But I didn't want to count Victor, with his shirt unbuttoned to reveal a bronzed but strangely pigmented chest, and that glint of opportunism in his opaque black eyes.

Purely because I was the only unattached woman on the bus, Victor made his way along the aisle – tacking expertly each time the bus swerved on a tight mountain turn – until he reached the seat behind me, where he settled himself, then leaned forward to rest his chin on the seatback beside mine. "My country, she is very beautiful, no?"

Well, maybe it wasn't quite *that* hoary a come-on, but damn close.

"You are your first time in Meh-heeco?"

"Yes, and you're right: It's very lovely here."

"Yes, much to see. I will show you."

Uh-oh. "Uh, actually, I'm kind of here to get some work done . . ."

"Yes?" Victor didn't look as though he believed me, and I couldn't blame him. Who books a week-long package holiday for any reason other than to collapse in a lounge chair, *cerveza* in hand, rising only to wade into the ocean, dive into the hotel pool, or amble over to the breakfast buffet for another helping of *huevos rancheros*?

By the time all we guests were assembled in the hotel lobby to hear about everything available at the resort – from hang-gliding lessons to car-rental arrangements – I was frantically figuring how to keep Victor from following me around for the rest of the week, inquiring at intervals about my affinity for the beauties of his native land. I was heartened to see him hovering attendance on another apparently single woman, younger and far prettier than myself, who must have arrived at the resort on an earlier bus but ended up at the same "get acquainted" session.

But then, abruptly, Victor was back at my side, throwing me meaningful looks and flashing his bare mottled pectorals in my direction, even as he handed around vouchers for one free drink apiece during Happy Hour. What had gone wrong in his courtship of the younger, prettier woman came clear when she took advantage of Victor's temporary preoccupation with some lost luggage to approach me.

"'Scuse me, but you're here by yourself too, right? I wondered if you might wanta team up to do stuff – you know, get a cab into the village, hit some hipper bars, get *real* Mexican food and whatever?"

"Sure," I said eagerly. "It's not the greatest place to be a woman alone, is it?"

"Yeah, my fiancé warned me about that. But shoot, the tickets were non-refundable and I decided to come, even if Jimmy – that's my fiancé – had to cover at work at the last minute."

Ah. Now I understood Victor's sudden defection, and equally sudden return to my side. And just as the absent Jimmy had served to protect his fiancée from Victor's unwanted attentions, so would she serve the same turn for me. Who knew? If I played my cards right, Victor might end up concluding she and I were lesbians, Jimmy or no Jimmy.

Even so, I couldn't help envying my new woman friend a little. A fiancé back home – both to act as a buffer and to put the seal of respectability on her temporary singlehood! Why hadn't I told Victor that my fiancé had been called to active military duty, or to Europe on business, or to his Eternal Reward, courtesy of a previously unsuspected heart condition? Anything to keep him from dogging my every step with his flat, intent stare and progressively less-buttoned shirt.

As it turned out, my new friend gave me impetus to get away from the resort compound and an excuse to get away from Victor for several evenings running. Then she went home, leaving me to ingratiate myself with the attached women in the hope of being asked to join them and their partners for drinks or dinner or both. One night, I espied another woman obviously by herself, and invited myself to sit down at her table.

"Oh, I'd like that!" she sighed gratefully. "I hate to eat alone, and my husband's sick as a dog upstairs."

"Sick?"

"Yes, the usual thing they warn you about. I told him not to order that salad in town. Victor told me our very first day: No fruits or uncooked vegetables, except here at the buffet. Don't you just love Victor? Isn't he the most wonderfully attentive young man?"

Isn't he just? "But that's awful, about your husband. Spending his vacation in bed!"

"It is, and it's awful for me, too, walking the beach by myself, going to town by myself, and eating my meals all alone. I told him I'd bring my meals up on a tray to keep him company, but even the sight or smell of food is more than he can bear. Well, you know how it is with these Mexican things."

I didn't, but I wanted to. Lucky woman, I thought, with her sick husband up there in the room to give her aloneness legitimacy. Why, a sick husband in the room was even better than a fiancé back home. In fact, for all anyone knew, there *was* no husband up in the room or any place else. The woman might very well have made him up – as a way of fending off Victor, or the pitying glances of other guests, or both.

Not that Victor would be easy to fool. He worked here after all, and no doubt had met the plane on which the woman and her now-ailing husband had arrived. But for the purpose at least of fooling other guests, who'd have no way of authenticating the existence of a husband they'd never laid eyes upon . . . ?

I left that thought alone for the rest of my stay in Mexico, but some years later, I took another solo junket to the tropics – this time eschewing the package deal in favour of taking my meals wherever I wanted. On the very first night, no sooner had I sat down at my table-for-one – predictably conspicuous among honeymooning couples – than a predatory waiter appeared.

"So, you like my country, yes?"

"Yes, so far it seems –"

"So far? Ah, you just arrive? So much to see! I be so glad to show you."

"Well, I'd –"

"Where you stay? I come take you dancing, after my shift."

"I'm sure that would be very nice, but I'm not sure my husband would like it."

"Husband? I . . . do not see him."

"You can. He's back at our hotel, sick as a dog. When you come to pick me up to go dancing, you can stop in and give him your regards."

The waiter surveyed me with the suspicious scowl of someone who'd had sick husbands sprung on him before. "So . . . you married. Where's your ring?"

"I lost it down the drain, not two days before we flew down here for our anniversary. Maybe it was an omen that we shouldn't be making this trip. Honestly, I was sick about it. And now my poor husband is just plain sick!"

Such was the compelling power of my narrative, that I actually felt sad about my lost wedding ring, our blighted vacation, and my sweating, groaning husband, back in our room. God, marriage was a wonderful thing – for better or for worse, for richer or for poorer, through sickness and in health. But especially in sickness.

"That is too bad," said the waiter flatly, and left without bothering to take my order.

As he disappeared, I marvelled at how much less substantial he'd turned out to be than my imaginary, yet highly palpable husband. Leaving me with a paradoxical piece of wisdom to ponder for all the years that lay ahead: How much easier it is to lie about a man who doesn't exist than to tell the truth to a man who does.

JUDE THE OBSCURE

SIMPLY BY DEFINITION, there are a whole lot of us who know how it feels to be part of a baby boom. In this case, that post-Second-World-War reproductive glut that has meant, for us Boomers, a lifetime of never being alone, any place – except, too often for our liking, in bed. And precisely because we are so numerous, every step of our overcrowded lives has been well-documented, whether in parents' home movies or on the cover of *Time* magazine in its Sixties' salute to the youth generation.

One way or another, we've remained in the spotlight, from kindergarten, where there were never enough slides and teeter-totters, to grade school, where some of us had our desks out in the hall. And even beyond, to university, where we arrived in such awful profusion that the principal or president, surveying the freshperson hordes overflowing that first assembly, invariably felt moved to toss aside his speech of welcome and scold the general multitude: "Look to the left of you; look to the right. Next fall, one of you isn't going to be here. In fact, you'd better *not* be, because we've got too damn many of you to graduate."

For female Boomers, travelling down the road of life as part of a mob scene has felt even more *de trop*. Why? Because, as more than 51 per cent of the population, women of that post-war generation are, inescapably, a majority of a majority, and have gone through their twenties, thirties, forties, and even fifties finding men as scarce on the ground as those swings back in the schoolyard.

"My God!" wail a bazillion women with but a single voice, "They can't all be gay!" No, ladies, not all. Just the good-looking, interesting ones went that way. And added to the insult to women of greater numbers at birth is the injury of living longer than their male contemporaries, thereby virtually guaranteeing they'll end up facing the final curtain as a solo act.

Men, meanwhile, can hardly be expected to feel flattered when they realize it's merely skewed statistics that have rendered them objects of such intense female interest – like a two-headed calf, let's say, remarkable for its rarity, rather than its intrinsic appeal. You're not likely to meet a man willing to concede that when it comes to getting lucky, he's merely lucky.

"Whaddaya mean, 'Where are all the good men?'" he'll demand, peevishly. "What am I here, chopped liver?" No, darling, not at all. And not to worry. Whatever kind of delicatessen meat you might resemble, rest assured you can be counted on to find *some* woman sufficiently statistically snookered to date you – well, at least once.

Unfortunately for Boomer-age women, the effect of this imbalance in the numbers is, to put it mildly, a diminished sense of specialness. Which, when you think about it, is a crying shame, since, for women, the desire to be regarded as special easily trumps the need to seem important. Instead of exulting in the strength of their numbers, women wind up feeling a dime a dozen.

"Done because we are too menny," was the text of the sad, succinct little suicide note scrawled by the eldest child in Thomas Hardy's *Jude the Obscure*. Having discerned his parents' plight in having too many mouths to feed, this preternaturally aged little boy hangs his siblings and then himself, leaving just one line of ill-spelled explanation that says it all. For the co-ed portion of the many overpopulated college classrooms of the 1960s and 70s in which the novels of Hardy were so closely considered, that poignant lament could have served as much as a comment on their social situation as on the financial concerns of Jude, Sue, and their abundant brood.

Another interesting side effect of women's sense of superfluity is the contradictory way in which they regard such men as *are* available. Women of the Boomer generation have an old-fashioned tendency to defer to men – as if men were dominant – yet at the same time to treat them as competitors in a thoroughly modern world, where nominal equality has at least done something to level the playing field, if not to even up the size of the two opposing squads.

In the previous generation, disparity in numbers didn't seem to be such a factor between the genders; nor did any issues of equality. Women of the 1940s and 50s seldom felt so compelled to compete with men. Not when they so clearly felt men to be their inferiors – kept in the merely titular role of "the stronger sex" by tacit agreement among the distaff ranks that the real power lay behind the throne.

I can remember, as a small child of the mid-Fifties, sitting under the kitchen table in some neighbour's house, listening to my mother and her peers at their morning *kaffeeklatsch*. The sharp, minky aroma of perked coffee mingled with cigarette smoke and the cottony smell of the fresh laundry the mums brought along to iron or mend. But even richer was the ripe, sardonic scent of their conversation.

"If those sissies had to have the babies," any one of the women would crack, "you can bet there'd be only one per family!"

A ripple of knowing laughter would follow – and, presumably, nods of assent all around the table. Down below, where my view was only of table legs and the women's thick calves in their pedal pushers, I had to make certain assumptions about the visual elements accompanying the conversation swirling above my head.

After a few more sallies at men's expense, followed by more snide chuckles of agreement, a brief silence would invariably ensue. And then, a sigh from some mother or another as she pushed her chair back from the table and rose. "Well, I best be gathering up and getting along. *He* expects his dinner hot on the table at noon sharp."

Murmurs of sober assent from the others, then a general scraping of chair legs, bundling up of laundry and assorted children – and the *kaffeeklatsch* was adjourned for another day. Men, it seemed, were laughable, but only up to a point – like the pea-brained but powerful masters in old Roman comedies. Our mothers, meanwhile, were cast as the clever slaves, rolling their eyes behind the backs of the mighty, and plotting busily behind the scenes. Until such time as the whip came down – whereupon it might become necessary to wheedle their way out of any serious punishment.

Such, at least, was the viewpoint from beneath the table. By the time I and all the other little girls of that generation grew up, there seemed no longer such a pressing need for women to bandy bold infield chatter among ourselves about the obvious inferiority of the sex that held the purse strings, the power, and all the cards. Now, much more of the loot had come up for grabs, making the competition for it – if not equal – at least more open.

Ours, however, was a transitional time, better equipped with open-ended questions than with definitive answers. Was it better to emulate men or to adulate them? Hard to say. While some young women of the sixties and seventies were making the case for following their male counterparts into the boardroom, others were still making plans to lead them into the bedroom, yet assuming leadership no place else.

Were men and women essentially the same, differentiated only in the unequal distribution of political strength and rate of birth? Or was there some innate difference between the sexes that somehow had contrived to keep women in a pristine state of moral superiority, which meanwhile – despite their greater numbers – helped continue to deprive them of the corrupting influence of power? Only two of many posers, to be argued by women long into the night, over cheap red wine and carbohydrate-laden snacks.

But perhaps the biggest conundrum of all for the Boomer generation – male and female alike – was this: How would it be possible for women to challenge men without scaring them off, and to gain men's respect without losing their admiration?

For their part, men mostly opted to shrug off the question with an apologetic grin. "Whooee, that's a tall order, all right. Sorry, gals. I mean, I'm sure you're entitled to be just as smart as us. Smarter, even. Only, whenever it happens . . . I don't know, I still wind up wondering where my balls went. Especially when the woman is, like, great-looking into the bargain? 'Course, maybe that's just me . . . Or maybe not."

Women, meanwhile, have found their own ingenious way around the age-old dilemma of how to suck and blow at the same time. What women in our culture have chosen to become is an oppressed minority – like people of colour, like the disabled, like – uh-oh. Except, wait a minute. Women are more than 50 per cent of the population, remember? Which means, of necessity, women in our culture must have chosen to become an oppressed *majority*. Quite a feat, especially in a society like ours, where the barriers most women still face are now almost entirely internal.

Think about it. Unlike the many places in this world where women are kept down specifically because they *are* women, the so-called First World is now largely populated by a privileged class of women compelled to take up the responsibility of oppressing *themselves*. Somewhat like self-cleaning ovens. "Never you mind," this large but self-effacing society of women in effect assures its men, "you're tired after a long day. Just rest. I'll oppress *myself*. Oh, and I'll press your pants while I'm at it."

It's a slick solution, when you think about it. Self-oppression not only helps keep large numbers of women away from the corridors of power, where we've always felt – and have always been made to feel – out of place, it allows us to continue to blame men for failing to encourage us to challenge their authority by swamping them with our superior numbers.

Men, meanwhile, have little idea what hit them. "Now wait a minute," they complain. "We gave you the vote, some seats in Parliament, including the odd Cabinet post, and the opportunity to do jail-time for insider trading, just like the rest of us. So what more do you want?"

Oh, not much. Women want to be important, but not at the expense of being special. They want to rejoice in their numbers, instead of lamenting how few men there are to go around. They want to point at some obstacle more significant than mere men as an explanation for their own continued failure to get what they want.

It's been exhausting for women of the overabundant Baby Boom generation to find reasons for the ongoing supremacy of a group so comparatively numerically insignificant as their male counterparts. On top of that, there's the effort involved in trying to figure out how to get a piece of that statistically limited action. Small wonder that, in recent years, women in search of men have found themselves resorting more and more to expedients left over from a far less liberated age.

Making Do is one such expedient, exemplified in my own experience by a woman I'll call Joanna. Joanna holds on to men she doesn't want, for fear of being caught without one for important occasions – like black-tie dinners, Christmas with her folks, and her own wedding.

Not that she's made it as far as the wedding phase. The trouble with Making Do like Joanna is that the man in question always *is* in question – constantly debated, doubted, discussed, and deplored. Until, eventually, he takes the hint and takes off. Whereupon, for the first and only time in the relationship, his stock rises so spectacularly in Joanna's eyes that she's suddenly convinced he must have been The One, against whom all future comers are to be judged and found wanting. At least, until such time as they, too, smarten up and start to walk away, thereby affording Joanna the opportunity, once again, to be reminded, regretfully, that men invariably look their best to her from the back.

Then, unlike Joanna, there are the women who go in for Holding Fast, come hell or high water. Another woman I know, named Kerri, has never quite let her poor fish off the hook, inadequate though she judges him to be. In fact, for what seems to her friends like forever, Kerri has been dating the same perfectly-nice-and-totally-wrong-for-her man, named Howard, while agonizing every step of the way over the prime time she's wasting on him.

Kerri loves to tour the galleries in search of small objects in porcelain; Howard's happiest at the bar, fishing pickled eggs out of a clouded jar. Kerri's lactose intolerant; Howard has all thirty-one Baskin-Robbins flavours memorized. The closest Kerri has ever come to involvement in athletics was once dating a man in a sports jacket. Howard, meanwhile, jogs religiously every evening of the year, except Superbowl Sunday.

Kerri is excitable, verbal, and staunchly committed to her psychoanalytic appointment three mornings a week. Howard is placid, accepting, and square – in other words, as utterly out of place in the closely considered universe that revolves around the woman he loves as a Barry Levinson character cast in a film by Woody Allen.

Yet he's too besotted with Kerri to give her up. While she's too terrified to toss away all those long, wrong years they've spent together.

And who can blame her, when the alternative is Soldiering On, lurching from one bad date to the next or – worse still – facing the fear of no dates at all? Life is often a barren affair in the barracks of the women who are Soldiering On, a constant balancing act as they seek to tread that elusive line between being too hard to get and too easy to forget.

One woman of my acquaintance, Amelia, assays the e-mails of men as assiduously as a prospector, in search of flirtatious meanings and promises of further parlay to come. Unfortunately – e-mails being as cryptically laconic as they are – Amelia strikes fool's gold all too often.

"Look!" she'll exclaim, producing another printout from her purse at dinner with a trusted female friend. "He's interested. He absolutely is, don't you think? How else do you account for that abbreviation for 'Indicating My Hopeless Obsession,' right above 'lk fwd to yr comments ASAP?'"

In the case of someone as eager as Amelia, it's hard to explain that e-mail is ripe with standard little acronyms like "IMHO" that have nothing to do with encrypted admissions of secret passion. And even in those cases where men *do* come on seductively strong in their e-mails, how do you make it clear to the Amelias of this world that e-mail embodies, to a generation of urgently sought men, what musk represents to a territorial tiger on the prowl: nothing more and nothing less than an effective way to disseminate a deeply intimate message through a highly impersonal medium?

Much to the confusion of women like my friend Amelia, e-mail has opened up opportunities in the arena of empty flirtation never before imagined by the mind of man – nor previously encompassed by the inboxes of unsuspecting female recipients. Women like Amelia seldom seem to realize how the comforting cover of e-mail serves to embolden some men to come up with come-ons online that they'd never ever commit to hard copy – nor even utter on voice mail.

Time and again has Amelia found herself falling for an amorous e-mail, only to end up out to dinner with its author who, in person, proves to be utterly out to lunch when it comes to making meaningful utterances for the record. Yet unable to abandon hope by abandoning her habit of grasping at straws, Amelia Soldiers On, in spite of all, misinterpreting the message "You've Got Mail" as "You've Got Male."

Last, and perhaps most confusing, on the list of tactics used by women to secure what they regard as their fair share of what feels like a perpetually short-staffed pool of men – is Stocking Up. I'm speaking here of women who hoard – which means, at any given time, keeping one or even more guys in reserve, just in case their main man should somehow drop off the map.

Needless to say, women who insist on exacerbating the Man Drain by Stocking Up drive the more allotment-minded women of their acquaintance nuts. "What do you mean Leona's setting you up with her cousin?" a good friend of the stockpiler will bleat with understandable indignation. "You've already got a boyfriend, remember? In fact, you've got *my* boyfriend. So why not let Leona set *me* up with the cousin, and we'll call it even?"

The sense of angry injustice most under-dated women express over Stocking Up and those who indulge in it is unmatched in the annals of indignation. Except, perhaps, by the wrath of any tall woman upon discovering that it's her teensiest female friend – the one who'd be dwarfed by a lawn jockey – who has managed to snag that new guy in the neighbourhood, nicknamed Stretch.

In either case, it's part of the same old story, as far as overly abundant Boomer-age women are concerned. And the name of that story is "Screwed by Statistics," in a world where the majority most certainly does not seem to rule. Or, if you're of a literary cast of mind, you could comfort yourself by retitling the story "Done Because We Are Too Menny," with a tip of the British bowler to Thomas Hardy, and the blind inequity that fuels the fates of the men and women who – in whatever equal or unequal proportions – populate the countryside of his nineteenth-century imagination.

KEN DOLLS

IT WAS BACK IN 1999 that this story begins, but the details are as clear as if it happened yesterday. Late at night, when I was on my way home from work, something prompted me to turn down a street I don't usually take and stop in for a drink at a place I'd never even noticed before.

A real hole-in-the-wall this bar was, where they apparently didn't care whom they served, because some of the clientele looked decidedly underage. Yet familiar. In one corner, I thought I spotted several Cabbage Patch dolls, although in the general darkness, it was hard to be sure. But the drinks they were giggling over were *not* Shirley Temples. That much I knew for certain.

Meanwhile, Tickle Me Elmo was becoming a little truculent with the barman, who'd evidently cut him off – and not, I sensed, for the first time. A family of Trolls took turns dangling each other by their hot pink hair from the mirror behind the bar, much to their own amusement, if nobody else's. Even My Little Pony was in evidence, lapping something out of a bucket that definitely did not smell like water.

My God, I exclaimed to myself. It's like an outtake from *Toy Story* in here, a place where all the forgotten toys have gone – in this case, to do some forgetting of their own.

No sooner had I formed the thought than I caught sight of a slim, attractive young man, somewhat vacant in expression and not even a foot tall, trying unsuccessfully to bend his moulded plastic elbow as he sat at the bar, belting back straight Scotch. Surely, it couldn't be. . . . And yet, I felt sickeningly sure that it was. Very tentatively, I approached and sat down beside him.

"Excuse me," I said. "But aren't you Ken? Barbie's boyfriend?"

Without turning his head (though it *was* movable) he continued to drink relentlessly. "I used to be."

"*Used* to be Ken?"

He attempted to twist his lips into a sardonic grimace, but as they were merely painted on, the effect was somewhat diminished. "That's right. Now I'm nobody. If you don't believe me, ask Barbie. Mind you, she may be too busy to answer. Seeing as this is her big day and all."

"What big –?" I started to ask, before recalling I had recently read a promotional piece about Barbie. "Oh, isn't today Barbie's . . . birthday or something?"

At that, Ken laughed. "Or something? That's rich. Barbie's fortieth birthday is only the media event of the century, that's all. This morning, she rang the opening bell at the New York Stock Exchange. All the traders wore vests of Barbie Pink in her honour. And she was togged out as Working Woman Barbie with laptop, cellphone, and CD-ROM, each sold separately. At this very moment, at the Waldorf Astoria hotel, there's a Barbie Ball going on, and the U.S. Postal Service has issued a Barbie stamp. Her birthday or something? I'll say."

As Ken recited this bitter catalogue of kudos to Barbie, a Betsy Wetsy doll close enough to overhear shed a real tear. I felt moved to sympathy myself. Who wouldn't be? A night of unparalleled triumph for his girlfriend, and yet where was Ken? Drowning his sorrows in an anonymous bar, lost and all alone.

"Not that I'm entirely alone," he continued, as though reading my unspoken thought. "Sometimes G.I. Joe drops by on his way home from the rifle range, or Raggedy Andy manages to shake his better half and stop in to hoist a few and reminisce about the good old days, when we boy toys were hot."

Hot? I couldn't speak to G.I. Joe, but God knows I'd never thought of *my* old Raggedy Andy doll as particularly hot. Nor had I thought of him much at all, except as an inescapable adjunct to Raggedy Anne – who was, after all, the main event, with her little appliquéd heart and its embroidered "I Love You" motto. Raggedy Anne had Raggedy Andy the way the Queen had Prince Philip: an official escort for public engagements who knew his place, a few paces behind.

Much, in fact, as Ken had always functioned in Barbie's life, for all of the thirty-eight years he'd known her by the time her forti-eth birthday rolled around, on that fateful March night in 1999, when I ran across him in a nameless bar, drinking regret and resentment to their bitter dregs. After all, by the age of forty, Barbie had already had something like seventy-five careers, from Astronaut Barbie, to Barbie the Dentist, to Medic Sergeant Barbie, to Barbie the Vet. Ken, meanwhile, had had . . . what? A camper van, some scuba-diving gear, tennis clothes, a Hawaiian shirt, and a few pairs of bathing trunks. Ken, in other words, had never been dressed for success – only for fun.

"Barbie may not get to make as many of her own choices as you think," I suggested. "For all you know, it's a marketing thing on Mattel's part, putting her forward as Working Woman Barbie on her birthday, all corporate and independent and –"

"And uncaring and cold and rich," Ken concluded. "I, mean-while, don't even have a decent place to live in." He gestured to the barkeep for another round. "You should see it; it's a shoebox."

Poor Ken. I could tell he meant it really *was* a shoebox. By contrast, it was impossible not to recall Barbie luxuriating in her very own Winnebago, or in a well-appointed poolside cabana, or in any of the many other glamorous dwellings she'd acquired over the past forty years.

Once again, even as the thought formed, Ken seemed able to intercept it. "So there it is: How could I ever expect a successful career type like Working Woman Barbie to lower her standards to the level of my current life?" As he ran his hands despairingly through his hair, I was at least glad for him that it was made of moulded painted plastic that could tolerate such treatment without looking disreputably tousled. Otherwise, though . . . not much uptick in being Ken, standing stiff-armed and rigid behind the same woman for so many years, only to wind up cast away in a shoebox at the bottom of some dark closet like a worn-out pair of Hush Puppies.

"She . . . she still might change her mind," I persisted, but without much conviction. "It's a woman's prerogative, after all. Even a working woman, like Barbie."

"Not a chance. Not at this stage. It's too late for her to settle down and slip into the background and let *me* be the breadwinner."

I saw his point. Breadwinner Ken? In all his incarnations over the years, what had he ever done, except to relax and smile, and lounge and smile, and play and . . . smile?

"Besides," he continued glumly, "if I know Mattel, they're already coming up with new versions of Barbie for her twilight years that'll also exclude me: Peri-menopausal Barbie, Elder Stateswoman Barbie, Raging Granny Barbie . . ."

What could I say to that? As I left him in the bar, droning on to whoever would listen, I reflected more intensely than I ever had before on the world of toys he came from – perhaps the only world in which dolls were so clearly favoured over guys that a dumb blond chick like Barbie could wind up feted on Wall Street while her discarded male companion bought rounds of drinks he probably couldn't afford for every other second banana fallen to obscurity from the top of the Toyland tree.

And yet, I further pondered all the long way home, why *should* poor Ken be perceived as such a laughable loser, instead of as a progressive prototype of self-assured New-Age masculinity? After all, the same egalitarian impulses that had brought Alan Alda and others of his gentle ilk into prominence in the Seventies and Eighties had undoubtedly inspired Mattel to keep Ken smilingly self-effacing in the background, while Barbie increasingly expressed her independence as a woman of travel, of adventure, and, eventually, of business. At the same time as life-sized men were being encouraged to cook, to clean, to commiserate, and to cry, ten-inch-tall Ken was playing the part of a similarly support-ive spouse, in whatever new domestic drama starred Barbie, her retinue of female associates, and her apparently endless parade of work or pleasure-related accoutrements, costumes, and cars.

By the time I was unlocking my front door, however, and preparing to head off to bed, I was beginning to look at the whole question of the benign Background Man in a slightly different light. Perhaps what had happened to Ken, on his miniature scale, was no different than the gradual decline and fall of the sensitive New-Age human guy from a revolutionary male role model in the 1970s and 80s to a contemptible wimp by century's end.

It was, after all, 1999. Who any longer respected men who could cry? The grunting, club-wielding hunter type seemed back in vogue – TV remote in one hand, can of brewski in the other, and an endless string of derisive cracks about his wife's shopaholic habits on his lips, to be dispensed at intervals between burps and guffaws and swigs of beer. Small wonder Barbie's real-life coun-terparts – similarly evolved from Malibu beach-bunnies into inde-pendent women of substance – had chosen, just as Barbie had, to go it alone, leaving behind the soft-centred Kens of their acquaintance as they walked onto Wall Street to face the bulls and the bears – and the boors – by themselves.

I felt sorry for Ken, I have to say. In fact, I may even have shed a furtive tear or two of my own for that small, broken vinyl figure on a bar stool I'd last seen drowning his he-man-sized sorrows with the other lost boy toys.

But as it turned out, I had kissed off Ken too quickly. For lo and behold, only a couple of years later, what did I discover in my e-mail inbox but an invitation issued by Mattel to an event head-lining him as the guest of honour? It was true. While the evening would also feature yet another unveiling of Barbie in yet another incarnation, this time she was slated to be a mere female sidekick to Ken – who was depicted on the invitation suavely decked out as Agent 007.

My God, I thought. Could it be that Ken, the perpetual second banana, has suddenly slipped one over on Emma Peel?

Yes, it apparently could. When I arrived at the event, there was Ken, holding court in satin lapels. It's no exaggeration to say he left the invited audience both shaken and stirred by the impression he made as the self-satisfied Bond. Barbie, meanwhile, deferentially held up the rear, while a garter held one of her inevitable cell-phones, right next to her stockinged thigh.

So much for Ken's dire, slightly drunken predictions of a life of continued second-string schlepper status. So much for my own tacit concurrence with his pessimistic view of himself as a guy doomed in a world where dolls held sway. What on earth had moved Mattel to promote shrinking-violet Ken at brash Barbie's expense? And yet . . . surely toy companies do their research. For all I know, recent surveys of pre-selected preteen Barbie-doll fans have begun to show that little girls of the twenty-first century have grown sick of Barbie at centre stage, and long to see Ken in the starring role – preferably as an unreconstructed man's man, like James Bond.

I would certainly have taken these matters up with Ken, had he given me the chance. But so caught up was he in demonstrating the many ingenious features of his fleet of cars and cunning array of concealed weaponry that he didn't even seem to remember he and I had ever met, let alone recall my sympathetic concern for his situation.

Under the circumstances, I saw little point in asking him if he'd heard anything lately from Raggedy Andy, or whether his old friend G.I. Joe was finding himself similarly in hot demand again, in a Toyland seemingly so newly charged with testosterone. Instead, I merely excused myself from Ken and sidled over to the open bar to lay hands on a couple of Pink Ladies, just in case poor Barbie might be looking for a chance to bend a friendly female ear.

But before I got anywhere close to the bar, I spotted Barbie, earnestly involved in conversation with her best friend Midge, who'd come to the event, I could only assume, as moral support. Well, good. If ever Barbie needed someone on her side, this was the night. Without giving much more thought to the matter than that, I betook myself home.

How much time elapsed before Ken – and by extension, Barbie – came back into my consciousness yet again? Six months, a year at most. It was a chilly winter morning – I do recall that – and I'd just settled down to breakfast with the paper, when a banner headline leaped out at me: "Barbie and Ken Call It Quits."

There was no mistaking the couple in the photo, smiling fixedly for the camera, though it was clear their hearts weren't in it.

"After forty-three years as the world's prettiest pair," ran the lead paragraph, "the perfect plastic couple is breaking up." Barbie and Ken, it seemed, had appointed a spokesman from Mattel to explain their situation to the world. It was the vice-president of marketing.

"Like other celebrity couples," he was quoted, "their Hollywood romance has come to an end. Though Barbie and Ken will remain friends."

For some reason, I was staggered by this news. Even more surprised than when I'd first encountered Ken, sloshed and sloppy in that neighbourhood bar, and certainly more startled than I'd been by his glitzy resurrection as 007.

Numbly, I continued to read what the vice-president had to say about the separation, including his sly suggestion that Barbie may have been pressing Ken too hard to take her to the altar in one of her many, many bridal ensembles.

Oh, Lord, I thought, I should never have left her without a word of comfort at that awful 007 do. I'll bet that might-as-well-be-married idea originated with Midge, desperate to see herself in the Maid of Honour outfit, as well as angry at Ken for letting Barbie get relegated to second banana without the cushion of matrimony to fall back on.

It was early in the day, far too early for a drink. Still, I needed something to steady my nerves. I thought of that hole-in-the-wall downtown where I'd first met Ken. It seemed like the right place to go. Nobody in my regular life – that is, nobody who came more than halfway up my calf – would be likely to offer anything but a chuckle, as they paged past the news about Mattel's two biggest stars headed for Quitsville. Whereas down at the bar, I might find G.I. Joe or even a Cabbage Patch kid or two, in for an eye-opener and a commiserative chat about the Barbie-Ken debacle.

When I got there, the place looked empty, and even dingier than I remembered. But I tried the door, and was surprised that it opened. Inside, it seemed much the same, except for the absence of clientele. Nobody at the bar, nobody at all, except . . . Ken, nursing a Scotch.

"Ken!" I said. "What are you doing back here?"

He didn't even bother to turn around. "What does it look like I'm doing?"

"But why? The way the newspapers tell it –"

"– I'm the one who busted up with Barbie? I'm the one who backed away from permanent commitment, right?"

As my eyes adjusted to the low light, I began to see how dreadful he looked: pale under his plastic tan, his unblinking eyes bloodshot, his clothes stained and dishevelled.

"Ken, that bespoke James Bond outfit you had, your new career, Barbie as your smiling sidekick. What on earth has happened to all of it?"

"Oh, that!" Despite his perpetual smile, Ken managed a laugh entirely devoid of mirth. "I can't believe I didn't see it coming for miles. I mean, hey, it's Mattel, right? Since when is anything about me *actually* about me?"

"You mean that big promotional 007 event, with you in the spotlight, and Barbie bringing up the rear . . . ?"

"Nothing but a way of getting Barbie's dander up so she'd dump me and they could stick me back in my shoebox, once and for all."

"I'm sorry, I'm afraid I don't get why Mattel would go to the trouble of bringing you out of obscurity, building that Bond campaign around you, simply to piss off Barbie."

"Because Barbie, for all her tough vinyl finish, is a softie at heart, that's why. And as conventional as they come. You think it was her own idea to freeze me out, back in '99 when that turning-forty marketing frenzy went on? Nah. Mattel talked her into it. But not for long. Eventually, Barbie started asking questions. 'Where's Ken? How can I turn my back on a guy I've been dating since 1961? Why do I have so many bridal outfits, when I'm too busy changing careers to ever settle down?'"

"Ah," I said. "So that vice-president from Mattel was telling the truth: Barbie really does want to tie the knot."

"Of course she does." Ken was helping himself to Scotch right from the bottle now. "Conventional as they come, just like I said. Only Mattel . . . they've seen how this same-sex marriage thing is taking off. They see little girls being raised to believe in sisters like Rosie O'Donnell and Ellen DeGeneres doing it for themselves . . ."

"You mean . . . Mattel is trying to turn Barbie *gay*?"

"Figure it out. Who did she end up huddling with that night of the 007 launch?"

"Well, Midge. But since Midge is Barbie's very best friend, I . . ." The penny finally hit the floor. "Oh Ken, come on! You're not suggesting that –"

"Barbie and Midge? Why not? Look at it from the marketing point of view: Twice as many engagement diamonds, twice as many bridal gowns, twice as many going-away outfits, twice as many trousseaus and bridal bouquets – all sold separately."

It made a certain kind of ludicrous sense. Still, the way Ken was knocking back the booze, how could I be sure he really had – had *ever* had – any real idea of what he was talking about?

"Ken, you've got to lay off the Scotch."

"Why?" he snorted. "Because martinis are 007's drink?"

Suddenly, I felt tired. Not only bored with Ken and his drunken self-pity, but exhausted by the entire world from which he'd sprung, with its synthetic values, false smiles, and small-minded behaviour. Before I even realized I'd made up my mind to leave, I was halfway to the door.

"So long, Ken."

For the first time since I arrived, he turned from his drink to look directly at me. "Where are you going?"

"As far away as I need to get, to find something *real*. Someplace where people stand tall, are able to bend a little, and care about changing the world instead of their careers and their clothes every five minutes!"

It was a pretty speech, but I didn't stick around to wait for Ken to applaud. I headed off without a backward look, and as I hurried home I vowed never to find my way back to that dreary little dive again.

Yet, by the time I got home, I'd begun to feel, in spite of myself, sorry once more for that poor, polystyrene creature on his barstool – as well as for Barbie and even Midge. None of them, I believed, was to blame for their cynical exploitation by Mattel. In fact, the manufacturer deserved an angry email from me to that effect.

But when I logged on to the Barbie.com website, what did I discover? Barbie wasn't about to make same-sex history by wedding Midge after all. Instead, what Mattel now had in store for her was a brand new boyfriend named Blaine, chosen to replace Ken – so the site said – by more than two million fans worldwide! And what a replacement: Blaine was Australian, enjoyed muscle shirts, hanging ten on his surfboard, and scarfing chili dogs. Worst of all, he boasted sunstreaked, rooted Saran hair, unlike Ken's rigidly moulded mane.

Oh well, then. Mattel I might fight, but two million fans? I clicked off the Barbie.com website and resolved once and for all to get on with a larger life. As I'd told Ken, there had to be something bigger out there, for those of us flexible enough to get out of our own litle box, and grasp opportunity with our two prehensile hands.

LISTMAKERS

FOR A NUMBER OF years now, I've suspected that many of the alleged differences between men and women are more imagined than real. But it took an encounter with, of all things, a bottle of hair dye to make me realize that, however imaginary – and however arbitrary – such distinctions are, one trifles with them at one's peril.

You might recall a commercial that used to run on TV advertising a tinting product called Just For Men. The one in which the wife ran her fingers admiringly through her husband's glossy new locks and cooed: "Such natural-looking hair colour, and in only five minutes! Meanwhile, I spend hours fussing with messy dyes and rinses!"

Now, wait a minute, I thought, when I first saw that ad. In fact, wait five minutes. How is it that, now that *they've* got into dyeing their hair, men have managed to improve the process, solely for themselves? Hair is hair, after all. Surely it must follow, as the black the grey, that a woman should also be able to touch up *her* tresses in record time. Just For Men, indeed. Says who?

That very day, I snapped off the TV set, marched to the nearest drugstore, and plunked my money on the counter, in exchange for a package of Just For Men. One small squirt of the dye-bottle for a woman, one giant blob of fast-acting colour for womankind.

True to the claim on the packet, it did only take me five minutes to cover the grey in my hair. And, as I gazed at the result in the bathroom mirror, my reflection did seem more youthful, more vital-looking, exactly as the commercial had promised *men* who used this product.

In fact, I felt like a different person. At first I couldn't quite put my finger on what that difference was. One obvious symptom, though, was a light-headed buzzing in my ears. This I simply ascribed to the giddy sensation of triumph any woman would feel, having seized a privilege formerly reserved for the opposite gender – as defiantly as Prometheus, stealing fire from the gods.

"Just for men? Not!" I gloated to my reflection in the mirror. Still towelling my hair dry, I strode out to the kitchen for something to eat.

Yes, strode. For not only was I feeling a little unlike myself, I appeared to be walking like someone else.

"Hmm," I murmured, tossing my damp towel on the kitchen floor. "Something is definitely going on here."

I opened the door of the fridge to stare pensively into its depths, and as I made inventory of the mayonnaise, mustard, ham, bread, pickles, onions, coleslaw, cheese, olives, turkey, tomatoes, and left-over chili that I had identified as the minimum initial elements required for the construction of any reasonably substantial sandwich, I began to scratch my stomach in an absent-minded way.

Somehow, the consideration that I'd finished breakfast only an hour before gave me no pause. Heck, I wasn't even worried that the turkey I was slicing might be slated for guests, or that the chili had been around a tad too long.

I wolfed my sandwich and gulped some milk straight from the carton. I belched with gusto, wiping milk from my mouth with the back of my hand. To search out a napkin struck me as a waste of time, and my time was worth quite a lot, right? After all, if I'd managed to cut to five the number of minutes it took to colour my hair, it didn't make much sense to squander all that time I'd saved on hunting for serviettes, rinsing glassware, cleaning up the counter in the wake of my sandwich-making, or even picking up the towel I'd dropped on the floor. The hell with all that.

"Gosh!" I thought. "This doesn't sound a bit like me. In fact, this doesn't sound like any woman I've ever met. What on earth is happening here?"

It occurred to me that I should have checked the product-warning label on the package of Just For Men more carefully. Perhaps I'd been wrong in my airy assumptions and there actually *was* some difference between the constituents of male and female hair . . .

Oh, well. What was done was done. Second-guessing was for wienies. No use crying over spilt milk – and if I'd spilled it by drinking right out of the carton, too friggin' bad. Somebody else could clean up the mess. Somebody like . . . my mother. Not that my mother had given any previous evidence of being willing to act as my unpaid maid. Still, it suddenly seemed like a good idea to give her a call, thereby making her day.

"Why, sweetheart!" Sure enough, my mother sounded over-joyed on her end of the phone. "How nice of you to call! And in a no-discount period!"

That was not at all typical of her. Usually, she'd spend the first part of the conversation chewing me out for never being in touch. Before going on to chew me out some more for phoning before the rates went down.

"Of course, you can afford these prime-time calls," she continued, purring into the phone. "You've made such a success of your career."

This conversation with my mother was going so well I didn't

have the heart to remind her that she had been urging me for years to give up my dead-end job, no doubt in order to spend more time on the phone with her.

"Speaking of careers," I said. "I'd better get to the office."

"Yes, of course, sweetheart! I know you have so many more important things to do than talk to me. By the way, if you're too busy to do your laundry, why not mail it home and I'll do it for you? My baby's time is precious, and what's a mother for?"

Wow. What had got into her? "Hey, thanks, Ma, but I gotta run." Her reference to laundry had reminded me that I had clothes to pick up at the cleaners' on my way to work.

Unfortunately, I'd lost my cleaning ticket again, and I could already hear the irascible old dry cleaner scoffing, "Just like a woman!" as he witnessed the familiar spectacle of me pawing frantically through my purse.

But when I got there, empty-handed, his response was entirely unexpected. "No ticket?" he smiled. "No problem. I have your clothes all ready for you."

Even more amazing, the bill was less than half of what I normally paid for a bundle of blouses. Today, he'd written them up as shirts.

I had no time to ponder the implications of that. I was already late for work, for which I expected the customary dressing-down when my boss met me at the door of my office.

But instead of scolding, he clapped me fraternally on the shoulder and announced: "Good news! HR's come up with an assistant for you!"

"A . . . an assistant?" I stammered. "There must be some mistake. I *am* an assistant."

"Not any more." The boss directed my attention to my door, where the words "Administrative Assistant" had been replaced with "Assistant Administrator."

"We can't expect someone in your position to make their own coffee and do the filing," beamed the boss. "So we've got you a girl to handle all that. Otherwise, your duties are the same as before – with a raise in pay, of course, to reflect your new title."

Well, what could I say? By this time, whatever doubts I'd experienced about the rashness of appropriating men's-only hair colour had been washed away in the tide of good fortune now engulfing me.

When lunchtime rolled around, I decided to celebrate my promotion by going out instead of gobbling the usual quick yogurt at my desk. So I told my girl to take my calls without explaining where I was going or when I'd be back. Then I headed down the street to a quiet little bar that was a favourite noon-hour haunt of us executive types.

"What'll it be, sport?" the bartender greeted me.

Sport. I liked that. I liked it so much, I decided against requesting a wine spritzer with an apologetic little giggle, as though there were something improper about a drink in the middle of the day. "Bring me a whiskey, Chief. A double," I ordered firmly. Never before in my life had I asked for a double anything for lunch. Or addressed the barman as Chief while doing so.

The rest of the day – and indeed the week – went pretty much like that. Like a charm. When my car engine began knocking, I didn't panic. Instead, I changed the oil. Myself.

Meanwhile, on the social front, invitations of all kinds began pouring in at an unprecedented rate. What's more, nobody seemed to mind if I showed up late for dinner, and without a bottle of wine. To hear them tell it, they were just thrilled I'd managed to turn up at all. The dinner-table conversation tended to revolve around me, and once the meal was done my hostess would merely gape in disbelief if I offered to help clear up.

Soon my calendar became so crowded there was no longer time to defrost my fridge, hem new curtains, wash out my delicates, re-pot the schifflera, or do any of the things that had formerly filled my weekends. Now, in addition to social functions, there were Bruce Willis flicks to take in, fights to watch on the jumbo screen at the sports bar, bets to be made on football games, and air guitar to play in the aisles at rock concerts.

In fact, I probably could have gone on indefinitely, revelling in the perquisites that are reserved just for men, had not the unexpected downside slowly started to present itself. My first indications of unattractive new elements in my character emerged at the office, where I overheard myself remark of a female colleague, "It must be her time of the month."

That same day, I laughed with genuine sympathy when my boss referred to his quite nice wife as "the old ball and chain." From there, it was only a short slide down a slippery slope to the point where I began shouting "Hubba, hubba!" out my car window, tossing litter carelessly on the street, and answering the phone with "Whassup?" instead of "Hello."

Now that the novelty of male privilege had begun to seem old hat, I was becoming aware of some of its inherent problems. Hockey broadcasts on the TV in bars where guys hung out were invariably cranked up to top volume. When my birthday rolled around, all my friends chipped in to buy me a drill. Worst of all was the eerie hush that fell one day around the office water-cooler when I happened to mention I didn't have a favourite old sweater.

Quickly sensing my mistake, I opened my mouth to take it back. But just as quickly closed it again. In that moment, the truth of my situation hit me harder than a playful punch in the ribs from a bar buddy. Dyeing was no better than lying. For all the advantages I'd gained, I'd also traded away my best asset: my own true self.

It was with a heavy heart, but with a sense of inner peace, that I made up my mind to renounce it all – cheaper dry cleaning, higher wages, better tee-off times – to go back where I rightly belonged. To a world where to speak of "turnovers" sparked an exchange of recipes rather than reminiscences about great grid-iron moments.

The only question was: Could I go home again? Or would the effects of my foray into a forbidden world prove more permanent than the dye I'd cast?

With my hair washed free of colour, I hung up my towel, put on flattering but uncomfortable shoes and a wool dress that looked great, but itched like hell. Then I headed to the snootiest restaurant I knew for a light but overpriced lunch.

Seeing that I was a woman alone, the maître d' seated me in a dark corner, where the swinging kitchen door riffled the pages of my menu each time a waiter went in and out. I relaxed, smiling, as nobody came over to take my order. I'd begun to suspect all was well.

Sure enough. The next thing I knew, a man who'd also arrived by himself was shown to a good table, right by a window. His salad arrived long before mine. "Yes!" I whispered to myself jubilantly. "I'm back where I belong!"

Thrilled as I was, I made sure to keep my voice down. Anything I said aloud might be interpreted by my waiter as a plea for service, which would only serve to send him in the other direction, as far as he could get from me, a woman whose time had little value, and whose tip would likely reflect an income to match.

All that, as I've said, was some years ago. Yet, it's taken me a long while to recover from the dramatic effects of changing my status so drastically, merely by poaching a product intended for the opposite sex. At the same time, that experience only underscored my earlier suspicions: How trivial, insubstantial, and capricious are the barriers that divide the male gender from mine.

Single men, for instance, always stock their shelves with tons of toilet paper. Check at the supermarket, if you don't believe me, and count the rolls of Cottonelle each guy's got in his cart. Or, next time you're alone in his place, start opening some cupboard doors. See? Rolls and rolls of the stuff, stacked to the eaves in every conceivable closet and cranny.

In fact, the only spot in his dwelling where you won't find a scrap of toilet paper is on the dispenser next to the toilet. Nobody knows for which nervously anticipated worldwide shortage single men are hoarding all that toilet tissue, even to the extent of never replacing the bathroom roll.

All we know for certain is that this difference between the sexes, while curious, is ultimately not significant. Especially when compared to the manifold ways in which men and women are startlingly alike.

Nevertheless, vast fortunes have been, and continue to be, made by authors of inspirational books, impresarios of the lecture circuit, and toasts of TV talk shows, all dedicated to the proposition that men and women may have been created equal but otherwise have no more in common than a cauliflower does with a calliope. Maybe even less.

You've seen those books. We all have. *Men Are from Manhattan; Women Are from Broadway*, or some similar assertion scrawled on the cover. And inside, a slew of pseudo-scientific explanations of why it is that males and females do things so differently.

Men hog the TV remote, for instance, flitting from channel to channel like bees pollinating a field of flowers, because of their essentially nomadic nature. Women, meanwhile, prefer to do their flitting from shop to shop, in pursuit of some platonic ideal of the perfect pair of pumps, because expressing themselves through acquisition is encoded in their DNA.

Men are too territorial to ask a stranger for directions; women are too trusting to ask a blind date for proper credentials before letting him offer investment advice. Even apparently contradictory claims are readily entertained. As expressive of their emotions as women allegedly are, they are also, inexplicably, assumed to be more given than men to deceit. Men, on the other hand, manage to find themselves charged with being both intimidated by and abusive of women.

Contradictions notwithstanding, it somehow seems that these listmakers find solace merely in bifurcating the boys and the girls into their separate columns of non-meeting twains. As, for instance:

MALE	FEMALE
List-making	Lace-making
Flashlights	Candles
Ball caps	Ball gowns
The Rat Pack	The mudpack
Gone Fishin'	*Gone With the Wind*
Hostile takeover	*Glamour* makeover
La-Z-Boy	Lazy Susan
NASCAR	Mascara
Chunnel	Chanel
Coach's Corner	Coach handbag
Short nap	Long lunch
Riding mower	Riding habit
Shinny	Shimmy
The Bridge on the River Kwai	*The Bridges of Madison County*
Joe Louis	C.S. Lewis

Naomi Campbell	Kim Campbell
WD-40	V-8
high-tech	low-cal

Ah, yes! Reassuring isn't it, to sort men and women on either side of some psychological Great Divide? Just as if there were something inescapable and irrevocable about their two different destinies, and therefore no compulsion on either side of the aisle to change, improve, adapt, soften, or diminish any of the identifying characteristics that, presumably, preserve the two sexes in their two solitudes.

Some men, I'm becoming more and more convinced, don't really want to see women as anything other than the Other. At the office, I often overhear male co-workers grumbling amiably among themselves about the chores their wives "make" them do around the house, or the lack of personal space they are "permitted," or the enforced marches they're "obliged" to make to relatives' homes, lawn and garden stores, and neighbours' barbecues.

The way they tell it, they're as much henpecked, helpless creatures of compulsion as Dagwood or Jiggs from the old comic strips. Yet I wonder what the wives would say if they heard their husbands handing them all responsibility for domestic decision-making, with the clear inference that women are whimsical, tyrannical, implacable entities who cannot be comprehended but must be obeyed.

I particularly wonder what they would say given the tendency of some of those same women to depict themselves as the ones forced to bend out of shape, in order to accommodate to the contour of the palm of the hand of whatever man holds them in thrall. In either case, it seems easier to blame the opposite sex for one's acquiescence than to stand up for oneself and defy the sexual stereotypes.

Besides, where would we be as a society without those demarcation lines between the genders, those little litanies of our differences to keep the status quo intact, like so many sets of picket fences? Imagine a world in which nothing was designated Just For Men or restricted to Women Only. With merely our complementary sexual organs to distinguish us, how could we continue the age-old debate about which sex is stronger, wiser, more innately moral?

I don't know about you, but I'd personally miss festering in front of the TV set as a hair product commercial grants to men in five minutes what women can barely attain in hours – and all, apparently, just *because* they are men. Certainly, I sleep better at night knowing those arbitrary little distinctions are still intact.

Of course, one day, I might rethink my position on that. Even in a man's world, it's a woman's prerogative to change her mind, right?

MEN O'PAUSE

LET'S FACE IT: THE advance word on middle age has never been particularly positive. Not for women, anyway. I can still recall, as an impressionable adolescent, being riveted by an otherwise unmemorable movie *The Roman Spring of Mrs. Stone*, in which a young Italian gigolo named Paolo scornfully chided the much older Mrs. Stone (Vivien Leigh) for her superannuated presumptions.

The fact that Paolo was played by Warren Beatty, uneasily sporting a "Ciao, bella" species of Italian accent, rendered his judgment no less scathing. "Rome ees a very old ceety: three thousand years. How old are you – feefty?"

Feefty. Ouch. At the age of twelve or so, that struck me as possibly the worst thing you could say about anybody. Mind you, Paolo's collateral point about the age of Rome I didn't quite get, and even all these years later I'm not entirely sure where he was going with that. But I have never forgotten the sight of a still-beautiful Vivien Leigh crumpling as the word "fifty" pierced her like a poisoned arrow.

Right then and there, I made a note to myself that I'd never end up fifty years old and at the mercy of some young gigolo with a noisy Vespa and a serious lack of tact. (Actually, I made a note that I'd never end up fifty, period. My plan, in those days, was not to make it past twenty-nine. Somewhere close to the eve of my thirtieth birthday, I decided, I'd line up a hit man who'd catch me in an unsuspecting moment and gun me down. When I made my idea the theme of a school assignment on "My Plans for the Future," I attributed the teacher's negative reaction to the fact that she was well past the twenty-nine mark herself.)

Subsequently, as I've progressed through twenty-nine, thirty, and far beyond, the concept of fifty has, predictably, lost much of its shock value for me. But the notion of resorting to men who have to be paid to play the part of escort continues to smack of something sadly akin to the no-longer-in-season Mrs. Stone. Even when the men insist they're *not* gigolos, like those Gentlemen Hosts who are allegedly supplied to solo women on cruise ships – along with the deck chairs, the fresh towels, and a formal invitation to dine at the captain's table.

It was in a newspaper article that I learned about the Gentlemen Hosts organization and the middle-aged and older men who sign on as companions and dance partners for the overabundant ranks of women of a certain age who are willing and able to travel alone, so long as they do it deluxe, but don't want to be alone in the dining room and at shipboard dances. The men in the article sounded nice enough. They don't get paid for their work as part-time partners, beyond a small stipend from the company that allows them to buy lonely ladies a drink. Nor are they permitted to make any moves, except on the dance floor.

Nothing sleazy or cheesy, in other words, and these nice, older gentlemen obviously have their own motives for signing on to cruise the seven seas – motives no doubt similar to those of the single women they service on the ship, with a foxtrot, a dinner date, or a gin fizz. They're alone; they've got time on their hands; they're keen to do some travelling before it's too late.

The only difference is that the men are in demand. According to the article I read, those who pass the screening process, and prove they can dance, might end up outnumbered twenty-to-one by female passengers, impatient to be partnered and determined to dance, dance, dance all night.

It's not a snapshot of ladies in later life that thrills or inspires one to join their ranks. Nor, I imagine, would it be any picnic for an older guy to spend his declining years and waning strength making dance-floor chit-chat with masses of clamouring women upon whom he's supposed to attend, but not too attentively. Yet here they are, post-menopausal women and after-andropausal men, continuing to enact the time-honoured pattern of the courtier and the courted – despite the disproportion of their numbers and the artificiality inherent in the idea of stocking a ship with men the way an ornamental pond is stocked with koi.

Oh, well, I figured, as I folded up the newspaper article and put it aside. Fifty was fast approaching, and menopause, when it came to me, would no doubt live up to its name: an activation of the Pause button on the love machine; a long lapse in the ready availability of men; a slow cessation of the sultry sizzle of the dating game.

Trouble was, already in my forties, I'd found the supply of available men was drying up, even before I did. My friends started reporting the same fearsome phenomenon. Long-time couples were splitting right and left, the men pleading "mid-life crisis" as an excuse for their impulsive defections – often in the company of telegenic twenty-something beauty queens. Long-time single sisters who'd never before been more than a month between involvements now complained that men found them invisible, or even risible. Biological alarm-clocks were going off all over town, with no man on hand to roll over, reach out, and grope to stifle the shrill clarion call.

Feefty? Forget it. As far as we forty-five-year-olds could tell, the full catastrophe was already upon us, the so-called pause in men already elongated to a span of time that felt as endless as . . .

well, the Eternal City of Rome came to mind – three thousand years and counting. As for menopause? What the heck, bring it on. At least we'd have our hot flashes to keep us warm in our newly empty beds.

Besides, I told myself, how bad could the change of life be? Despite the faintly lycanthropic image I'd always had of menopause, I didn't *really* imagine that I'd sprout furry paws, start slavering at the full moon, or run feverishly mad in the market square. The way I saw it, it was only a matter of hanging tough for a decade or so, after which I'd emerge into some gauzily backlit post-menopausal paradise, populated exclusively by wisely smiling and radiantly beautiful elder stateswomen beckoning me to join their seraphically aging circle.

I knew this, because prominent post-menopausal women told me so. All over the media, the likes of Shirley MacLaine and Gloria Steinem and Lauren Hutton were popping up to proclaim the manifest pleasures awaiting us on the other side of that womanly watershed. Their skin was fresh; their eyes were bright and clear; their brows unfurrowed by frown-lines of failure and feelings of self-doubt.

If fifty was a stake to stab in the heart of an aging coquette, then sixty, to hear Shirl and Glo and Laurie-baby tell it, would be a healing balm to a newly respected dowager's dignity. "Just you wait," these wise women's serene smiles seemed to say. "We know what it's like to be free of periods and the tyranny of having to look young."

But what these elegant elders did *not* tell me – and what unexpectedly turned out to be true – was that almost as soon as the periods stop, the supply of men that dries up in our forties comes back. Just like that.

Why? Do guys just sense that the need for birth control is past? Or does a woman of fifty look inexplicably better to a man of fifty than does a woman of forty-five? For whatever reason, the men came back, suddenly and mysteriously, like the swallows to Capistrano, like the buffalo thundering back across the Great Plains in the Indians' dream, like the cat in the NFB short-subject film. All that my formerly frustrated friends and I could do was shake our heads in wonderment, and kick back to enjoy our renewed good fortune.

In fact, in the early weeks and months of menopause, sex, it seemed, had never been better. Relieved, at long last, of the anxious possibility of pregnancy, I felt, for the first time ever, able to enjoy eroticism for its own sake. It didn't matter what time of the month it was. Why should it? Any time of the month was fine with me – time after time after time. Feefty? Fine.

"Ay em in may prrrime," I now purred to myself in the mirror, Miss Jean Brodie-style, no longer fearful of seeing the reflection of Mrs. Stone staring back at me, hollow-eyed, haggard, and humiliated.

At work, a perennially sex-obsessed male colleague of my age ruefully remarked to me that I appeared to be "blooming."

Still purring, I agreed with him. "Menopause," I confided, breezily and brazenly. "There's nothing like it."

"I'll say," he grumbled. "My wife has the window wide open, even on the worst winter nights, and at that, she's *still* kicking off the covers, claiming she's boiling to death."

"Ah, yes," I nodded, like the sagacious Dr. Ruth I had recently become. "Those'll be the hot flashes. More like a . . . warm electrical sensation, actually. Quite titillating, if you ask –"

"Uh-huh? Well, I've given up asking my wife altogether. Sex? 'No fun any more,' she says. 'Too painful.' Okay, so how's about a friendly little cuddle? No dice. 'Too hot,' she says. 'I'm sweltering.'"

I felt sorry for my colleague and his sexually sapped wife. Sorry, and smug – until I experienced for myself the downside of

menopausal mating. After those heady, hedonistic early weeks
and months of anxiety-free eroticism, other, less desirable, symptoms began without warning: the rolling, roiling waves of internally generated sweats, day and night; the embarrassing lack of
lubricity I'd heard rumoured in ladies' locker rooms; the middle-
aged midriff bulge, and a general podgy, blodgy, stodgy lack of
sex appeal.

Oh, God. In panic, I thought of my randy male co-worker,
despairing of his sex life's decline into nocturnal *noli-me-tangere*
nothingness, all because of his wife's menopausal miseries. Was this
befalling me? And if so, whither my ripening relationship? Would
it wither on the vine, leaving my man o'pause to drop into some
other woman's – some younger woman's – more luscious lap?

Luckily, no. My man, it turned out, was willing to take on my
menopause without taking off. Like concupiscent Curies in the
lab, he and I began to experiment with unguents, floundered
through creams, and when conventional techniques came up
short, tried as best we could to come, regardless. It was all very
interesting, he insisted. Even fun.

For me, what it was actually like was a return to all the messi-
ness of birth control. But God love the guy for putting a positive
spin on it – and for staying the course with me, come hell, high
water, or hormone replacement therapy.

Maybe there's some magic inherent in meeting men in middle
age. Maybe those men o'pause have had their fidelity forged in
the furnaces of other earlier, edgier involvements. Maybe the men
who come on the scene in the second act are the ones who have
worked through their own mid-life crises with somebody else,
and thus are now able to survive the rigours of menopause with
women like me and my fiftyish and even sixtyish friends, who
seem to have lucked out, man-wise, only in our later lives.

These are guys, after all, who'll never get to know how much cuter we looked when we were younger, slimmer, and sprightlier – and will therefore never have any idea of what they missed. Nor did we know *them* with hair, discernible waists, jutting jawlines, or decent hearing.

There are blessings to be counted by all parties concerned. Thank heavens, my middle-aged female friends and I agree, that we thought to burn those ancient snapshots of ourselves in hot pants, or hippie communes, or Dynel wigs – lest the new companion of our later years look upon those earlier likenesses and laugh himself into cardiac arrest. How lucky for us – and for him – that he didn't have to know us when we cried at the drop of a hat, spent money like drunken sailors, and altered our convictions as often as we adjusted our hemlines.

For our part, we're fortunate not to have met the man while he still kept all his old *Playboy* magazines carefully collated in a binder with the trademark bunny emblazoned on it. We feel grateful to have missed out on his little-black-book phase, or his period of principled refusal ever to pick up the tab, or that epoch of weekend custody of his four-year-old – the one with the short attention span and the long list of allergies. Indeed, when all is said and done, we don't mind admitting that we're downright delighted that the guy with the lime-green leisure suit and the wispy ponytail belonged to an earlier era, and to another woman.

Best of all, from a middle-aged female's point of view, men o'pause seem more willing than previous guys to look on life as a shared struggle. You and he can go to Weight Watchers together without concerns about loss of mystique – or, in fact, much hope of loss of *avoir dupois*. You take turns hunting for the magnifying glass. Dining out, he lets you figure out the tip, and dining in, you let him plan the menu and pick the guests.

Arguably, of course, none of the above is barred to couples who've been together all their adult lives — the ones whose joint memories go back several dozen years, to encompass kids and cottages and countless car trips. But I wonder if men and women with a long shared past might not be more real to each other *in the past*? For instance, my colleague who complains about what menopause has done to his marriage keeps a strip of photos on his desk of himself and his wife in their early twenties. In neither fresh face is there any hint of his future impatience, her impending resistance to his amorous advances.

For those of us whose lives have actually changed for the better with menopause and the men who came with it, the entire concept of "change of life" seems more appealing than ominous. You and your middle-aged man may be advanced in years, but you're both brand-new in terms of starting afresh along a conjoined path.

Once you're fifty, the future starts shrinking into something so inconsequentially short that at long last you're free to live entirely in the present. Shorter on time than you used to be, but so much longer on patience that if now is all you've got, it seems worth the wait.

Especially — should you happen to pause on the brow of one of the seven hills to look back at the grandeur that was Rome — if there happens to be a man to pause at your side, who makes three thousand years feel . . . well, like a mere fifty.

NONCOMMITTALS

IN THE MID-1980s, noted social commentator Barbara Ehrenreich wrote a best-selling book entitled *The Hearts of Men: American Dreams and the Flight from Commitment*. It was, I thought at the time and still do today, a wonderfully evocative title. Especially that "flight from commitment" part, which makes men as a group sound like some great, thundering herd of horses, plunging away in panic from any female foolish enough to believe she could approach them, coaxingly, with a hatful of oats in one hand and, in the other, a halter hidden behind her back.

So catchy did I find Ehrenreich's subtitle, in fact, that I never bothered to investigate the contents of her book. Instead, I satisfied myself with feeling grateful that someone had finally found a phrase to summarize what men had been doing for centuries – and what women had been worrying about them doing for just as long.

Women throughout history have not been without their resources – such as tears, sexual bribery, emotional blackmail, and public opprobrium – to keep their men, if not in line at least in sight. And on those occasions when psychological pressure came up short, there was always the expedient of grappling him to one's soul with hoops of steel, or some other more glamorous but equally durable metal: the diamond-studded engagement ring;

the plain gold wedding band; even the humble high-school pin
has had its part to play in impaling the female's prey.

I wonder if teenage sweethearts get "pinned" any more? Already,
in my own bygone day, the concept was dwindling into a kind of
quaintness, with its implied image of a boy and girl jointly shish-
kebabbed – like a pair of unwary butterflies – on the business end
of his high-school pin. Which she, of course, would be the one to
sport, along with his letter sweater, as mute testimony and eloquent tribute to her precocious ability to catch and hold her man.

Men, it was well understood in those days, required some
catching, not to mention holding, by any means possible, all
their lives long. Even men as unappealing, say, as Alfie Doolittle,
the aging dustman in *My Fair Lady*, who sang with a sagacious
wink about how, with a little bit of luck, "you can 'ave it all and
not get 'ooked."

By "it," he meant sex, and by "hooked" he, of course, meant
married – the more mature version of getting pinned, and similarly to be avoided by any red-blooded male. And even once
"roped, tied, and branded," as men in those days sometimes liked
to describe the matrimonial state, there still lingered some chance
of going astray, given the terminally restless nature of the male of
the species.

Looked at from a female point of view, it all struck me as rather
depressing, and hopelessly against the grain. If men didn't want to
be caught, why bother to chase them? If no combination of
pinning, hooking, roping, tying, or even harpooning would truly
hold them, what was the point in applying your brand to their
ornery hides? And if commitment represented some sort of
unreasonable imposition, why go through the motions of extract-
ing their worthless pledges and empty vows at all?

There seemed no clear answer to the question, except some
vague, adult allusions to "human nature," many of them proffered

– à la *My Fair Lady* – in the form of a song. One that peeved me particularly cropped up in another Broadway blockbuster, *The King and I*, when the King puzzled tunefully – and somewhat disingenuously if you asked me – about the seeming inability of the imported governess to comprehend that the role of woman was to stay rooted like a flower, waiting for man to come buzzing along like a bee, from blossom to blossom, gathering nectar at random before moving on.

Puccini's *Madama Butterfly*, though more exalted, didn't state the male case any less smugly with Lieutenant Pinkerton's musical musings on the life of "lo Yankee vagabondo" casting his anchor in every port of call, and doing what he pleased with whatever girl, then sailing smartly away. Even Shakespeare seemed in on the act, with droll ditties that cautioned "Men were deceivers ever, / One foot in sea and one on shore, / To one thing constant never." Interestingly, it always seemed to be men singing this stuff, just as it was men who wrote it, sounding more self-congratulatory than sorry for their wandering ways.

Later on, in the Sixties, the same buyer-beware disclaimers were issued in the acoustic anthems of the free-loving folkies. "Like a Rolling Stone." "That's What You Get For Lovin' Me." "It Ain't Me, Babe." Well, we women got the male drifters' drift, as we sat on the sidelines with sombre expressions, drinking in their ramblin'-man philosophy, along with the bad black brew and swirling smoke of the coffee house.

In my last year of university, along with a "steady" boyfriend I acquired the opportunity to spend time with his three roommates and observe, at close quarters, the way the "it ain't-me-babe" ethic informed their oft-stated preference for philandery over fidelity. Their ever-present *Playboy* magazines strewn on the sofa, a virtual landfill site of empty Pepsi cans advancing across the living room, and the queasy drone of Dylan arising from their record

player, the roommates would smoke, toke, and talk – pausing only
to inhale deeply of the dope or to toss another dead soldier onto
the Pepsi-can pile before picking up their never-ending discourse
on the theme of their own romantic inconstancy.

Frankly, it amused me to hear the three of them styling themselves as such college-level Casanovas. Only one of them had a
girlfriend, on to whom he'd been holding for dear life since grade
school, and whom he called every night in her college dorm
down at SUNY New Paltz. Neither of the other two ever went
out, except with each other, and then just to restock the apartment with Pepsis, tokes, smokes, and Bob Dylan albums. One of
them, as I recall it, fretted bitterly that my boyfriend's fraternity, to
which the roommate had aspired to pledge, had turned him down
– which suggested, at least to me, more of a craving for commitment than he seemed ready to own.

By the end of the Seventies, however, I'd ceased being so smug
about men – or being married to one, for that matter. Now the
men I was meeting, as just another newly single woman in a sea of
same, really *were* attachment-averse. Talk about your flights from
commitment. There seemed to be, on average, at least one leaving
the airport every hour, to hear me and my gob-smacked girlfriends tell it, as we sat up late at night with each other, picking
through the wreckage of the most recent romance with the sad
efficiency of aviation investigators looking for some small clue to
what had brought on the disaster.

There seldom was any evidence to find. Men who'd chosen
against commitment had not done so by any apparent rational
process. Non-commitment seemed more like a religious calling –
some sudden, emphatic, and utterly inexplicable epiphany, in the
manner of Saul summoned by God on his way to Damascus. One
minute, there'd be the guy, ardently looking into your eyes, and
the next minute – pouf! An expression of impatience had crossed

his face, and he was tying his shoes, gathering up his car keys, and heading for the nearest exit, never to be heard from again. At least that was how we women always told it to each other, shaking our heads in bewilderment, adding a snap of our fingers to indicate the rapidity with which he'd left.

It was, we would venture to each other in hushed and anxious tones, as if these guys were on a special wavelength emanating from outer space. As if, on some order from High Command, they'd dropped us like hot rocks, donned their protective gear, and obediently made tracks back to the mother ship. So eerie and automaton-like did their defections seem that only the intervention of aliens could explain it.

In my own case, the worst of these close encounters occurred at a point when, for once, meeting a man was actually the last thing on my mind. It was Christmastime; I'd just been through a heartbreaking obsession that had blown up in my face; I was almost literally on my way to the airport for a late-night flight, not from commitment, but to my parents' place, out West. Mere hours before departure, I stopped in at someone's Christmas party and ended up embroiled in an intense conversation with a man I'd never met before.

I wasn't immediately sure that I liked him – certainly not nearly as sure as he seemed to be that he liked me. By the time I broke the news to him that I was heading out of town, he'd decided that he wanted to marry me and insisted on my parents' phone number so he could call me while I was away.

A little dubiously, I gave it to him. Normally, guys who proposed marriage on two hours' acquaintance were anything *but* normal, and smelled of desperation, or something worse. But this guy wasn't like that at all. He was good-looking, well-dressed, fluent, funny – just the sort of beau from the blue that any single woman would welcome when on her way home for a family

Christmas bound to consist of such questions as: "How come you haven't met anybody since you and that no-good husband of yours called it quits way back when?"

For the entire week I was at my parents', my new admirer called faithfully at least once a day. Despite our absurdly short acquaintance, our conversations were animated, intimate, full of promise. Cradling the phone, I began to wonder more and more if this, at last, might be love at first sight – the sort of instantaneous attachment I'd only ever encountered in movies.

Not that I could honestly claim to love this stranger back. But each time he called, I felt myself a little more willing to entertain the idea that he was in love with me. After all, daily long-distance calls in prime time to Calgary, with no apparent concern about the length of our conversations. . . . If that wasn't plight of some kind of troth, I was damned if I knew what else it might be.

"Who *is* that fellow?" my mother inquired pleasantly, after three or four days of fielding his calls and summoning me to the phone. "He sounds awfully nice."

"I hope he is. I only met him a couple of hours before I caught the plane."

"Oh Toad!" said my mother, with the characteristic mixture of admiration and amusement my adventures seemed to inspire in her. "How *do* you do it?"

"I didn't actually do anything. He did it all. He says he wants to get married. He's even told his long-time ex-girlfriend all about me, and he says I'm the first woman he's talked about since they broke up that she thinks is a potential successor. But don't worry, Mum. I'm not about to rush into anything with some guy I hardly know."

"Of course you're not. Mind you, he does sound awfully nice . . ."

Yes, he did, and for that alone, as well as the cachet that his faithful phone calls conferred on me that Christmas, I was more than willing to give the relationship a chance, as soon as I returned to Toronto. When I did, there followed a couple of weeks of what seemed like a fulfillment of the promise hinted at in those daily long-distance calls. So far, I thought, so good. . . .

I can still pinpoint the exact moment I knew something was wrong. It was only a few weeks into our involvement, which had more than made up in hectic intensity what it lacked in longevity. At his insistence, he and I spent (well, *he'd* done the spending) a pricey and rather pointless weekend at one of those out-of-town retreats with faux-country wallpaper, designer dinners, and confusing snowshoe trails populated by valiant couples trying to find their way back both to the lodge and to the sort of joyous togetherness they'd lost the hang of, many years before.

Still supposedly in the first blush of my brand-new romance, I nevertheless remember failing to feel as smug about those couples as I wanted to. Some element of lustre was decidedly absent from our own getaway weekend, some species of ardour and energy was definitely lacking in my heretofore passionate partner. And when I realized only a mile or so down the road, after checking out of the resort, that I'd left something behind in the room, he seemed barely willing to turn around and head back to the desk to inquire.

When next I saw him, something had changed even more drastically, though I didn't immediately detect what. It was like walking by a house you routinely pass on your way home and suddenly one night realizing it no longer has a lamp shining from a certain window – a lamp you hadn't been aware of until it had ceased to glow. That was it exactly: The light had gone out of him. The light of love that I had supposedly inspired was now extinguished.

The day that he chose to make it explicitly clear to me that the party was over, he invited me out to lunch. Uh-oh. Bewildered though I was by the unhappy turn of events, I knew what that meant. Lunch, the meal of non-commitment, designed to be got through and, once the bad news was broken, got over with as expeditiously as possible, leaving the rest of the day open for life to begin anew. No tearful lingering over late-night drinks, no private recriminations in a public place, no threat of ill-considered sex as an impulsive but awful aftermath.

He was, he told me over his caesar salad, going through a very difficult time. So difficult, he'd been forced to seek the advice of a psychiatrist, who'd advised him in no uncertain terms that, if he wanted to avoid a complete nervous breakdown, the first thing he needed to do was eliminate complications from his life. By which I understood he meant me.

"But you said you were in love with me. You said you wanted to get married. There doesn't seem to be anything complicated about that."

He looked pained as he flicked a pouch of Sweet 'N Lo with his forefinger before tearing it open to pour in his coffee. "I am this close to an ulcer, *this* close. Simplify my life. Those are doctor's orders."

"He'd do better to order you to cut out coffee. Besides, what does a psychiatrist know about ulcers?"

There was, however, no point in mounting any further argument. Stone-faced, my erstwhile admirer paid the check and helped me into my coat. Stone-faced, he drove me home. And stone-faced he waited for me to get out of his car, and out of his hair, for good.

And that was that – effectively, if not actually. Because I continued to struggle for quite some time to comprehend what had happened. How could someone fall in love so suddenly, and then – just as speedily – turn cold, indifferent, even hostile?

I tried writing him letters in order to pose just such open-ended questions. I tried leaving the kinds of messages on his answering machine calculated neither to threaten nor to reproach. When all else failed, I sent my best friend to find out from him why he'd dropped me, just like that, from his dance card.

That, at last, drew a response. My best friend came back to my place to report that he'd asked *her* out and was, in fact, somewhat in love with her.

They did go out – for a few weeks, until his ulcer and his incipient breakdown came back, and he had to drop her too, for the sake of his health. It did no good to remind myself how, initially, he'd been smitten with me, while I'd been the one who was tentative, even bemused, in the face of his sudden and unbidden declaration of love. Now that he'd gone off me for good, and fouled up my relationship with my best friend on his way out the door, I was the one left holding the emotional baggage.

Although that was by far the most extreme example of a flight from commitment I've personally waved goodbye to, it was by no means the only one. And all kinds of other women of my acquaintance seemed equally prone to collisions on the rocky road to love with men who swerved to avoid only *after* impact.

No wonder, at a certain point, married men started looking to some of us like a better bet. Unavailable they might well be, but at least it was only legally rather than emotionally. At some point in the past, they'd made a lasting commitment to *some*body – the proof was on the third finger of their left hand. Where that hand had strayed since wasn't the issue. Protected as he was by his Ring of Power, a married guy could feel free to surrender himself utterly to a dalliance of the moment – secure in the knowledge it was a lending arrangement and not a non-refundable sale.

You could call that chronic non-commitment, I suppose, but with the Marrieds, *over*-commitment was more what it seemed. Married philanderers tended to overbook, often quite literally: One set of records kept for the world to see, with dental appointments and dull business dinners all duly marked; and alongside, a secret stash of little black books, full of names and numbers and dates and details of an entirely alternative life.

In neither world was a birthday ever overlooked. No meeting was missed, no preferred perfume or favourite flower ever forgotten. It was hard, looking at those overly organized men, to imagine them as careless crushers of hearts, inveterate avoiders of consequence, or the kind of cads who'd run a mile from any promise they'd made. It was hard to imagine them as they perhaps had once been: impetuous, unreliable, evasive, and flight-prone.

For all I knew, every one of my reliable married philanderers was a noncommittal at heart, and every single guy I'd met who'd begun red-hot then blown ice-cold was now settled into a stable marriage, in addition to keeping company on the side with a stable of girlfriends. For a long time, that intriguing speculation merely played around the edges of my mind. Until – as is so often the case – a Movie of the Week came along on network TV to bowl me over with a flash of true insight.

Typically, the movie's name was instantly forgettable. But what I do recall is that, like any MOW worth its salt, it purported to be based on a true story (!) and starred Jack Ward in the role of a man who specialized in leading women to trust him for no reason. (Yes, that would be the same Jack Ward who always matched Heather Locklear for blond, suntanned sociopathy on *Melrose Place*, a perfect conniving Ken to her bad-assed Barbie.)

In this made-for-TV movie, Jack Ward played an airline pilot – an occupation made for the flight from commitment, if ever there was one. First we saw him meet and marry an attractive flight attendant. Then he got involved with a pretty passenger and married her too. Then a *third* woman came along from some quarter or other and . . . yep, he wound up wed to her as well. Which would, I guess, make him a "trigamist," even though that sounds more like someone who dedicates his life not to love but logarithms.

Of course, none of the three women knew about either of the others, and each of them lived in a different city. The logistical nightmare this created for Jack Ward, you can only imagine. He was forever stuck on a layover in Hawaii with Wife Number One when he had a dinner party to attend with Wife Number Two on the U.S. mainland. Meanwhile, the wife he kept stashed in Europe someplace was forever showing up to surprise him at the most awkward moments . . .

I knew I was meant to find him selfish and heartless, a half-baked excuse for a man obsessed with Having It All. But in fact, watching Jack Ward's conjugal contortions was, more than any-thing, nerve-wracking – like enduring a segment of *The Ed Sullivan Show* involving some frenetic fellow trying to keep an array of plates twirling on sticks to the strains of "The Sabre Dance." As poor Jack Ward strove, with less and less success, to keep straight which wife liked beluga caviar and where he was with the renovation plans on one or other of his troika of dwelling places, and under what sofa cushion in which living room he'd stowed what incriminating proof of which perfidy, I could only marvel at how someone supposedly so strenuously in flight from commit-ment could have wound up spiralling right down into it.

Like a righteous polygamist from some fundamentalist reli-gious sect, his was not the behaviour of a bold swinger but the modus operandi of a man who craved order, social definition, responsibility – and constant company. If married men, as surveys say, do indeed number as the most personally satisfied and most long-lived members of male society, then that polygamous pilot played by Jack Ward had to be one happy, healthy fella – until, of course, the wives found him out.

Which made it crystal clear to me: The men who proclaim the loudest their freedom to philander are also the men most likely to embrace entanglement with a vengeance. Looking back at Alfie Doolittle in *My Fair Lady*, what do we find? The same devilish dustman who contrived to have it all without getting 'ooked ultimately prances about in tails and top hat as he proclaims "I'm getting married in the morning!" Lieutenant Pinkerton, once he's impaled his Butterfly and then moved on, returns to Nagasaki with his American wife to claim his child and go home. The King of Siam – far from buzzing amorously from flower to flower like a bee hopped-up on Spanish fly – in fact never stirs a step from his palace containing his retinue of wives and children until Anna Leonowens comes along to get him up off his duff and onto the dance floor.

Even that guy who dumped me over lunch had, after all, embarked upon our encounter by expressing a desire to change my name, almost before he asked me what it was. Is that the mark of a man not at all into commitment, or the mark of a man so committed to the idea of commitment that he's incapable of simply having a casual relationship?

To think that I owed so much insight to a made-for-TV movie about a multiply-married airline pilot! At the time that film appeared, I was watching a lot of TV, in the quiet countryside of eastern New York State, with a male partner for company on weekends and our two dogs as my only menfolk the rest of the week. For two middle-aged, human curmudgeons – not so much noncommittal as just desperately ambivalent – this part-time partnership proved to be the most workable way we could find to live together yet save our respective sanities.

It was all *très moderne*, in a very Victorian *Parallel Lives* kind of way. Even though there were numerous banal chores to share, like stacking wood and shopping for groceries and worrying about the state of the septic tank, our scheduled separations Monday to Friday kept our mutual fear of the mundane somewhat at bay.

Previously, we'd tried living together seven days a week in Westchester, and failed. Then we tried having a long-distance relationship, with me in Toronto and him in New York, and failed at that as well. Like the bears in "Goldilocks," ours was a case of too much of this or too much of that – fretting either because of excessive distance or over-proximity before finally finding the combination of both that was just right.

Eventually the relationship foundered, though I'm convinced the semi-detached way we lived extended its lifespan. There was a sense of occasion on those Friday afternoons when he would arrive from Westchester, laden with laundry, the H&H bagels, the whitefish salad and coffee procured from Zabar's in the city, and all of the books, videos, CDs, and back issues of *The New York Review of Books* that he intended to get through before the drive home on Monday morning.

"Home." Interestingly, he reserved that term for the apartment in Westchester. Inevitably so, perhaps – given the weekly schlepping back and forth to and from the little country house he owned but left up to me so much of the time, along with the dog walks, the weekday shopping trips, the connections with neighbours and everything else that contributed to making that little place at the foot of the Berkshires my home rather than his.

There was also my sense of proprietary domain, which may have made him feel like a visitor to his own house. All week long, I worked on my writing, did a bit of decorating around the place, planted some impatiens or pulled up some weeds or raked some leaves – depending on the season – and spent those short winter evenings cuddled up with the dogs, nodding off by the fire, or imbibing fresh insights from the Movie of the Week.

I was alone a lot, and missed him a lot, and made a point of talking to him on the phone every day. But there was a luxurious quality in that sort of missing – knowing that the lack would be filled, come the weekend, and knowing that, in the meantime, my craving for solitude could be gratified. It was, I felt certain, the same for him, with his teaching, his modest social circle, his long hours spent on the phone, usually while supine in a rapidly cooling bath that he had to keep constantly topping up with hot water. He had his own life as well as the life he shared with me, with no incumbency to commit to the one over the other.

To our critics on either side of the U.S.–Canada border who saw the ambivalence implicit in our arrangement, I extolled the ever-fresh virtues of living together but only partly. And from the long-time couples of our acquaintance who were a little weary of too much togetherness over too many years, I modestly accepted coos of congratulation ("Together only on weekends? In the Berkshires? Lucky you!") as I endeavoured to explain how a mode of existence that might appear like a sudden stroke of brilliance had, in fact, been arrived at through trial, error, adjustment, readjustment, and constant retooling.

In the end, no amount of any of the above could paper over more essential problems. But at least I moved back to Toronto believing that our Berkshire Compromise had served to sustain our relationship, probably beyond its actual sell-by date. For someone as increasingly skittish as me, I told myself, any out-of-town alliance was doomed to fail, simply because one of the two parties was required to make a commitment to live in the other's domain. The fact was, I further told myself, I'd come to the point where I wanted only to live on my own, and even if I ever managed to meet anyone again, cohabitation of any sort would be out of the question.

That was not, I knew, how women are supposed to wind up feeling. Women are supposed to be grateful for any alleviation of their awful aloneness, fearful of the future in an empty nest, and terrified at the prospect of being left by their menfolk for other, younger women.

The thing was, most of the older, single women I actually knew did not feel the way they were supposed to; they felt the way I did. We all wanted men in our lives much more than we wanted live-in men. In our twenties, we'd embarked eagerly enough on marriages and other cohabitational arrangements. After that, we'd suffered through some unspeakable cads and endured constant reversals, as well as long stretches on our own, or alone with kids. Perhaps for those reasons, or perhaps because of something even more deeply ingrained, we'd ended up protective of our own time, stingy with our space, and selfish about our solitude.

Talk about your flight from commitment. Or, at the very least, an ever-lengthening postponement of permanence. Now it's the *men* in the older couples I know who want to move in together or get married, and the *women* who sit up late at night with their female friends, no longer blubbering in panicked bewilderment over the men who'd inexplicably got away, but nattering nervously about losing a life of solitary satisfaction and gaining a guy who'd be there *all the time*.

It is, of course that terror of the quotidian, which is perhaps more deeply rooted in some women than in most men. For my part, I know what I want: to keep it forever fresh, like a movie which, no matter how many times I've seen it, seems as crisp and colourful as on the day of release. I shrink from the spectre of staleness, the horror of humdrum sex, available at several convenient locations in my own home, togetherness always on tap, but no longer ever on the edge.

At the same time I struggle to exorcise my ambivalence, to embrace the present moment and the present man, with the kind of energetic enthusiasm that characterized my younger years – only, please God, minus the desperation that often underlay my motives then. Is that a full-fledged flight from commitment, or merely a nervous sidling away from sameness? The female equivalent of what Barbara Ehrenreich mapped in the hearts of men?

Perhaps I'll ask her, or better yet, ask one of those guys I used to date – like one out-of-town guy I remember who was so wary of shackles that his visits to me in Toronto would be punctuated by angry phone calls from women all over the rest of the country. Maybe I'll call up that feckless out-of-towner-turned-long-distance-friend and find out how it is that, in late middle-age, he's actually recently gotten *married*, for God's sake, for the very first time. Yes, maybe I'll ask him, or any of the men I've known who finally outgrew that impulse to plunge away in panic at the first hint he was being approached by someone with a halter in her hand.

Who knows? Those men may well have something wise to whisper to me, something that will gentle me for a life in loving harness with a true gentleman looking for a long, long ride into an eternally technicolour sunset.

OUTLAWS

WHEN THE FILM *Butch Cassidy and the Sundance Kid* came out in 1969, I was in graduate school in Toronto, feeling suffocated, lost, and somewhat as if my life had – prematurely and without warning – packed it in. With another similarly disaffected female student friend, I headed off to the movie theatre to find what respite from scholarship we could in the pleasant faces and manly graces of Paul Newman and Robert Redford.

At a certain point in the movie, having burned their bridges as train robbers in the American West, Butch and Sundance decide to go to Bolivia for a fresh start robbing banks. Rather charmlessly, Sundance (played by Robert Redford) invites his girlfriend Etta Place (Katharine Ross) to come along – provided she's willing to handle the housekeeping without whining too much.

Etta deliberates, and then accepts, declaring, "I'm twenty-six years old, I'm single, and a schoolteacher, and that's the bottom of the pit . . ." At that line, my fellow female graduate student and I whooped with self-satirizing laughter. Although we were merely twenty-two ourselves, we were also single and, unless some miracle intervened, slated to be schoolteachers too. Given the choice, what woman of any era wouldn't opt for the outlaw life in the company of two good-looking gunsels, against whom the actuarial odds may have been stacked, but who were at least guaranteed in the short term to show a girl an exciting time?

Besides, in the film Etta seems smart enough to buffer herself against the inevitable outcome. "I'll sew your socks," she goes on to promise the boys. "I'll stitch you up when you're wounded, and I won't whine. But I won't watch you die. I'll spare myself that scene, if you don't mind."

In fact, she does much more than refrain from whining and keep the hosiery darned. As Butch and Sundance's career in bank robbery in Bolivia begins to unfold, Etta is right in the thick of it, teaching them simple Spanish commands like "Put up your hands!" and "Get over against the wall!"

She accompanies them on heists, either as a well-dressed *Americana* luring an unwary bank manager into the vault, or as an accomplice disguised in men's pants and boots, waiting with horses for their getaway. Through it all, we watch her enter into the entire venal spirit of the undertaking, smiling broadly when she joins in a toast to a robbery well done and helping to plot the next campaign against the next hapless Bolivian bank.

Only when a Pinkerton man arrives from North America to spoil the fun does Etta's anxiety about the fate of her two desperadoes come to the fore. She attempts to persuade the outlaws to go straight, to try farming or ranching, at least until the hired heat takes a hike. But Butch says he's too old for the drudgery of ranchwork, while Sundance, an easterner, professes to know nothing about it.

When the two outlaws seek to go legit as payroll guards, they immediately get robbed, by local *bandidos* – then end up killing them and finding themselves on the lam again. Butch, a gentle, philosophical soul who's never before had to shoot anyone, sums up the irony of their latest plight: "Well, we've gone straight. What'll we try now?"

The unspoken answer is in Etta's face as she lies in her bedroll, her back to Sundance, out under the South American stars. "I'm thinking about going home," she offers quietly into the darkness.

We know that she's actually thinking about the urgent need not to watch her men die.

Nor does she. By the time the inevitably bloody ending occurs, Etta is nowhere to be seen, and the film offers no suggestion that she ever did find out what became of the bandits she'd lived with and loved. Instead, there, in the final frames, are Butch Cassidy and the Sundance Kid, all by themselves in San Vincente, in an adobe building surrounded by police, with a huge band of reinforcing soldiers amassing in the background.

An arriving officer is himself stunned to discover how much military might the situation requires. "Dos hombres?" he asks the local constabulary incredulously. "*Dos* hombres?"

With that, it's obvious the mythologizing is already beginning. Two amiable but essentially aimless young men, who turned to robbery as the only means of survival they could manage, turn into legends of the fading frontier West. Even as the camera catches them charging with foolish gallantry out of the doorway and into the onslaught of armed opposition, they have no inkling of what awaits. The frame freezes on them, eternally alive, while the soundtrack crackles with repeated rounds of gunfire.

Back in the late Sixties, to my friend and myself – going down the wrong road to academic respectability and God only knew what else, desolation and death seemed like a small price to pay for the careless rapture of robbery that preceded it. As women, we were particularly interested in the supporting but substantial role of a combination mistress, partner in crime, and den mother to desperadoes played by Katharine Ross.

Sure, her character got written out of the picture well before the end. On the other hand, hadn't Etta Place set the terms of the limited partnership, and chosen her own exit strategy? In the lopsided world of men-on-the-lam-and-the-ladies-who-love-them, Etta appeared to us to have fared better than most.

Take Wendy, for example, in *Peter Pan*: a humourless hausfrau
in little girl's clothing, presiding over Peter and all the Lost Boys
like the matron of a British boarding school rather than a partner
in piracy. Maid Marian in *Robin Hood* seemed a little more game
in that old TV series of the 1950s – although, I can't recall ever
seeing her burgle a baron or help out in a single highway robbery.
Mostly, she was there in the background, offering apple-cheeked
approbation and not much else to Robin and the rest of the *pueri
aeterni* of Sherwood Forest.

In literature as well as in life, there's always been an undeniably
attractive element to outlaws that sucks in the ladies, will they or
no. From Bess, the landlord's lovely daughter plaiting a knot in
her dark hair for love of a highwayman, to the Woman in Red,
who, as legend tells it, fingered her lover John Dillinger for the FBI
right in front of a Chicago movie marquee advertising *Manhattan
Melodrama* with Clark Gable.

Certainly, the Woman in Red story was one that, as misfit teenagers, my best friend Ruth and I mulled over, along with numerous other tales of barflies, bimbos, showgirls, and cute coeds taken
in by the dark domain of racketeers, overlords, and hit-men-for-
hire. But at that age, despite our own outsider status, Ruth and I
were rigid moralists, firmly on the side of law enforcement. We
were more or less immune to the mesmerizing appeal of good old
bad boys, like Butch and Sundance, who were simply ill-suited to
regular wages and pedestrian plans, rather than criminals for criminality's own savage sake.

It was only later in life – on the straight-and-narrow of graduate school – that I became susceptible to the attractions of the
doomed desperado. Which may make a certain sense. As one's
own existence more and more attains a sort of orthodoxy ("I'm
twenty-six, I'm single, and a schoolteacher . . .") one more and
more needs an outlet, however vicarious, for one's own outlaw

impulses. How else to explain the demure daughters, lady literati, and dependable dowagers who kick over the traces for the love of some convict in irons, some handsome hijacker, or some lowdown black sheep on the lam?

I have never (to my knowledge) kept company with a career crook – not, at least, while he was actively engaged in unlawful pursuits. But I do remember the fascination I used to feel for the bad old days of a boyfriend of mine, long before I'd met him, as an armed robber of singular ineptitude.

Inevitably, ineptitude led to arrest. It was the kind of experience, as he described it to me, that was both hideously immediate and yet oddly unreal – dreamlike, in a waking-nightmarish sort of way.

In a scene more familiar to him from television than any place else, he watched the arresting officer snap the cuffs on his wrists. Then – as one of the cops pressed down on the top of his head and pushed him into the back seat of the cruiser – he saw a woman watching from the opposite curb, her hands clapped to her mouth in an involuntary show of horrified compassion for his plight.

His impulse, he said, was to smile at her, shrug, or even wave as best he could. Anything to assure her: "Don't worry, lady, this is not the worst thing in the world. This is just something happening to a guy you don't know. It's all going to come out okay in the end."

Yet even as the thought was forming, he said he had no idea why he might feel inclined to utter any such thing aloud. Because this *was* the worst thing that had ever happened to him, and he really had no reason to assume it was going to come out anything like okay in the end.

Nonetheless, he felt the instinctive need to reassure the female bystander, to somehow acknowledge her apparent sympathy. And when he told me the story, some of that sympathy seemed to transmit itself to me. I felt a rush of compassion for that long-ago

boy, with his stolen handgun, his blighted future, and his igno-
minious arrest with no witness other than a passing woman who
had no reason to care yet apparently did. While a man looking on
the same scene might have shaken his head in reproach or disgust,
almost any woman would be likely to feel for the hapless young
felon and wish him well.

Maybe it's the sort of women forced to live lives of quiet, desperate respectability who are the most drawn to outlaws, the most
susceptible to the eternal-boy types inclined to inhabit Sherwood
Forest, Never-Never Land, and the backwaters of Bolivia. Mind
you, it was men who dreamed up Robin Hood and Peter Pan, as
well as the women who tagged along with them. Even Etta Place
– an actual person – exists for most of us only in the film about
Butch and Sundance. Her words and feelings have been supplied
to us by writer William Goldman, whose screenplay of *Butch
Cassidy and the Sundance Kid* made Sixties folk heroes of two
almost forgotten figures, and explained Etta's involvement in their
crimes as a woman's only available escape from a dead-end female
career and certain spinsterhood.

In reality, Etta Place may well not have been a schoolmarm. She
may not, for that matter, have been Etta Place, but Ethel Bishop. If
she taught at all, one theory has it, it may have been piano lessons
– in a brothel in San Antonio, where patrons also got breakfast and
their pants pressed, along with the more usual amenities.

Possibly, it was in that full-service whorehouse in Texas that
Ethel (or Etta) met a young drifter and sharpshooter named Harry
Longabaugh, already dubbed "The Sundance Kid" in honour of
an early horse-rustling conviction in Sundance, Wyoming. What
we know more or less for certain is that when Sundance departed
San Antonio, Etta was with him. And by the time they got to
Pennsylvania, where he had family, the Kid was introducing Etta
as his wife.

Several years after that, when Etta and Sundance, along with Butch Cassidy, set sail for South America, it was not Bolivia but Argentina they chose as their destination. Nor was bank robbery the initial point of the excursion. Their plan was to homestead.

Homestead they did, and for a while quite successfully, outside a place called Cholilo in Argentina's Chabut province. Once the quiet farming life ceased to interest Butch and Sundance, they went back to robbing banks. There are reports of that period to indicate Etta went along with them on those heists, certainly in Argentina, and maybe later in Bolivia as well.

Yet there are other, equally reliable reports of her enjoying her role as a lively but entirely reputable member of that ranching community outside Cholilo. Allegedly, Etta (or Anne Marie Place, as she was known by her neighbours there) cut a splendid figure, both on horseback and on the dance floor – on at least one occasion with the governor of Chabut province as her attentive escort.

If Etta did indeed revel in the respectability she briefly found for herself in Argentina, it suggests that her original purpose in teaming up with Sundance and Butch had not been to inject some excitement into the staid, schoolmarmish life scriptwriter William Goldman later wished upon her. What seems more likely is that the real Etta Place was, by her early twenties, a woman already in search of a way back, from beyond the pale, to the safe side of the law, yet was compelled by circumstance to choose as her travelling companions men unable to go straight for any length of time, to any place apart from hell.

For all anybody knows, she may have longed for some quiet, cultivated man to free her from the two career criminals with whom Fate had forced her to cast her lot. Certainly, among the stories about Etta's time in Argentina is a persistent rumour of a romance with just such a person, a bookish Scot named John Gardiner, who ranched nearby and was her open admirer.

In the absence of evidence that Etta remained behind in Cholilo, it seems likely she left with Butch and Sundance, possibly pressing on to Bolivia as their accomplice in crime. But surely not without a lingering allegiance to the genteel world represented by John Gardiner, and the hope it had offered her of moral improvement by association with what must have seemed in him so decent, so sane, so high-minded, and so fine.

Of course, that may not have been Etta's dilemma at all. It's not every woman who finds herself torn between the earthy outlaw and the sort of spiritual allure offered by a bona fide gentleman. The kind of woman both these species of men attract – and find attractive – is inclined to be bold but oddly conventional, independent yet strangely submissive, and ferociously strong, in spite of her iron-clad determination to be seen as weak.

On the one hand, she requires a renegade if she's in the mood to break a few laws. On the other hand (the one extended so chastely to be kissed), there's the need for a nobleman on-site to provide her with some fine old tradition to which to adhere.

In such situations it's usually the outlaw who's the more interesting man. Just as frequently, that truth escapes the woman until it's too late.

Who can blame her? The poor woman hasn't enjoyed the advantages the rest of us have had, including the opportunity to sit through *Gone With the Wind* a time or two or ten, silently willing Scarlett O'Hara to smarten up and pick that reprobate Rhett Butler as her soulmate instead of throwing herself away, as she invariably does, on anemic Ashley Wilkes. And the reason that poor woman hasn't had that opportunity is that she *is* Scarlett O'Hara, forever fated to misread her own character and to miscalculate which sort of male suits her best.

Too bad for Scarlett, missing out on the movie that's taught the rest of us so much. In my own case, that course of tutelage began when I was thirteen, seeing the film for the first time in the company of several other little girls, on a birthday party outing.

Gone With the Wind had been re-released that summer for the first time, I believe, since the Second World War. My mother, a passionate devotee of the film since its premiere in 1939, leaped at the opportunity of that birthday party to send me off to the re-release as her advance scout.

"Now, when you come home, you must tell me the truth," she said. "I'm so afraid it won't stand up to my memories. I'm so afraid."

I have no recollection what the other girls thought of *Gone With the Wind*. I know only that I was enraptured from beginning to end. I'd never seen anything like it: A heroine who was brave and foolish, shrewd and stupid by turns, and two men who each accommodated a different aspect of her variegated self.

"Well?" my mother demanded tensely the moment I walked in the door.

"Oh, Mum," I sighed. "It stands up."

My mother sighed as well, in vast relief. "Good. I'll go tomorrow. Do you want to see it again?"

That was the beginning for me of many, many viewings of *Gone With the Wind* over many, many years, through my adolescence, young married life, and ever more mature adulthood. Throughout the successive decades, my admiration for the shrewd depiction of Scarlett O'Hara has only increased.

Here is a woman raised in a rigid tradition of simpering Southern belles, dedicated to little beyond maintaining the lily-whiteness of their soft, idle hands and learning the management of the staff of household slaves. Yet even before the Civil War comes along to up-end everything in her restrictive world, Scarlett is somehow outside the mould, already some sort of maverick in the making.

It's not a side of herself she likes to acknowledge. As the film opens, her only ambition is to align herself with Ashley Wilkes, the gentle heir to a nearby plantation, and the epitome of cultured civility that was the American Old South at its best.

Ashley, however, has other matrimonial plans, involving his cousin, whose mild nature and quietly ladylike ways mesh perfectly with his personality. At the same afternoon barbecue where Scarlett learns this devastating news, she also meets the man who's *her* ideal match, the renegade Southerner Rhett Butler.

"Who is that?" Scarlett inquires of another belle at the barbecue, after she spots Butler gazing up the stairs at her. "He's staring at me as if he knows what I look like without my shimmy."

The other girl is only too happy to confirm Butler's a man of bad reputation, rumoured to have "ruined" a girl in Charleston merely by taking her buggy-riding in the late afternoon without her chaperone or her shawl.

For his part, Butler instantly recognizes in Scarlett the rebellious traits that complement his own lawlessness, but Scarlett resists any inference that the two could be in any way alike.

"A gentleman," she tells him, after he's unintentionally eavesdropped on her failure to woo Ashley away from his intended, "would have made his presence known. You, sir, are no gentleman."

"And you," Butler says approvingly, "are no lady."

On that same eventful afternoon at the Wilkes plantation, a rider on a lathered horse rushes in to announce war has been declared. This changes everything in that genteel society, except the personalities and relationship of the three principal characters. Ashley immediately joins up, Butler breaks all the rules to keep the Southern aristocracy supplied with contraband goods, and as war whistles all around, Scarlett finds herself forced time and again to call upon her own strength to protect the weak, including Ashley's wife.

Scarlett next encounters Rhett Butler at another social event. This time, it's a fundraiser for the war effort, where well-to-do men of the Confederacy bid to dance with a particular woman. As the widow of a soldier she married impulsively, Scarlett wears mourning. When Captain Butler offers a sizable sum to dance with her, he is rebuked by the auctioneer. A woman in mourning will surely not dance.

"Oh, yes she will!"

Scarlett's retort startles the crowd, as well as herself – but it does not in the least surprise Rhett Butler. As they bow to each other to lead off the reel, he grins at her like someone confident that this is just the first step in a lifetime together of outrageous defiance.

That confidence, alas, is not borne out. Himself the ultimate outlaw, Butler fails to take into account the side of Scarlett that still aspires to remain a Southern belle. That's the side of her that holds utter allegiance to Ashley Wilkes, and the gentlemanly ideal that he continues to represent, despite the devastation the war wreaks on their way of life.

To keep her kinfolk and herself from ever being hungry again, Scarlett vows to go to any lengths to survive, and she does. She cheats, she lies, she schemes, she scams, and undertakes anything that will help the cause of saving Tara, the family plantation, and all the people who come to depend upon her – including Ashley and his wife. She will stop at nothing, whether it's doing business with the very Yankees who ravaged their homestead or stealing her own sister's beau because she needs his money to set herself up in business. Even employing sick and starving convict labour to run her sawmill is within Scarlett's expedient ethic, much as it horrifies everyone else, especially her beloved Ashley.

Even so, Scarlett keeps her own version of faith with the side of herself he represents by keeping his picture close to her heart, and by urging him to help her get away from her sordid enterprise by running off with her to Mexico. Noble but somewhat feckless soul that he is, Ashley finds himself feeding off her strength, while at the same time shrinking from escape, or even anything resembling outright adultery.

For Rhett Butler, who succeeds, as he says, in catching Scarlett "between husbands" long enough to marry her himself, this ongoing idolization of Ashley is infuriating, hypocritical, and, above all, baffling. He has never had any trouble identifying Scarlett as a strong-willed outlaw just like himself. What on earth compels her to continue to pine for a man too timid to embrace her and too weak to let her go?

Yet there's a certain psychological sense in what Scarlett, if unconsciously, has elected to do. The sweet Southern belle in her, snuffed out both by the war and by the demands of her truly rebellious nature, lives on in her idealized view of Ashley, to whom she dedicates herself with all the fervour of a medieval knight dedicating his deeds to his Lady Fair as a means of personal ennoblement. The farther her actions take her from antebellum stereotypes of Southern womanhood, the greater her need to ally herself with Ashley and the immutable values of the departed world he represents, as a means of washing away her sins.

The film presents a startlingly advanced perspective for 1939. Scarlett treats Ashley the way men have traditionally treated women, as a mirror in which to look for an acceptable if inaccurate image of herself. Even Rhett Butler's role is largely assigned by her. When money is needed, he's there to provide it. When sex is what's wanted, he provides that, too. Above all, when she requires a companion in bad behaviour, he is up to the challenge like no other man she will ever know.

Perhaps not surprisingly, it's only when Ashley becomes widowed, and therefore technically available, that Scarlett realizes she prefers him out of reach. And it's only when Rhett Butler declares himself no longer capable of giving a damn that she longs to draw him close. All he can give her at that point is a handkerchief to dry her tears, and some good advice about going back to Tara, the source of her strength.

What happens to Scarlett O'Hara after that is as much a mystery as the upshot of the real-life adventures of Etta Place. Depending on my mood when I see *Gone With the Wind*, or how old I am, or what shape my own psyche is in, I alternate between assuming Scarlett gets Rhett Butler back, and imagining her caretaking Ashley for the rest of their lives at Tara, refurbished to its antebellum glory.

On the screen, of course, the film always ends – as does *Butch Cassidy and the Sundance Kid* – with the outlaw heading out the door. Leaving those of us who care so desperately for desperadoes and the women whose hearts they steal with no choice but to watch it over from the top, in hopes of a different outcome the next time around.

Priests

IT'S BEEN MANY years since I had any direct contact with the Roman Catholic Church. So many years that the current crisis involving (mostly male) victims of sexually predatory pastors, and the ongoing debate over clerical celibacy, seem entirely removed from what I remember from my childhood as the unswerving esteem in which priests were held.

I doubt the actual circumstances were really much different then, or that there wouldn't have been secret speculations and *sotto voce* concerns expressed by adults about the rigours of the celibate life and their effect on the conduct of the clergy behind closed doors. All I'm saying is that in those days the mystique of priests – including parish priests – still seemed largely intact.

Those men were treated like gods. More specifically, like God. Like Jesus Himself, as a matter of fact, because, according to the liturgy of Holy Mother Church, each and every priest ordained was Christ's chosen deputy on earth – a member of that exclusive, you might even say *con*clusive, club which, once joined, you could never, ever leave. Much like the Hotel California.

In my childhood, whenever the parish priest chose to drop in – unannounced – at our house, his arrival had a seigneurial quality. My mother, normally no fan of impulse visitors, would leap to the ready with an offer of coffee or tea – which my dad would dutifully trump with the suggestion of something stronger.

"Must be short on rye at the rectory," he would observe, after the good Father had departed, leaving my parents' liquor cabinet somewhat depleted.

Nevertheless, it was unthinkable that a man of the cloth should not be asked in and accorded unstinting hospitality, whatever the motive for his arrival. The rectory was right across the street from our house; ours was the only Catholic family on the entire block, and Father Feeney could always find something to say to my parents about the latest Knights of Columbus "Smoker," or the upcoming parish hall bake sale, over a rye-and-ginger and a few of my father's Buckingham cigarettes.

The fact that he, like most parish priests, seemed to like his little nip and a butt to go with it was not at all viewed as a shortcoming. Catholics generally prided themselves on the cheerful venality of their faith, as opposed to the anemic observance of the nearby United Church, where, it was said, grape juice served the turn for wine in what passed with Protestants as the ritual of Holy Communion.

Sure, sex before marriage was a mortal sin for Catholics. Yes, fish on Fridays was still *de rigueur*. But there'd been wine on the table at the Last Supper, hadn't there? And if tobacco had existed back then, who was to say Our Lord might not have encouraged the apostles to try one of His, at the end of their final repast?

In the case of Father Feeney, there was a secular one-of-the-boys quality to him that he seemed determined to cultivate – which in no way diminished the persuasive power of his clerical calling. If there were Roughriders tickets going the rounds, Father would make clear that he wanted in. What's more, he implied, he was *entitled* to such temporal perks, by virtue of the hard, lonely, underpaid life he led.

No doubt he was. Hearing endless confessions, keeping track of contributions to the building fund, training a constantly green contingent of altar boys to replace those who continually grew up and moved on, chasing the Ritters' big grey cat out of the sacristy, sorting through the articles of apparel invariably left behind after Mass. . . .

"This week, in the Lost and Found box," Father would announce sternly from the pulpit of a Sunday, "There's one lime-green ladies' glove and one pink one." (Pause for maximum comic effect.) "I'd wear them myself, but the colours don't jibe." (Acknowledgement of the congregation's obedient titters with the merest flicker of a smile.)

Predictable folksy jokes apart, Father Feeney always struck me, in my childhood, as a frightening, almost angry, figure. My uneasiness went beyond his cordial loathing for our cat and the way he'd strong-armed my unwilling mother into becoming the Brown Owl of the parish Brownie pack – prompting her, in turn, to strong-arm me into joining so she wouldn't have to suffer the sunny Brownie ethic all by herself. Father Feeney, I felt, merely acted the role of the with-it, wisecracking padre. Inside, he was as tightly wound as a watchspring.

At our elementary school, he had a way of materializing, unannounced, in the doorway of our classroom, as though hoping to surprise some unwary student in the act of worshipping false idols or consorting with money-changers from the temple. Sometimes, his plan was to confront us all with a snap quiz on our catechism.

On other occasions, a more urgent agenda underlay the visit – such as the morning we learned that the most popular boy in our class had died, just like that, of strep throat over the weekend. Such was the terrible speed of Jimmy's death, that his parents hadn't had a chance to get his Last Confession heard or the Last Rites administered before he was gone.

"Now, I know what you must all be wondering," Father Feeney

declared, solemnly surveying our class. "What about the sins on his soul at the time of his death?"

Actually, some of us were wondering no such thing. What some of us, with far greater urgency, were wondering ran more closely along these lines: If a healthy, happy, nice kid like Jimmy can just up and die like that some Saturday afternoon at home with his family, what guarantee do any of the rest of us have that we'll live to see Grade Eight graduation?

"Well," the priest went on, in response to his own, very different, question, "of course, we can't know what the Creator has in mind when He makes certain choices for us, or what His plan is for young Jim. But I can tell you this much: As sure as God made little green apples, Jim will make it to Heaven, with the help of your prayers."

It wasn't that I didn't feel somewhat relieved to hear that the prognosis for Jimmy was more or less positive. It was just that the "little green apples" allusion struck me as somewhat hokey and false – more the kind of a thing a priest in a movie or on a TV show might say. Besides, how could Father suggest even for a second that someone as good-hearted as Jimmy wouldn't go straight up to Heaven on his own steam, even plus or minus his Last Confession?

Now that I'm so much older, I can look back and label that priest a "control freak," determined to dole out the good news and the bad news to us kids in such a way as to give himself the role of magnanimous, God-like judge, dispensing homey maxims and hard facts of faith with the same even and inspired hand. At the time, however, all I was able to sniff out was a sense of theatricality that smelled insincere, for all Father's well-wielded dramatic effects.

The worst part for me, on such occasions, was the impossibility of telling if anybody else felt the same way. The other kids in class paid the priest automatic deference, like eager-to-please dogs, while the all-female staff of teachers would literally fall back in awe whenever Father loomed suddenly into view. Particularly those teachers who happened to be nuns.

Nuns had a way of flapping and scattering like a flock of frightened starlings at the mere glimpse of a clerical collar, a way that even I, an easily intimidated child, found excessively servile. Impossible to canvass *them* for an objective assessment of that peculiar mixture of benignity and belligerence dispensed by priests like Father Feeney.

The older I got, the wider the gap between priests and nuns began to yawn. While their vow of celibacy lent priests much of their allure, on nuns the mantle of chastity looked quaint, timorous, even absurd. Oh sure, there were Sisters among the staff in my high school pretty and enigmatic enough to bespeak a romantic past and a tragic tale adumbrating their decision to take the veil. Mostly, though, they seemed silly, childlike, simply not up to independent adult life.

It was, God knows, a depiction of nuns that priests liked to foster. Especially those visiting stars who arrived, frequently from the U.S., to lead us girls in our annual retreat.

A Retreat was a special sort of event in the Catholic calendar, a few days' dispensation from regular classes so that we might meditate in silence on our sins, pray for the souls of other sinners, pore over a ready supply of religious tracts, and – above all – attend to speeches about spirituality, and carnality, delivered by the priest in charge, usually with a mixture of humour and hellfire.

It took a special sort of priest to run a retreat, someone with the unflagging energy of a motivational speaker and the chummy compassion of a Father Confessor, as well as the oratorical wattage required to train the glaring spotlight of Truth on the shrinking souls of a pack of convent-schoolgirls, unwilling to face head-on the horrific possibilities of eternal doom.

For such a task, no mere parish priest or familiar Fatherly figure would suffice. Hence, the emphasis on imported talent, and the need for the rigorous imposition of silence, the disorienting suspension of normal routine, the tightly scheduled rounds of lectures by the retreat leaders, the protracted sessions of soul-searching, and unlimited opportunity for Confession. Eventually, under such a regimen, even the hardiest among us would crack – and end up sobbing (silently) in some dark cloakroom, or sitting alone in the chapel, calm in the despairing knowledge that we were in the passing lane on the road to perdition.

Even more effective than a few days of Retreat within the familiar walls of our own school, and within the normal confines of regular classroom hours, was the pilgrimage reserved for Grade Twelve girls to an out-of-town establishment consecrated to the purpose. The village of Lumsden is that rarity in flat southern Saskatchewan: a valley town. And the Catholic Retreat House was (and, for all I know, still is) a mecca of serene solitude.

As a small child, I'd often driven by with my parents and brother to go tobogganing on Lumsden's snow-crested hills. The Retreat House, with its sharply pointed spire, was a familiar sight from the car window. Little had I suspected then that I'd eventually wind up incarcerated inside the place for three endless days, gazing wistfully out a window at the same sloping highway our family car had travelled, topped by the toboggan.

When the nuns instructed us to pack for Lumsden, a number of us Grade Twelves were dubious from the start. Our convent school was a day school only, and many of us had never spent more than a night away from home, apart from vacations with our parents. The prospect of days and nights away from everything familiar, under constant religious supervision, constrained by silence and subdued (as we'd heard) with saltpetre struck us as nothing like a vacation and suspiciously like an attempt to induce a vocation.

"It's how they brainwash us into taking the veil, you know," the better-informed among us counselled the others. "They get us way out there in the middle of nowhere, feed us on overcooked macaroni laced with drugs to lower our sex drive, lull us with sacred music, scream at us about sins one minute, then coo at us about becoming soldiers of Christ the next, and – bingo! Ready-made vocations. It's a poor excuse for an out-of-town Retreat that doesn't net at least a couple of fresh recruits."

Personally, I didn't think there was much danger of anybody at Lumsden trying to turn me into a nun. Going mad from boredom was my only urgent concern. I was determined to combat that by regarding the Retreat as a literary assignment: I would pretend I was taking some time for myself at one of those art colonies in the eastern United States I'd read about, where painters and writers were glad to pay for the privilege of secluded surroundings, the promise of peace and quiet, and the prospect of meals provided by a silent, unseen kitchen staff.

I was relieved to find that our time at Lumsden was fairly unstructured – offering more freedom, in fact, than what we'd been used to in the highly supervised atmosphere of our small girls' school. There were scheduled events, but otherwise we could read; we could visit the chapel; we could nap in our rooms for all anybody knew or cared. The only catch was that we couldn't leave – not because anybody had forbidden us to do so, but because it was February in Saskatchewan, and making it as far as the highway to hitch a ride without freezing to death seemed doubtful.

With a spiral notebook and a ballpoint pen, I spent my first morning looking out the window and waiting for literary inspiration to strike. Ice crystals sparkled in the air, lending a quality of cinematic unreality to the scene outside – where a few straggling, infrequent vehicles made their laborious way up the steep, slippery slope rising from the depths of the valley.

I moralized, of course, on the Sisyphean struggle of those trucks and cars as a metaphor for the human condition. But after making that obvious allusion, I bit on the end of my pen, uncertain what else to say. Eventually, I wound up doodling a version of the winter landscape, complete with declivitous road and boxy little automobiles, trailing plumes of exhaust behind them as they took on the sharp incline of the hill in the sub-zero cold.

Suddenly, I felt sad, in an aimless way that seemed part of a larger sadness that hung in the air as palpably as the smoke in the wake of those cars out there on the highway. Forgetting my fantasy of myself as a member of a professional writers' colony with work to do, I began to brood as one only can at the age of seventeen or so.

It didn't seem at all natural to me that a bunch of convent-school girls like us should be herded together in this remote Retreat House to contemplate our sins and set a future direction for our lives. What sins? Thanks to the vigilance of our parents and the interventionist attitude of the nuns, most of us hadn't yet had a chance to come a cropper. As for the future . . . Personally, all I hoped for was to get as far away as possible from the dreary introspection brought on by the penitent atmosphere of the Retreat.

Nor did some of my fellow contemplatives seem to be faring much more cheerfully as the long first day journeyed uncertainly toward even lengthier night. Although the food turned out to taste somewhat better than the saltpetre-laced pasta predicted by the pessimists in our ranks, it was served by impassive, almost impossibly self-effacing nuns, and consumed, of course, in silence.

In such a sombre atmosphere, none of the more devilish dared to meet each other's eyes for fear of either breaking out in giggles

or breaking down in tears. Tears, in fact, seemed unavoidable for
one of our classmates. More than once, passing the closed door of
her room on my way to Mass or a meal, I distinctly heard the
sounds of sobbing within. Weeks afterward, once were we safely
back in the city and back to our chattering, secular lives, I learned
that she'd discovered around the time of the Retreat that she was
pregnant, and had been forced to address that realization, while
being bombarded alternately with sermons and with silence, as an
increasingly tortured captive of her own reproaches.

At the Retreat House, I remember two priests operating in
standard good-cop-bad-cop configuration. One, tall, forbidding,
and a bit desiccated, spoke to us gloomily of our many shortcomings, the limits of even the infinite patience of the Almighty with
unrepentant sinners, and the particular proclivities of members of
the female gender toward temptation. On the other hand, the
good-news guy was – as if sent by Central Casting – a round,
robust, and wholly happy Father with a fund of self-confidence-
inspiring tips and a host of good jokes.

The jokes were often at the expense of nuns. Not only the
silent wait staff on hand at the Retreat House; every nun who'd
ever dared to don a habit and identify herself as a Bride of Christ
was fair game.

"Oh, those sweet, simple Sisters, back in Grade One!" the fun
Father quipped, enlisting our allegiance with a conspiratorial
wink. "Remember them – passing out the holy cards with the
picture of the Christ Child on them whenever you got an answer
right in catechism class?" Here, the priest would pause to purse
his lips in imitation of some bygone, slightly batty nun, dealing
out the sacred images like a hand of poker. "'One Baby Jesus for
you . . . one Baby Jesus for you . . . and one for you . . . Who wants
a Baby Jesus?'"

We girls were grateful for a laugh in such solemn surroundings. What a perfect takeoff of every nun we'd ever known! How cool of Father, even while representing a religion that seemed mostly about men, to act as if we had more in common with him than with those poor, witless Sisters!

It was only once some of us had sobered up and stopped laughing that it occurred to us how cynically the fun-loving Father had sought to ingratiate himself, by flattering us girls at the expense of the women we might well become. After all, if any of us did decide on a vocation in the Church as a result of this Retreat, what role would be available to us, other than as the object of similar ridicule?

In our lives back then, the priests who most embodied the antiseptic, anti-female arrogance of men of the cloth were the Jesuits who ran the boys' high school next door to ours. Jesuits, of course, were the intellectual elite of the Catholic clergy, but the Fathers of Campion College were equally renowned among both boys and girls as brutal enforcers of a species of discipline totally beyond anything even the nastiest of nuns had ever been known to administer.

From earliest childhood, my brother and I had been regaled with my father's stories of his own days back at Campion, where – as in the Old West – the only law was apparently a hook and a draw. Those tales of the Jesuits' penchant for physical force caused our blood to run cold as our father relayed, with nostalgic gusto, the array of punitive instruments the priests in his day had at their beck. Straps and paddles and switches and rods were among the most conventional weaponry. Boots, books, bits of chalk, and innumerable other airborne objects seemed to find even greater favour among the Fathers.

Even an excellent student like my father seemed to come in for his share of sadistic torment, and at times he would recall the injustice with real resentment. It came as an enormous surprise, therefore, when he decreed that my brother would follow in his footsteps to Campion's door. Brought up on those stories of the Jesuits' bloodthirsty ways, my brother, naturally enough, had no desire to spend his high-school days dodging blows and verbal abuse. But like his father before him, he was offered no choice.

Not much had changed since my father's schooldays, except, possibly, some refinements in the weapons of choice. One of the teachers – whether a priest or a lay Catholic, I can no longer remember – affected darkly tinted eyeglasses, my brother told me, and a sawed-off pool cue that he brandished like a billy stick. Another preferred the simple expedient of throwing misbehaving or academically inadequate boys through the cheaply plastered walls of the classroom.

Living the comparatively civilized life of the convent school – where the nuns' cruellest corporal punishment was to seize a girl sharply by the wrist, or perhaps slap her smartly on top of the head with a yardstick, thereby driving the plastic tines of her hairband into her scalp like a latter-day Crown of Thorns – we girls could only shudder at what our brothers and boyfriends faced from the Jesuits. On occasion we were forced to witness some of these brutalities for ourselves, whenever the lack of a priest to say a separate Mass at our own school compelled us to troop over to Campion College instead.

There, down on our knees, praying through fervent and trembling lips, we would silently beseech the Blessed Virgin to protect us from punishment at the hands of the priests. Meanwhile, the Jesuits and lay teachers alike prowled menacingly all during Mass, flexing their leather straps, or tapping some truncheon-like instrument meaningfully against a chairback. On one occasion, I remember the entire student body, male and female, congealing in terror as a Jesuit voice rang out like a pistol shot in the midst of the

Elevation of the Sacred Host: "There is a boy with his hands in his pockets. If that young man does not instantly remove his hands from said pockets, I will make sure those hands of his will no longer fit into his pockets for some days to come."

Knees knocking, we girls whispered all down the line to each other through paralyzed lips. "They aren't allowed to hit *us*, are they?"

Possibly not, but one thing we knew for sure: the Jesuits took a dim view of the female sex generally. On the positive side of the ledger, obviously, there was the Virgin Mary – a virgin, and, paradoxically, a fertile one at that – who'd somehow managed to comply with God's directive regarding fruitful multiplication while at the same time avoiding the normal, regrettably carnal, preamble. But as far as the rest of womankind went . . . well, the farther a good Catholic boy got away from us, the better, according to what the Jesuits preached and presumably practised.

Which struck us girls as something of a joke, when set alongside the nuns' dark opinion of the male of our species. "Girls, if you're in a car with a boy, and if he brings that car to a stop any place other than in front of your parents' home . . . As soon as he reaches for the ignition key, you reach for the doorhandle!"

Either it was boys who led girls astray, or it was we who pointed the way down the primrose path of dalliance. Why couldn't nuns and priests get on the same page of the hymn book and figure out once and for all where to place the blame?

Of course, when it came to those few students of either gender in whom both priests and nuns sensed the sprouting seeds of a vocation, the incentive to inveigh against the corrupting influence of the other sex acquired even greater urgency. For the nuns, it was not so much a quest for the brightest and the best among us girls, as for the sweetest and the saintliest – the girl most likely to succeed in a life where the emphasis was on obedience.

When it came to the priesthood, however – especially aspirants to the elite ranks of the Society of Jesus, or Jesuits – the bar was raised much higher. Holy Orders was, after all, no mere calling like the convent, but a sacrament. It was the very permanence of the priesthood that made it both unbearably romantic to us girls and totally terrifying to the kind of scholarly and sensitive young man the Jesuits were most intent on recruiting to the ranks of the Soldiers of Christ, fit to handle the Holy Eucharist, forgive others their sins, and wield the Word of God like a weapon – meanwhile going without sex (or so they said) forever and ever.

Shortly before our class was to graduate, one of my best friends lost her boyfriend to the Jesuits. Pat was exactly the studious, scrupulous sort of boy who could be made to believe that his superior intellect, as a gift from God, should be returned to Sender in the form of fourteen years of unremitting study at the seminary, followed by a lifetime of celibate service in some realm of Catholic scholarship.

Sorry as I was for my girlfriend, I felt as well a stab of envy. How lucky, in a way, to lose the love of your life, if it meant having him forever frozen in time as the perfect paramour, plucked in his prime and sealed in the vault of your memory as the beatified boyfriend against whom all future comers could be judged, and found wanting, along with the current boyfriends of your friends. Mine, for instance – an ordinary, lumpen sort of lad, a member of good standing in the Sodality of the Blessed Virgin but not likely to attract the attention of anyone in search of the brightest or the best at anything.

Right after graduation, Pat was sent on his way to the seminary, where he was forbidden to so much as write a letter to the girl he'd left behind.

"Look on the bright side," I counselled my girlfriend, who was sobbing into the telephone after she and Pat had parted. "He might wake up in a week, wonder what in Hell came over him, and get himself sprung before anything irreversible happens."

"N-no," my friend hiccupped tearfully. "Not Pat. H-he's out of my life forever."

"Poor you," I said, while feeling sorrier for myself, cast in the far less attractive role of the consoling companion to whom nothing remotely as interesting was ever likely to happen. "But at least Pat loves you, and you love him. Nobody can take that away."

"I'd rather they'd t-taken that away and left *him* behind."

Still, she got to wear her loss like a war widow's star, and it was impossible not to crave that species of tragic nobility. As unsusceptible as I was to much of conventional Catholicism, I was, at the age of seventeen, still a sucker for the romantic idea of young men seduced by the sanctity of Holy Mother Church. The film version of *Becket* had come out that year, and the agony of asceticism as practised by the unlikely likes of Richard Burton drove me almost insane with a conflicting desire to be both devout and debauched.

Oblivious to the movie's explicit elements of homoeroticism, I identified avidly with the all-too-mortal man upon whom holiness had been thrust willy-nilly. I plunged myself up to the neck in the Middle Ages, with its attendant images of sexily suffering saints, its gaunt, suggestive spires, and – mostly – its incense-scented emphasis on self-abasing sacramental devotion.

At home, I taped my bedroom windows with squares of tissue paper painted to look (a little) like stained glass. I copied scenes from the Bayeux Tapestry with painstaking precision in pen and pink. At school, I showed a surprising new attentiveness to the rites of the liturgy, which the nuns found impressive, if somewhat mysterious in origin.

Within myself, however, I knew none of this apparent religious revival was likely to last. It was the doubting Thomas quality of

Thomas à Becket that attracted me – the sensuality that had preceded sainthood and not been quite successfully suppressed. This
was just another teenage phase I was in – quite possibly my last. At
the first opportunity to practise some sensuality on my own, first-
hand, I knew any interest in sainthood would be right out the
faux stained-glass window.

Acting on that awareness, I took my concerns about myself to a
priest. As a rule, confession had always been a ritual from which I
shrank. Abject, odious, vaguely neurotic at its worst, confession
sometimes felt like kissing the feet of the crucifix at the sombre
Good Friday service, or presenting your forehead for the priest to
smudge with ashes at the beginning of Lent. At its best, it was
merely depressing, like a visit to the doctor or dentist – just
another in a series of compulsorily intimate encounters with
gruff, scary, much older men.

On this occasion, however, confession finally felt as if I was
calling the shots. I'd safely survived the Retreat House at
Lumsden. Graduation and the prom were in the past. The last
departmental exam was written, and though we did not yet have
our final grades, we seniors were, in effect, already on our way. I
had secured, *mirabile dictu*, a scholarship to a university in the
fabled East come fall. Now, before I headed out of the sphere of
anybody's spiritual influence for once and for all, it seemed
important that some things got said.

"Father," I confided to the anonymous priest, "it's not so much
that I feel I'm losing my faith as I feel that I never had it to begin
with. It's like an inoculation that didn't take, or something – if
you see what I mean."

But through the screen that divided us, it seemed he didn't
quite see. I would need to elaborate.

"It's as if I were heading out into a world full of all kinds of infec-
tion, except I was never properly immunized. It's not anybody's

fault. I mean, I got the . . . required shots, just like everybody else. Weekly Mass – *daily* Mass during Lent – regular confessions, catechism classes, the works. But, here's the thing, Father: a little more than two months from now, I'm going to be a couple of thousand miles away from here, in a big university, in a big city, with nobody but me around to tell me what to do. Now, what do you suppose is going to happen?"

"I don't know. What?" On the other side of the partition, the priest suddenly sounded rather interested.

"I'll stop going to church. I'll quit worrying about Holy Communion and making my Easter Duty. It's not like I'm *planning* it, Father. It's just what I know is going to happen. Because, deep down, I never have, somehow, bought this, not any of it."

I could not see the priest clearly, and his voice didn't sound as if it belonged to anyone I knew. But I could tell from the long pause and the way he shifted on his chair that he'd been warned in the seminary that there might be days like this.

"Oh, now," he murmured at last, "I don't imagine that's actually true. You may *feel* this way right now, but the roots of your faith are probably deeper than you realize, and your faith, you know, will see you through."

But he couldn't have been entirely complacent on that score, because later that morning, when we Grade Twelves were all assembled for some sort of farewell address from the nuns, and the anonymous priest stepped out of the confessional to say a few final words of his own, he chose as his theme the tests of faith we could all expect to endure out in the real world.

"Just because there may be nobody on hand to make you go to Mass, or check up on the date of your last confession, that's no reason to assume you should see what your life would be like without those things. Keep on going to Mass every Sunday; take Communion weekly, and keep up the habit of regular confession.

Because it's habit that'll get you through, even when your faith fails, or seems to. And once Faith returns to greet you like an old friend, you'll find you won't need the habit of faith any more, and all will be well."

It probably was good advice, advice that may have satisfactorily served any number of other girls in the assembly room that day. For my own part, I did stop going to Mass almost as soon as I arrived in Montreal that fall, and I never went to confession or took Communion again.

Early in my days at McGill, at a dance at one of the men's residences up the Mountain, I met a boy who owned a recording of dialogue highlights from *Becket*, starring Richard Burton and Peter O'Toole. I necked with the boy solely so that he'd give me the record, which he did.

But by then, my brief infatuation with the ruthlessly sexy aesthetics of asceticism was almost over. I still loved to hear the well-crafted voices of Burton and O'Toole, fervent, playful, and petulant by turns, in a relationship that was more about their romance with each other than the dictates of Roman Catholicism. But I could no longer remember why their words had ever fired up in me a kind of fervour for the privations of the priesthood. I was exactly where I'd predicted I'd be, months before, in the confessional back at my old high school: adrift in a world of secular temptation without the necessary religious immunity.

It wasn't, God knew, for lack of effort on the part of the many priests who'd made their way in and out of my life. It was more because, though many are called, there are always the obdurate few who will simply decide not to pick up the phone.

QUIPSTERS

ONE GOOD THING – possibly the *only* good thing – about being a writer is that you can try out almost anything in the name of research, and no matter how badly it goes, you still wind up with something useful somewhere down the line. That, at least, was the basis on which I undertook my brief and undistinguished apprenticeship in stand-up comedy.

Whoever said comedy is serious business wasn't kidding. What I remember most about my summer of weekly stints onstage at Yuk Yuk's Comedy Cabaret in midtown Toronto was the terrible stage fright that would kick in at around three o'clock on the afternoon leading up to my evening performance, while I was working to memorize my routine with the aid of a tape recorder.

By nine p.m. or so, as I headed to the club, my innards would be in the clutch of the cold hand of doom. By ten o'clock, for good or for ill, I was onstage, rattling through my material, more or less by rote, in front of an audience consisting mainly of polite if unimpressed high-school kids who were waiting either for one of their classmates to take the stage or for the advertised headliner to close out the night.

I was far older than most of the other comics, and certainly older than the vast majority of the audience. I felt, in fact, more like their teacher, there to hand back papers or announce an exam, than like someone with comedic insights to dispense. Once in a while, a joke of mine might score, and I'd make a note to myself to keep it in the act. Mostly, though, I strove simply to get through my stuff unscathed, and counted myself lucky not to get derailed by hecklers, or even by an unexpected laugh, which – while welcome – always threatened to throw me off my script.

But however the routine went over, I would, as I stood up there, become aware of the gradual easing of the cold fingers gripping my gut, and a rising sense of grateful relief as my ordeal came to its close in a smattering of good-natured applause. *Never again, never again* was the refrain my jubilant blood sang in my ears. I may have lived to fight another day, but I didn't *have* to fight if I didn't feel like it. After all, this was research, right? Nobody was paying me to stand up there and make a fool of my –

"So, you signed up for next week?"

That would be Mark, the diminutive despot who controlled both the crowds and the comics he employed with the same mixture of pleasantry and persecution. "You didn't stink so bad. A couple of your bits almost worked, even. You can't get it right if you don't go up there. So, here's the pen, here's the book, here's next week. You gonna sign or what?"

Almost against my will, I'd feel the pen between my fingers and find myself writing my name in the book, like a soul seemingly determined to seal the terms of its own damnation. Comedy was indeed serious business. You hoped to kill, but if you failed you died. Still . . . I hadn't stunk so bad, according to Mark. If I could take a couple of those bits that almost worked, and combine them with something new and boffo . . .

In my own defence, I can only say there was something of the exultation of the matador who survives the bullring, something of the skydiver who floats to earth intact, in that rush of euphoria that succeeded the sickening flop-sweat and somehow induced me to defy my own best judgment and get out there again, determined to kill or be killed in the attempt. As an unpaid performer, certainly there was little other inducement to keep me going up there week after week.

Of course, for some of the other comics – the *real* comics – the motive to perform must have come from some other, far more authentic, though far more frantic, place. The women, of whom there were few in those days, were the more flamboyant performers. Full of self-deprecating shtick ("How about this nose? In sailing season, I go down to the yacht club and rent myself out as a rudder") or full of peculiar skills, like the ability to fast-forward through the entire film of *The Wizard of Oz* in ninety seconds flat. It was those female comics who gave me tips on how to deal with hecklers. ("Point to him and say, 'Hey, whaddaya know! A talking urine sample.' Or say, 'That's a great shirt, sir. How long you gotta wear it before you win the bet?'")

The men, on the other hand, were far more likely to offer advice on my material and technique. ("Don't show fear, okay? Don't ever show fear, or they'll turn on you like a pack of dogs. If you say the line and nobody laughs, you don't rush on to the next bit the way you did tonight, okay? You wait for the laugh. Just wait. Eventually, it'll come. Or not. If not, well *then* you move on. Before they turn on you like a pack of dogs. No, just kidding. The trick is, show them you're the one in control. Not them. You. You got that?")

It wasn't so much that the guys cared more than the women did about helping me develop my act. It was more that analyzing comedy was part of its appeal for them. A stand-up routine – anybody's routine – was like a watch, or a train, or a pocket puzzle: half the fun was in taking it apart to see how it worked, then putting it back together.

Backstage and after-hours, much of the discussion that went on among the guys revolved around truisms of the trade: "Funny always comes in threes. That's why the three-point gag is the classic gag." Or: "Odd numbers are funnier than even. Eleven? Pretty funny. Ten? Not so much. Don't ask why."

There was a kind of uniformity about those boys – and they mostly were still boys. Jewish in the main – though not exclusively – and often from Forest Hill Collegiate, a good high school in a good part of town. Neatly turned out in sports jackets and jeans, with a stock of jokes on the theme of high school, teenage sex, teenage angst, and toilet humour. Even some of the older regulars – one a self-described substitute teacher named Steve – made the requisite high-school jokes ("Hey, how come when you're sneaking in late at night, there's *always* this one loose floorboard right outside your parents' bedroom that squeaks like a son of a bitch? And next time, when you try to avoid it, there's a *different* one that squeaks. I mean, does your mom spend her afternoons *loosening* them, or what?")

In an earlier generation, Steve and all the future Steves who nightly took the stage at Yuk Yuk's might likely have learned ventriloquism, or the musical saw, or magic tricks – anything to attract attention and give the folks a real good time. There seemed to be no other agenda in their comedy, no trenchant politics, no plea for understanding, no desperate cry for help. While the few female comics seemed to fulfill the role of kooky outsider, or insecure self-critic, the guys on the whole seemed pretty much okay with society and their own role in it, give or take the odd bad night onstage, with too little energy from the audience, or too much, or the wrong kind.

After-hours, it was mostly the guys who got together at a neighbouring delicatessen – just the way the professionals presumably did in places like New York – to go over the evening's experiences, swap or sell a few jokes, or simply spritz with each other, around a mouthful of pastrami on rye washed down with Diet Coke. They were, for the most part, slightly doughy and definitely schleppy young men, with quiet jackets and loud mouths, trading insights and insults at Manny's Delicatessen with all the buttoned-down businesslike efficiency of a convention of chartered accountants on the brink of tax season exchanging the latest on income averaging.

Even so, these young stand-ups clearly got girls, and cute girls at that. The only girls I ever observed in attendance (apart from myself, and at my age I hardly qualified) were the pretty, almost interchangeable, blond or brunette babydolls who came along as mute consorts to the male comics much in the manner of pro hockey wives or members of a rock star's retinue. Except, of course, these guys weren't sports celebrities or rising pop personalities. Women, apparently, were attracted to funny, much in the same way money or muscularity or political power appeared to act as an aphrodisiac even for guys who lacked conventional good looks. It was the Woody Allen principle given proof in real life.

For female comics, however, a sense of humour seemed to have no similar effect on male sex-hormones. Seldom did I see any of the women who worked regularly at Yuk Yuk's escorted to or from the club on the arm of a man. Nor, God knows, did my own modest efforts onstage that summer net me any stage door Johnnies who were anything other than decidedly weird.

If, for those mere boys, funny business had proven so sure a route to romance, I was inclined to imagine the seasoned pros who topped the bill forced to use a firehose to fend off the females who must besiege them at their hotels. Yet, when I did once get a chance to spend time after the show with a headliner at Yuk Yuk's, he seemed like the loneliest, least glamorous guy imaginable.

He was a comic from LA, who invited a bunch of the young kids from the club back to his hotel room, presumably to alleviate some of the isolation of his life on the road. Because I happened to be on the bill that night, I got invited too, and I braced myself for a very drunken, very male sort of party.

In fact, the evening proved fairly subdued, even desultory, despite the abundance of alcohol and, if I correctly recall, a fair amount of pot making the rounds.

The room was a mess. Obviously, the headliner from LA had ordered pizza at several points in his stay, because the place was littered with dried-up old crusts and Styrofoam coffee cups and cigarettes stubbed into blobs of dingy mozzarella. But the comic didn't seem to care; he just sat there in a corner with a stopwatch and a notepad and played a tape of his act.

At first, the young male comics eagerly attempted to make the most of this heaven-sent opportunity to banter about the business with a seasoned pro. But all the headliner from LA would do was hit the Pause button on the tiny, tinny mini-recorder every so often to ask in a general way, "What about that? Was that at all funny?"

The headliner's act hadn't gone very well that night, but he *was* the headliner from LA. So, on every Pause, somebody would be sure to say, "Sure, that's a funny bit, man. That's very funny."

Gradually, the headliner began to pay more attention to the fact that we were all there. He started throwing out new lines he'd spun off from the material on the tape. And after every new line, he'd stop and ask, "What about *that*? Could *that* be funny?"

Still eager to make an impression on someone so much more advanced in the game, the young comics tried their best to offer sincere answers. But some of it was funny, and some of it really was not, and after a while anyone could see he wasn't really listening to what they had to say. It wasn't ideas he was interested in – it was reassurance. Simple, straightforward, continual reassurance that he was funny.

As more and more alcohol was consumed in the hotel room, and more joints were rolled and smoked, the comic's improvisations of possible new material became increasingly desperate.

"Ship of . . . shit!" he said at one point, snapping his fingers and clicking on the tape recorder once more. "How about that? Ship of Shit. A disaster movie, right, about this ship in danger out on the high seas, and it's . . . full of shit. Literally. Ship of Shit. Could *that* be funny?"

No, never in a million years, but there was something about the man's quest to nail the essence of "funny" that was unbearably poignant. Funny was his stock in trade. Funny was all he had to sell, and when the sample cases were empty, as they seemed to be tonight . . . well, it was impossible not to ache for his obsession. Like a violinist nervously flexing his fingers, or a boxer worried about his footwork or his reach or the fragility of his jaw, the headliner from LA was fretting about his one talent which was death to hide, yet impossible to simulate when absent, recapture when lost, or even explain in so many words.

"Ship of Shit?" Politely, the young comics pretended to consider the merits of the suggestion as they downed the headliner's liquor and availed themselves of his dope. "Yeah, with the right crowd, Ship of Shit could maybe be funny. Maybe."

Later on, when we were all on our way out of the headliner's hotel, they exchanged despairing glances in the elevator. "Ship of Shit? Hoo, boy. Is that not el stinko or what? Poor schlub. What the hell was he *thinking?*"

It was, it seemed to me then and still seems to me now, an entirely male interaction − both the headliner's naked terror of ceasing to be funny, and the younger comics' admission to each other that he had a right to be scared. Women comics also fret about the ineffable nature of "funny," but surely not with the same desperate demand for reassurance that they've still got it – especially once they know it's gone.

For a man, of course, when humour is gone so much else goes along with it, whether he's a professional comedian or just a guy who gets girls because he's quick with a quip. Men know this, and it must make them very tense. I've gone out with men who became angry when I didn't find them funny, especially in front of their friends. The angrier they got, the less funny they became. And the less funny they became, the harder they tried to get their groove back.

As with sex, there are no points awarded merely for trying. Quite the reverse. Humour, like sex, just has to happen. And the more a man has to call attention to the fact that it's happening, the more embarrassing it gets for all concerned. "Look at that! Look at the size of this joke. Is this not the biggest, most impressive joke you've ever come across?"

Equally, it's anger-making for him if he's forced to explain. "That was a *joke*, goddammit. I don't know why you can't appreciate that. Every other woman I've ever been with was always very, very appreciative of my jokes."

Worst of all, for a woman, is when he apologizes. "I'm sorry. I don't know what's gone wrong with my jokes tonight. I've never had this problem before . . ."

And she is forced to assure him that it's perfectly all right. "Now, don't give it another thought. Making me laugh isn't everything. There are lots of other ways we can have a good time together. Please, just relax, and it'll happen, I'm sure. I mean, the worst thing you can do is get all self-conscious about it and try too hard."

But both men and women know that at the base of all this angst is one indisputable fact: Women value a sense of humour in men far more highly than men value it in women. Is there a woman in the world, I wonder, who would choose a good-looking, vapid stud over a funny guy not nearly so attractive? Oh sure, there's that famous example in the film *Broadcast News*, when Holly Hunter breaks Albert Brooks's heart by falling for the empty-headed blond TV anchor played by William Hurt. But the problem with that example is that Holly Hunter mistakenly believes that the anchorman is sensitive, and she turns away from Albert Brooks because he's a cynic. Once truth levels the playing field, she sees the funny guy as the better man.

Men, meanwhile, are cut from other cloth. There's no man I know, however high-minded, who would be congenitally capable of picking a plain but funny female ahead of a comely yet comedically challenged babe. In the old movies, in order to offer the witty woman the edge over her dishy-but-depthless rival, she had to turn out to be at least as beautiful, once her glasses were off. While in films of more recent vintage, everybody's so good-looking anyway, that male characters cannot lose, however they choose, and women often wear glasses simply to make themselves look cuter still.

Meanwhile, back in real life, the kind of humour that men practise can be as important to their attractiveness as the fact that they are funny in the first place. For the young comics back at Yuk Yuk's, the mere fact that they were funnymen seemed sufficient to get the girls. But in the adult world of everyday relationships, it helps when a guy can make jokes at his own expense. Smart men know how to use this technique advisedly, in a way that smacks of sensitivity, not of desperation.

One of the funniest men I've ever been involved with had such a disarming gift for self-deprecation that he was able to keep the allegiance of almost every woman he ever broke up with. Much of the time, he managed to do it by pretending that it was always the woman who broke up with him.

"No matter what you say," he used to tell me – both before, during, and after the period of time we officially spent as a couple – "breaking up is murder on guys. Breaking up, in fact, is almost always way harder on any guy than it is on any woman. Really. You run into a woman whose boyfriend has just handed her the mitten? She never looked better. She's been to the hairdresser; she's signed up for tango lessons; she's gone out and got herself a whole new wardrobe. Meanwhile, a guy whose girlfriend is gone? He's a mess. In his bathrobe at four o'clock in the afternoon, with a three-day growth of beard, drinking milk right out of the carton, his eyes all red from blubbering, 'I can't go on without her!' Forgetting he's the one who walked out on her."

In the realm of professional comedy, however, it is mostly the women who practise self-put-downs as a way of getting laughs. Even those female comics who dish it out to other women tend to do so with an implied acknowledgement that those other women – too pretty, too rich, too thin – are the true representatives of their sex. The trick is to enlist the allegiance of females in the audience as fellow schleps – "Don't you hate the kind of itsy-bitsy little girl, you lend her a bracelet, she wears it as a belt?" – but with the clear understanding that those itsy-bitsy little girls are more to be envied than mocked.

Joan Rivers, in her prime (i.e., long before the silly excesses of Oscar night) was a past mistress both at skewering the concupiscence of the competition – "My friend Heidi Abramovitz? She's had more hands up her dress than the Muppets!" – and sending-up her own insecurities – "My body has fallen so far, my gynecologist has to wear a hard hat!" Nothing overtly angry in it, no particular quest for power or for any other kind of apparent gain. . . . Humour, I would hazard, for its own sake, as a coping mechanism, a quest for reassurance, an ingratiating plea for public approval. "Can we *talk?*" was the famous tag line, but "Can you *listen?*" was the question underneath.

Men, I think, undertake professional comedy for reasons less to do with personal therapy and more to do with social advantage. Not only does the funny guy, however schleppy, so often get the girl, he frequently gets the goat of his male antagonist, whether with a Woody Allenesque aside, a mordant bit of Mort Saulish satire, or a Don Rickles-style Rottweiler attack.

Even where the worlds of male and female comedy intersect, there are significant differences. While female comedians like Lily Tomlin are prone to concern – "I worry that the person who invented stickers on fruit is working on something else" – a Jerry Seinfeld sort of stand-up is more likely to begin with a nonchalant "Did you ever notice . . . ?"

When it comes to anger, Roseanne Barr is easily as irritable as the late Lenny Bruce. Where that anger is directed, however, may be another matter. Roseanne's own multiple makeovers, regimes of facial reconstruction, and desperate attempts to diet herself into an utterly other person seem to signify a need to nullify not the world at large, but her own large self. Lenny Bruce, on the other hand, filled himself with drugs, candy bars, and self-recrimination, yet he reserved his real assaults for the hypocrisy of a society that he saw as equally obsessed with sex as with censorship.

Out in the larger comedy arena that is the world we all live in, humour, at some level, may in fact be neither male nor female but merely human. In that realm, men and women often laugh when they're hurt, and make jokes precisely *because* they are hurt, and are hoping to cover that up with a quip and a quick getaway. Comedy can be deceptive that way: The real agenda is often to fend other people off, while appearing, conversely, to invite them in.

Men are often wary of women who operate like that, but women are oddly attracted to the kind of man whose knowing wink beckons like an elusive will-o'-the-wisp. The kind of funny-man – professional or amateur – who seems to sense that, in a perfect world, there would be no need of his jokes, and who may actually have a vested interest in keeping things rotten, if only to keep himself in fresh material.

On the conscious level, that may be a conundrum too twisted for any quipster to dare contemplate. But it may also be true that the anger behind some of the best comedy comes from the awful awareness that the best comic business is built from the worst elements on earth, and the bigger the belly laugh, the more it resembles a roar of rage.

But beyond material that gets belly laughs, there are the wry, quiet comments that serve only to summon knowing smiles. Those kinds of quips are most often made by women, and most often made about men. Like the truism coined by an anonymous female cab driver, and more famously quoted by Gloria Steinem: "If men could get pregnant, abortion would be a sacrament."

That's a line that goes beyond most women's mild kvetches about male attitudes, beyond any sort of summational comment a male comic could make about his own sex, and instead gets straight to the heart of what still keeps men in official charge of human history and most other realms of endeavour: their skill at putting both biology and religion to work in service of their politics.

Could that be funny? Sure, it could. Particularly when you bear in mind that the comedy of men and women can be serious business indeed.

RERUNS

NEWLY RETURNED FROM a lengthy – and ultimately somewhat lonely – vacation, I'd been looking forward with particular anticipation to the next regular gathering of a group of my best girlfriends as an opportunity to catch up on all that had gone on in my absence. When I walked into our favourite restaurant, therefore, I was surprised, and disappointed, to see a number of empty chairs around our customary table.

"Where's Millicent tonight?" I inquired of the reduced ranks. "What about Toby? And Lena, for heaven's sake? I thought for sure *she'd* make a point of showing up, if only to twit me for squandering my life savings on yet another trip where I didn't encounter a single decent man. Or, a single indecent man, come to that."

"Lena's met someone," the women chorused as one. "So's Millicent. And Toby ... well, maybe. A boy she knew back in Grade Three phoned her out of the blue, and tonight's their first date."

"Grade *Three*?" I was incredulous. "It's taken him all this time to get up the courage to call?" Having gone to all the trouble to travel halfway around the world in search of a date, it didn't seem fair somehow to find out I should have stayed home by the phone instead.

"Well, I think it's romantic," offered Karina.

"Not half as romantic as what's happened with Millicent," Jackie corrected her. "You see," she said, turning back to me, "it

seems as if Mil– no, wait! You should give Millicent a call, and let
her tell you herself. It's the most utterly, incredibly lovely story
you've ever heard."

"Fine," I said miserably. "I will. So what about Lena? Do you
want to tell me who she's met? Or should I leave it to her to give
me the scoop?"

Lena, the others were happy to tell me, had taken a second look
at a guy she'd been set up with seven years before, dated once,
dropped, and then recently reencountered sporting fresh dental
work, a more convincing hairpiece, and a brand-new attitude
toward meaningful relationships. A nice enough story, but Jackie
was right: it was Millicent's tale of love rekindled that took the
three-tiered wedding cake.

Luckily for me, Millicent opted to give me all the details in
person, rather than squander such sensational material over the
telephone. She's always had a true sense of occasion, has Millicent,
as well as an insatiable craving for "afternoon tea," which she considers imbued with the sort of atmosphere appropriate to the discussion of social adventures of the Jane Austen kind. Accordingly,
at four o'clock precisely on the soonest mutually convenient
weekday afternoon, Millicent and I met at the Four Seasons (her
current favourite among a roster of competing Toronto tea-tables)
for a complete debrief on the new, improved state of her love life.

"He was my high-school sweetheart," she started, once we'd
ordered our tea and sandwiches and dispensed with the boring
details of my recent ramble into the dateless heart of Borneo. "We
went out all through our senior year – were even crowned King
and Queen of the prom – and then headed off to separate univer-
sities and separate lives. Totally. I mean, we're talking a period of
twenty-six *years* during which there was zero contact between us.
Not so much as a Christmas card, an e-mail, or even a friendly
Hello passed along by a hometown friend."

"Wow," I said. "That's zero contact, all right. So how did you ever manage to get back in touch?"

This was Millicent's story, of course, and along with an appreciation of the proper setting in which to tell it, she also had very definite feelings about the pace at which to deal out the elements of her narrative.

"It was as if he had dropped off the face of the Earth," she said with great emphasis, just in case I had not yet managed to grasp the absolute nature of their long separation. "I got married and divorced twice, as you know, lived in Europe for a while, went briefly back to the States, then moved here permanently. He, meanwhile, unbeknownst to me, had contemplated matrimony a couple of times, had even gone so far on one occasion as to get engaged, but . . ." and here Millicent paused for maximum dramatic impact, "but for some reason unclear to him at the time, *broke off the engagement because something about it didn't seem right.* None of his near-alliances ever seemed quite right.

"And then, lo and behold, I'm up in Ottawa at a symposium, giving a paper on "Currents of Coincidence in the Nineteenth-Century Romantic Novel," of all coincidental things, and who do I run into, of all people?"

"Your high-school sweetheart?" I suggested.

"My high-school sweetheart! Who wasn't even supposed to *be* at this particular symposium – which is why his name hadn't appeared on the list of presenters we got e-mailed to us beforehand. I mean, get this: he's stepped in as a completely last-minute replacement for another guy from another university, whose wife's mother has passed away unexpectedly in Toledo . . . And guess what's the topic of the paper he's pulled together in about six seconds?"

"'Currents of Coincidence in the *Twentieth*-Century Romantic Novel'?"

"What?" Millicent seemed miffed, as though she hadn't actually expected me to hazard a guess. "No, of course not! By the twentieth century, there's no real romantic tradition worthy of the name in contemporary novels. Besides, his field of study is Shakespeare. Anyway, the topic of his paper is – you won't believe this – 'Themes of Exile, Return, and Reclamation in the Reign of the Plantagenets.'"

"Gee," I said, afraid of making another gaffe. "That certainly sounds . . . informative."

"Pardon? Sure, I guess so. But don't you get the bizarre connection? 'Exile, Return, and Reclamation' – and there are he and I, running into each other at some stupid symposium in *Ottawa*, after twenty-some years of – if not exile exactly, then certainly complete separation."

"I get it," I said. "But where does the Plantagenet part come in?" Of course, by now I realized full well that the Plantagenets were in no way involved, but I was still feeling a little tender from the short shrift Millicent had given my suggested topic for a paper.

"You really mean to say you don't see it? How incredibly romantic all of this is?"

"Oh, all right," I admitted. "Yes, it certainly is incredibly romantic. Seriously. It is."

"Yes, isn't it?" Millicent agreed, pouring the tea with an air of quiet pride in her successful completion of a satisfying story, satisfyingly told. "And now he's planning to spend his sabbatical year here; we're looking for a place together, and we talk on the phone for *hours* every single night, just the way we did back in high school!"

On the subway home from the Four Seasons, I came across a story in that day's paper which, for sheer romanticism, put even Millicent's recent experience in the shade. An eighty-something man and an almost as elderly woman, who'd met in London during the Blitz and then been parted, had both married other people. After that, they passed most of their long lives on separate sides of the Atlantic, and in the fullness of time, each was widowed. It was at that point, somehow or other, that they managed to reconnect with each other, and – according to the article in the paper – "fell in love all over again." They'd got married without delay, and were now living together in what they described to the reporter as a "cozy" room in a seniors' complex in Brampton.

At a certain age, I mused on my way from the subway station to my apartment, romantic reruns seem to become, if not actually inevitable, then more and more likely. There were, after all, a finite number of new men any given woman was slated to meet in her lifetime. At some point – although, ideally, not as late as one's eighties – one was bound to reencounter someone somewhat suitable in a former time who'd for some reason become even more suitable in the here and now. Look at Toby, with her blast from her grade-school past! Look at Lena, reconsidering a one-time reject who'd reconstituted himself as someone far more appealing now. Look at Millicent, multiply-married and divorced, who'd recently had the great good fortune to run into – to *re*run into – an old boyfriend who, for his part, had clearly never quite moved on.

The question was, how was I going to get in on this apparently growing trend toward the relationship retread? One couldn't simply start flipping through one's old high-school yearbook, could one, in search of a bygone boyfriend? Especially when, as in my case, one had attended an all-girls school.

Of course, in the years since, I'd travelled far along the road of romance. It was littered along the shoulders and at the exit ramps with the wreckage of relationships that hadn't stood up to the rigours en route. But what exactly was I supposed to do?

Commence riffling through my entire romantic Rolodex, so to speak, then start cold-calling guys who hadn't really warranted all that much warmth the first time around?

Temporizing, I turned on the TV, as I often do when stymied by the sort of questions with which I seem uniquely able to stump myself. Oh, Lord. There on the screen were Judi Dench and Geoffrey Palmer in that venerable old British sitcom whose name I could never remember. The one about Jean and Lionel, a sixty-plus couple revisiting a romance interrupted almost four decades before.

Oh, swell, I thought. It's a veritable conspiracy of romantic reruns. In fact, this particular episode of this particular series had replayed so often on PBS, that you could call it a kind of rerun of romantic reruns. How many times, oh God, was I condemned to listen to Lionel explain to Jean that he never received the letter she'd mailed to him in the army thirty-eight years before? And how frequently did I need to find out that a late middle-aged man is as queasy about commitment as someone young enough to be his grandson?

On the other hand, the program certainly provided additional proof – if more proof was needed – that the sequel to a relationship can possess a piquancy equal to, albeit somewhat different from, the feeling engendered the first time around. As the closing credits churned along to a particularly treacly rendition of "As Time Goes By" – oh, right, I thought *that's* the name of the silly show! – my mind went back, as perhaps it was meant to, to the sizzling scene in *Casablanca* in which Ilsa walks into Rick's Café, and urges Sam the piano man to strike up the former couple's formerly favourite song.

Ah, Rick and Ilsa! Now *there* was the paramount example of lovers whose second act exceeded even the first fine careless rapture of romance's opening scene. But there again – just like

Millicent and her high-school prom king, like that old couple in the newspaper who'd found each other a lifetime after the London Blitz, even like Jean and Lionel on those endlessly repeated episodes of *As Time Goes By* – their reencounter was more or less accidental, was it not?

Clearly, then, no use for me to make a project out of looking up some long-lost beau in hopes of a spontaneous rematch. After all, if I'd learned anything from my effortful and ultimately fruitless single slog through the heartless heart of Borneo, it was how doomed to disaster are explicit attempts to get out there and meet somebody on demand. Satisfied with – if with nothing else – my resolve to leave bad enough alone, I snapped off the TV set and went to bed.

It was the very next evening, while on an errand downtown, that I found myself walking past a once-familiar bar. My God, Perry's Lounge! I hadn't even realized the old place was still extant, so long had it been since I'd made it a habit to have a "regular" drinking haunt. Perry's, in fact, dated from an earlier era in my life I'd mostly rather not remember – and indeed in some aspects *cannot* remember, thanks to the inordinate number of hours I'd logged on the third barstool from the left, imbibing sequential vodka stingers as I pretended not to wait for the man of my dreams to make his nightly entrance with the girl of the moment.

Self-inflicted pain, they say, is the worst kind. I really had nobody but myself to blame for my bootless crush on Carson Kilroy, all those years ago. God knows, he'd never offered much encouragement – just the precise dosage, in fact, carefully calibrated to keep me hanging on in hope.

And, God, how mortifying those months of futile infatuation had felt! Even now, so many years later, finding myself in the doorway of Perry's for the first time in such a long time, I was suddenly conscious of a deep, dull ache somewhere in the vicinity of my heart, and tears smarting at the corners of my eyes, as recollections of my past wretchedness stirred anew.

Not surprisingly, the last thing I wanted to do was walk into Perry's once more, approach the bar, order my one-time accustomed drink, and sit down at the third stool from the left to consume it. Yet I found myself acting on exactly that impulse. Even as my hand reached out to push open the old familiar door, I felt my nerves steeling themselves for the first night of this particular brand of excruciating disappointment in a long, long time.

Amazingly, the interior of Perry's looked exactly as I recalled it from so many years in the past. In fact, the sound system seemed to be featuring the very same tape that I could remember, back in those bygone days of tape, constantly playing a predictable selection of Billy Joel, Warren Zevon, and other pop performers of those now-distant days.

"Usual?" the man behind the bar greeted me, before I could even open my mouth. It was, I could swear, the same bartender. No great wonder in that, I supposed, except for the fact that he appeared not to have aged a whit in all the time that had elapsed since I'd last seen him measuring out the ingredients for a vodka stinger – exactly as he was doing now.

"Here you go, Toots." In mere seconds, he'd managed to mix up my drink and place it in front of me, just as he had every night for all those months so long ago. And "Toots"! My God, how could I have forgotten his habit of calling all women "Toots" and all male customers "Jack"?

"So, how've you been, Wes?" I asked him, pleased with myself for recalling his name.

He grinned. "Since last night, you mean? Oh, 'bout the same, Toots. 'Bout the same."

Last night? What on earth could he mean? As Wes turned to take another order farther down the bar, I realized suddenly that he was dressed precisely as he'd been dressed the last time I'd seen him – in what was now an outmoded-looking shirt in a floral pattern with a long pointed collar, and an ugly suede vest.

"Uh, Wes . . . When you say 'last night,' what exactly do –"

But before I could finish phrasing my question, Wes had clicked a new tape into the deck and pressed Play.

"Oh, no." As the too-familiar strains of Gerry Rafferty's "Baker Street" wafted through Perry's Lounge, my fingers squeezed convulsively around the stem of my glass. "Our" song – mine and Carson Kilroy's. How could it be that I'd forgotten all about the nightly ritual of "Baker Street," yet, seemingly, Wes the barman hadn't?

"'Smatter, Toots? Doncha wanna hear that song? Sheesh, I thought you *always* wanted tuh hear that song."

No, not in more than twenty years, I hadn't. But how exactly to explain that to Wes, apparently caught in some sort of late-seventies time warp? "Sorry. I . . . I guess I'm just not in the mood tonight."

"Sure, Toots. Whatever you say." With a women–who-can-figure-'em shrug, Wes ejected the tape from the antiquated eight-track player, and replaced it with the BeeGees at their most eerily shrill.

But the BeeGees were no more than halfway to wanting to know how deep is your love, before the song was brought to a premature finale by a sudden "Click!" of the Stop button.

"Aw, now, Jack," Wes protested feebly to the customer who'd eighty-sixed the Brothers Gibb. "How many times I gotta tell ya? Patrons are respectfully requested to keep their effin' mitts offa the sound system."

"And how many times do I have to tell *you*, Wes? Management is respectfully requested to can that castrated Saturday Night Fever shit and put on some real music. Come on, you know what I want to hear. Play it."

Unable to believe my ears, I turned to the source of a voice so instantly recognizable it might easily have been yesterday – yester-night, to be precise – since I'd heard it last.

"Aw, fer . . ." Wes protested. "Look, Jack, you're not gonna –"

"Play it, I said. You played it for her, you can play it for me. Now, play it."

With an apologetic shrug in my direction, Wes replaced the BeeGees tape with Gerry Rafferty, and once more the moody throb of "Baker Street" resounded throughout the bar.

As for me, I was sitting transfixed on my barstool gazing at someone I had never expected to behold again in my lifetime: Carson Kilroy, the owner of that oh-so familiar voice, now sitting at a table a few feet from the bar, clutching a highball glass with both hands and staring pensively into the middle distance.

I must say, he looked good – in a somewhat out-of-date way. His sideburns were unmodishly long; in the back, some sort of mullet-cut thing was threatening to happen. His moustache drooped well beyond the corners of his mouth. Like Wes, he wore an absurdly tailored and patterned shirt which, in Carson's case, was sufficiently unbuttoned to reveal a thin gold chain nestling amongst his curling blond chest-hairs.

How many times had I sat staring hungrily at that burnished glint of hair while dreaming about sliding my forefinger flirta-tiously up and under the fine metal links of that chain to caress the underside of Carson's perfect chin? Strange, though, how I'd never before noticed how cheesy that gold chain looked, all tangled up in his chest-hair like that. Kind of like . . . a Wheaton Terrier with a choker, I suddenly thought. All he needed was a licence and a name tag jingling against each other to complete the impression of a well-behaved canine bellying up to the bar, as in some classic joke. . . .

Startled by this reverie, I got a hold of myself and returned my attention to contemplation of the man before me. What a hunk, in spite of the cornball clothes and other adornments. No wonder I'd found myself drawn to Perry's all those years ago, night after night, if only to be teased, toyed with, and eventually left in the lurch.

Yet tonight, Carson Kilroy seemed entirely alone. A little lost, and somewhat defeated as he nursed his drink, stared into space, and let the sad sounds of "Baker Street" wash over him like a slow tide breaking on a melancholy beach.

Encouraged by the vulnerability indicated by this new attitude, I approached his table, and simply stood where the light behind me would act − I hoped − as a blinding, radiant aureole. "Hi," I said, in an understated tone. "You look like you just lost your best friend."

"Worse than that," Carson said, without looking up. "I lost my best girl. And even worse than that, I lost her through my own fault."

"Yeah? Now, how'd you come to do that? A smart, good-looking guy like you?"

Still not even bothering to meet my gaze, Carson indicated the empty chair opposite him. "Sit down if you like, let me buy you a drink, and I'll tell you the whole, sad, stupid −"

But as I moved to sit down, allowing him his first good look at me, Carson broke off abruptly.

"What's the matter?" I asked, reaching across the table to place my hand on his arm. "Seen a ghost?"

"My God," he whispered. "Of all the gin joints in all the towns in all the world, you gotta walk into this one."

"But . . . you did, too," I pointed out reasonably.

"Of course I did! Jeez, haven't I been walking in here every night, looking for you? Checking out that third barstool from the left to see if you'd maybe somehow, some way, come back. Making ol' Wes there put on the Gerry Rafferty, whether he wants to or not ... Don't you understand what I've been through?"

"Not quite," I admitted. "You mean, in all this time, you haven't stopped to rethink the Wyatt Earp moustache? Maybe update your shirts a little bit?"

"Look." Carson took both my hands in his. "The point is: I made an awful mistake with you, way back when – leading you on night after night, before going home with somebody else. I didn't blame you when you finally smartened up and stopped coming in here. Well, I lost you once, but I won't make that mistake again. Stay right here, will you? I'll bring you another vodka stinger, and then we'll sit and talk and catch up, and try to make up for all the time we've lost."

Wow. As he hurried over to the bar to place the order with Wes, I sat shaking my head in disbelief at this turn of events. Carson Kilroy – whom I'd all but forgotten as anything other than the source of one long-ago season of sadness and discouragement – had allegedly been trying and failing to get over the memory of the mistake he'd made in letting me slip out of his life way back then? And now, here we were again, at Perry's – just like before – but for one big difference: This time, I was in the driver's seat and Carson was along for the ride. All I had to do, to make it end happily this time around, was to relax, smile, sit back, and enjoy the trip.

Carson returned to the table with our drinks, eager to tell me, again and again, how sorry he was for all the pain he'd caused me, how desperate he was to make amends, and what a wonderful future he envisioned for us, now that we'd found each other again.

As for me, I concentrated on relaxing, smiling, sitting back, and enjoying the trip – meanwhile imagining how this story was going to spellbind my regular group of female friends. Especially Millicent, Lena, and dear old Toby.

"It was just like that great scene in *Casablanca*," I could already hear myself explaining to the open-mouthed assembly. "You know, the part where Ilsa walks into Rick's place, and good old Sam is at the piano, and she gets him to play the song that . . ."

Well, maybe not exactly like that, but damn close. Anyway, I could work on the details in advance of my next dinner date with my friends. The point was, at this very minute I was sure I already had enough terrific material to hold one entire restaurant table of women in rapt silence for at least ten minutes. "How often," I imagined myself launching into my account with élan, "how often in life do we get the opportunity to reach back in time, pluck an unsuccessful experience from the reel of life's projector – then rewind and rerun it? Only *this* time, altering the outcome, so that . . ."

So that what? Why, so that I could spend the rest of my life with Carson, of course, toying seductively with the gold chain around his neck, teasing him about all those other women he foolishly flaunted in my face, reliving with him, time and again, that climactic moment when I'd wafted over to his table like an illuminated angel, to the sweetly soulful strains of "Baker Street," and said to him in a sexy, sultry voice, "You look like you just lost your best friend."

The only trouble was, I couldn't fast-forward beyond that point, into the mutually meaningful future Carson was still rabbiting on and on about as he sat across the table sipping his drink. Boy, was he rabbiting on – acquainting me, in a rapid-fire way, with all kinds of facts about himself I hadn't been aware of when our conversation here at Perry's had consisted entirely of inane flirtation, laden with successive layers of sexual innuendo, X-rated allusions, and not much else.

Now, I was finding out from Carson much more, frankly, than I cared to know about narrow-gauge railways, the precise amount of gasoline required for his car to get him to work, to the gym, to Perry's Lounge, and then home again, and the very real possibility that Earth had long ago been visited by an advanced race of aliens who had brought us, among other things, the zipper, fitted bed-sheets, and a primitive version of "Twister."

Carson's lips kept on moving, but all of a sudden I realized I wasn't listening to him any more – indeed, had not been for quite some time. Nor, I also realized, was I any longer concocting in my head fresh and even more fascinating ways to relate this extraordinary adventure to my friends.

To be perfectly honest, I no longer cared whether reencounter-ing Carson Kilroy qualified as a bona fide rerun, on a romantic par with Toby's phone call out of the blue from the heartthrob of her third-grade classroom, or Millicent's coincidence-laden reunion with a large chunk of her past at an otherwise uninspiring sympo-sium, or even Lena's decision to refile a back number at the front of her folder. All I knew was that I, at this moment, was bored, bored, bored, and couldn't wait to get myself out of Perry's and home so that I could remove my odiously tight shoes and run a hot, comforting bath.

Meanwhile, over at the bar, Wes kept putting on "Baker Street," no doubt at Carson's request. Good God, what was the matter with me that I was so utterly failing to find the gesture romantic. Hadn't I been moving heaven and earth for months to meet a guy just like Carson? And what, I asked myself, could be more romantic than the trusty old scenario of *Casablanca*, in which the two lovers, deprived of their destiny back in Paris, are somehow flung together again by fate, and this time manage to find for themselves the happiness that –

But wait a minute! *That* wasn't how things turned out at the very end for Ilsa and Rick! They hadn't wound up chatting cozily at Rick's Café about the nice, boring life they were going to have, alleviated only by talk of wacky hobbies, how much depletion of the world's supply of fossil fuels was required on the drive to work, and crackpotted theories about visitations to our planet by Venutians.

No, damn it, in the movie, Ilsa had been prepared to throw over her entire life for Rick, but he couldn't let her. Victor Laszlo had been the problem in Paris, and Victor Laszlo was still the obstacle the second time around in Casablanca. Ilsa was what gave Victor Laszlo's work meaning; she was the thing that kept him going. And since Victor Laszlo's work was saving the free world, a deep-down patriot like Rick was hardly about to stand in the way for the sake of a selfish if lovely alliance.

Of course, I thought. That's what was so romantic about the story. Not the fact that Rick and Ilsa encountered each other again. But that they reencountered only to part a *second* time, leaving themselves perfectly preserved in each other's memory, to run and rerun as often as they chose. . . .

Carson Kilroy's mouth was still moving as I rose from my chair, picked up my purse, pulled some bills from my wallet, and lay them on the table. "That should cover my stingers, I think."

"W-wait a minute!" Carson looked up at me in alarm. "You're not leaving?"

"Look, Carson, the problems of a couple of little people don't matter a hill of beans in this crazy world –"

"Problems? What are you talking about? I told you, I came to realize my mistake ages ago. There won't be any more other women. Honest!"

"Believe me, Carson, someday you'll thank me for this. Oh, not now, maybe. Not tomorrow. But someday, and for the rest of your life."

"Is – is this goodbye? Is that what you're saying? That we're never going to see each other again?"

"Here's looking at you, kid."

"What looking? We're never going to see each other again! What the hell have I got to live for now?"

Smiling with a wisdom beyond even *my* years, I gave Carson's muscular arm a farewell squeeze and tugged playfully on the tacky gold chain around his neck. "Carson, you've got plenty to live for, and so do I." Tenderly, I looked around the room, and then back at him. "After all, we'll always have Perry's."

And with that, I left the bar, never to return again. Like, ne-ver. Reruns, I'd learned, can be wonderfully romantic. But only to a point.

Soldiers of Fortune

BACK IN GRADE SCHOOL, when we were still filling our fountain pens with bottled ink, I lost my heart to a particular shade of turquoise called South Seas Blue. It wasn't only the aesthetic pleasure I derived from practising my curly-tailed *a*'s and my flourishing signature in such a bright, vibrant hue; it was that label on the bottle, with its thumbnail depiction of exotic palm trees and rippling waves, which seemed to beckon to the ends of the earth.

Of all the places in the world I might visit once I grew up, I felt the most powerful attraction to the South Pacific. I imagined an enormous sparkling ocean the same colour as my favourite ink, and smiling, oiled natives in long dugout boats, paddling out to greet me with floral wreaths and joyous drumbeats – the way the Tahitians in the old black-and-white version of *Mutiny on the Bounty* I'd seen on TV had come from the beach to welcome Clark Gable, Charles Laughton, and the rest of the crew arriving to gather breadfruit and dally with native girls.

In fact just about all of what I understood back then about the South Pacific I'd picked up from that 1930s studio depiction of tropical splendour. And what impressed me most by far was the transforming effect that Tahiti and those Tahitian girls had on the sullen, pale, probably chilblained sailors of the HMS *Bounty*.

Imagine, I thought, going from those tight naval tunics and hot white stockings to nothing but a flowered sarong, some strange-looking amulet around your neck, and a gaudy hibiscus blossom tucked behind one ear. Gone were those sailors' white, lumpy torsos and pallid, pudding-like faces. After what seemed like mere minutes of sybaritic South Seas life, they were taut, tanned to leather, white-toothed, well-muscled, and endlessly smiling.

Somehow, that image of sailors gone salubriously native stayed with me into adulthood. I still wanted to go to the South Pacific and see for myself the effect of endless sea and sand and uncensored living on ordinary white men, turned into sunburned soldiers of fortune, living like kings on whatever remote reach they'd washed up on, underneath the stars that comprise the Southern Cross.

In my early thirties, by a happy accident, I was offered an opportunity to travel with a group of Canadian playwrights to Australia and New Zealand. From there, I thought it would be an easy add-on to my ticket to drop in on Tahiti on my way back home.

But too much, apparently, had been altered there since the *Bounty*'s crew of sun-starved mariners ran amok. Tahiti, I was sternly advised Down Under, had become shockingly expensive and utterly out of my league. Why not try some place equally enchanting but more offbeat?

Why not indeed? From Fiji, at that time, there was one flight a week to Rarotonga in the Cook Islands. Nowadays, I have no doubt, there are many more. But of all such things that have surely changed right across the South Pacific over the decades, I suspect the view on arrival at a place like that still catches the breath in the way I recall: the long white beach, the misted blue volcanic hills, the startlingly other blue of the sea, the barely discernible paths running into thick, bright green banana groves, never to re-emerge.

This, I thought, gazing down from the round window as the

grass airstrip approached, was even better than the label on the bottle of South Seas Blue ink. This was better than anything.

What must also remain immutable on those innumerable islands dotted across the South Pacific are certain tawdrier verities – like those ends-of-the-earth drinking establishments, almost invariably called The Reef. There – along with other such predictable fixtures as mileage posts pointing to places like Oxford Circus, examples of currencies of several dozen countries taped up behind the bar, and licence plates from Second World War-era military vehicles – you can almost always find at least one literal or spiritual descendant of Fletcher Christian, as well as other mutineers from mainstream civilization.

A faint air of failure often hangs around these men, like a drooping necklace of tropical flowers. In spite of that, they seldom seem in the least bit unhappy to have abandoned their (rumoured) careers as Cambridge professors, civil engineers from Sydney, or underemployed international playboys. On one of the many islands that make up Vanuatu, formerly known as the New Hebrides, I encountered a lean, laconic (rumoured) Scottish laird with white-blond hair, tobacco-coloured skin, and a gaunt jawline, who had tribal markings inscribed on his face and chest, and (also rumoured) a dozen or more young children with his three native wives, none of whom was even half his age.

"One Blong squaw I can understand," said the ex-pat Australian who'd filled me in on the laird's life and times. "But three? Randy as goats, but twice as rank, those women are."

"Blong," I'd already learned, was an indispensable word in Pidgin, the lingua franca of the islands. Shrunk from the English "belong," the word could connote simple possession, as well as serve the purpose of almost any preposition. But certain white colonials like David stretched its usefulness even farther, to refer disparagingly to the natives themselves. Despite his apparent contempt for the "Blongs," David, the ex-pat Australian, had gone a bit native himself, at least to the extent of speaking rapid-fire Pidgin to the Melanesian employees at his rundown resort. His scathing racial prejudice and sense of superior status were abetted by the biases built into the language itself, particularly the Pidgin word for "boss," which is *masta*.

Masta was the way David invariably referred to himself when he addressed his workers – generally at the top of his lungs, and with a few obscene Anglo-Saxon epithets that even I could understand, to fill out the rest of the sentence. I'd been living at David's resort, The Reef, located what would have been less than an hour's drive from the capital, Port Vila, had the road not been a rutted cow-track, and had the car I'd rented from the only franchise in town not been a spavined old Japanese coupe with gears that went wonky if you shifted beyond third.

The main attraction of The Reef was the rent – seven U.S. dollars a night for a plain but respectable cottage on the beach. Certainly David constituted no part of the charm of the place. Sunburned he was, but otherwise nothing like my image of a romantic white-hunter type, wasting away in the tropics. He was glowering, temperamental, bullying, scatological, and a bit mad, especially when pulling his Simon Legree act. It was still hurricane season, and he had few other tourists. For that reason, he seemed to like me – at least when he was sober – and also enjoyed the fact that I'd been a lifelong sucker for the South Pacific.

"You'll want to get the hell and gone away from Vila, then," he advised me, as he cooked – quite brilliantly – a coconut crab in a lethal curry sauce of his own devising, which had such inevitable consequences next day to the lower intestinal tract he'd dubbed it David's Ring-Burner.

"Come on," I said. "I *am* away from Vila. It takes three hours to drive here from town. Four, since the cyclone. Besides, there's a beach here, outdoor dining, a sky full of stars. If this isn't the South Pacific, what is it?"

"Civilization," he said. "Far be it from me to talk myself out of my only paying customer in a week, but take my advice and look over some of the other islands in the chain. There's over a hundred just in the New Hebrides, you know. Some of them even air-accessible and eager to accommodate tourist twits like yourself."

It was as a result of this good advice that I ended up on Erromango, a scrubby, jungle-ridden, mosquito-infested island of Vanuatu that got onto my list of ports-of-call only by virtue of its being what David had called accessible as well as accommodating. Merely offering a place of any kind to stay was something so rare among these islands that I didn't even bother to inquire what was in store before booking myself into Erromango's one and only "guest house."

When the small plane put down on the grass runway among pasturing goats, I wasn't concerned to find no one there to meet me as promised. By this time I knew enough about small South Pacific islands not to expect to be greeted by Bloody Mary and the entire ensemble singing "Bali Hai." Not at the pre-arranged hour, anyway. Since the airport building consisted only of a ticket wicket with a sign that read "Closed" in English, French, and Pidgin, I sat down on my suitcase in what shade I could find to wait for the guest-house proprietor to come along in his or her own good time.

It took only a half-hour or so for a shiny-looking Toyota truck, in startlingly good repair, to come bumping across the runway and screech to a halt beside me and my suitcase. From the cab emerged a very tanned, very blond, very attractive man of no more than thirty with a big, brash smile, a minimal amount of clothing, and an entirely trustworthy manner.

"Booked for the guest house, are you?" he asked in what I later learned was a New Zealand, rather than Australian, accent.

Good God. This was better than anything I'd dared to hope for – this handsome, wholesome-looking lad from Down Under as my handy host, as opposed to the scowling, belligerent David. Mind you, since it had been that same David who'd so wisely urged me to forgo the "civilization" represented by corrosively curried crab, Pidgin curses, and drunken diatribes against the "Blongs," I reckoned I at least owed him a silently telegraphed "Thanks" for the way my foray into the more remote islands was turning out.

"I'm Roger," the handsome apparition continued. "The guest-house folks phoned our camp to say their truck is crookt again, and would I pick you up at the airstrip." He patted one front fender of the Toyota with proprietary pride. "This here's the only working vehicle on the island, just at the moment."

Then, before heaving my suitcase into the back of the truck, he paused to give me an appraising glance. "Of course, I can easily drop you at the guest house, as arranged. Or... you'd be welcome to come up to the logging camp instead. Frankly, I think you'd find it more to your taste – hot running water, indoor plumbing, and a slap-up camp cook." He resumed loading my suitcase.

"Gee," I said. "I do have this booking..."

Roger settled himself into the driver's seat, then watched as I got in beside him, taking in my white wedge-heeled espadrilles, my neatly flowered skirt, and citified shoulder bag. "Frankly, I don't much like your chances at the guest house. There's rats, the food's bloody awful, and on the river as it is, the place is crawling with malaria mosquitoes."

"Wow. Do they know this is the kind of recommendation you give when you pick up their guests?"

"It doesn't happen often, believe me. The guests, I mean. Their vehicle, on the other hand, is broken down most of the time. Look – it's some government make-work project to help the locals, this guest-house caper. Nobody *ever* stays there. Not after a good look at it. But I'll tell you what: If you still want me to run you there, I will. Mind you, up at the camp, me and my mates will make you very comfortable, and . . . nobody will take advantage of the situation, either. You can trust me on that."

I sized up his smiling face and decided I would continue to believe in him. Tomorrow would be soon enough to face the rats, the malaria, and whatever other amenities the guest house might offer. For tonight, I would take my chances with an unspecified number of loggers, out in the middle of the jungle, on an island nobody back home had ever heard of, or had any idea I happened to be visiting.

On every score, Roger proved as good as his word. The loggers were a genial, gentlemanly band of white and Maori New Zealanders, genuinely delighted to have a newcomer – especially a female newcomer – in their midst. Of course, Roger took a fair amount of ribbing for bringing me there, particularly when he reappeared from his trailer after "freshening up" reeking of cologne.

But not one of the lumberjacks, Roger included, stepped out of line for a second. There was good grub, just as promised. There was a drunken after-dinner singalong, inspired by a pile of old rock-and-roll tapes loaded into a cassette recorder. There were photos of wives and kids and girlfriends back home to pass along the dinner table for my inspection, and there were stories about other logging adventures from Papua New Guinea to the Solomon Islands to the Australian outback.

Not one of the men could abide Erromango, but not one of them seemed unhappy to be there, harvesting enormous cowrie trees to float on barges to some distant port. The men had befriended a wild pony, who stuck his head in over the Dutch door and promptly bit me when I tried to pat him. There were bats whizzing casually in and out the same door all evening long – which, for some reason, didn't completely unnerve me as it normally would. And there were many jokes at the expense of one man in the group who'd come down with malaria after failing to get the recommended shot, and now sat limply in a corner, his teeth chattering audibly with every spasm of shivers.

I did, the next day, decide to brave the guest house for a night, out of rank curiosity, if nothing else. Bemused but without complaint, Roger dutifully drove me there, and with a farewell grin predicted I'd be phoning by dusk to beg to come back up to the lumber camp.

I did not phone, though I thought about it. As a matter of fact, I didn't even see a phone or anything like one. The guest house was everything Roger had warned me against, and worse. I was shown to a thatched shack, featuring a rusted oil drum full of rancid water out in the yard to serve as my sink. There was an outhouse that I never did investigate, since it seemed to be guarded by a large and very angry-looking pig. My only meal, left on the oilcloth-covered table in my shack, was some mushily cooked taro and a slightly mouldy stale bun. The kerosene lamp beside it was my only light.

Once I'd extinguished the lamp and crawled into bed, a rat began capering across the rafter above my head, his brown-and-white body visible in the moonlight from the open window. As I listened to him burrowing noisily in the straw thatch, I thought about the boys up at the logging camp and felt homesick for their music and their lively humour, and – a little – for their bad-tempered pony.

But the rat seemed like a chubby, cheerful little beast, more like a guinea pig than a slinking slum-dweller, and I didn't wish that

I'd elected to stay with Roger and his mates. I wanted them in my memory of that one, perfect night: A crew of colonials turned varying shades of red, copper, and brown by their labours on a remote South Seas isle – not unlike the men of the HMS *Bounty*, harvesting breadfruit a wide world away from home.

The key, of course, to any successful fantasy is never to linger long enough to take the bloom off the romantic rose. Maybe that's what motivated the men who stayed loyal to Captain Bligh to make their long way back with him to Old Blighty, rather than continue their lives as castaways in Paradise under the command of Fletcher Christian.

"Why don't you just stay?"

On an earlier trip of mine to the South Pacific, that had been the entirely sensible suggestion of a man I'd met and, in the space of a week, become attached to in the way one often can with a healthy assist from swaying palms, silken sands, and first-rate sex.

Clark did not, in some ways, fit my previous projections of the South Seas soldier of fortune. He was American, not English or Australian; he was neither a remittance man, nor a footloose adventurer, nor someone about whom wild rumours swirled. He was black, as opposed to some white colonial turned to shoe leather by the unrelenting sun. And he was too intelligent to qualify for one of my female chauvinist fantasies of a sweet, simple suntanned hunk of cured male flesh, disinclined to complicate the essential elements of life with too much cogitation. By the time he came into my ken, however, I was grateful for the arrival of any good man, especially one who provided promise of rescue, which I'd wound up requiring.

I was on my own in the (then) sleepy Cook Islands of the Polynesian South Pacific, and having an unexpectedly wild time at the very first of the many places I've encountered called The Reef. A self-described Polynesian princess – a huge woman who lived in a scabby stone palace nearby – came to party nearly nightly at The Reef, along with a flock of other locals, white or brown, in varying stages of inebriation. There hardly seemed to be any actual guests besides me and a prim pair from Wellington, who turned out to be spies for the hotel's offshore owner, sent to tattle on the crazy way in which The Reef was being run by the Australian couple who were its on-site managers. Even after the New Zealand spies had been outed and sent on their way, I continued to be treated like a fellow reveller by the staff, who didn't seem to care that, once the owner heard what was going on, the boom would shortly fall on their casual way of dealing with the paying customers.

Mostly, the staff consisted of pretty Maori girls who rubbed ylang-ylang oil into their marvellous hair to make it shine and smiled with the kind of unstudied, obliging sexuality that Margaret Meade had made so much of among the Samoans. Unfortunately, in addition to these wonderful women, The Reef for some reason employed a wine steward, of all things, who seemed unhappily out of place in the carefree ranks of the down-market and down-at-heel place the hotel had lately become.

The wine steward was a heavy-set, pouty, unattractive young white man, who reminded me of Charles Laughton – not so much as Captain Bligh, but as some even more miserably dyspeptic misfit. He was reported to be the son of the former premier of the Cook Islands, and how he'd ended up performing his rarely requested oenophilic function for mostly non-existent guests at a place like The Reef, I had no idea – and no interest in exploring.

But because I was there, fraternizing in a friendly way with all and sundry, when the former premier's son asked me for a dance after dinner, I obliged. And when he told me all about the accomplishments of his father, I evinced a genuine interest. Then he further informed me that tomorrow was his night off. Perhaps

I'd like to be shown around, perhaps even introduced to his illustrious father, who was still alive, although no longer often in evidence on the island. I said that perhaps we could talk about it tomorrow.

By that time, I was heading off the dance floor and toward bed, in my room in the back extension of the hotel, which overlooked the ocean. The wine steward was following me, still pressing his offer of an island tour. When I reached the door of my room, I paused pointedly, as a cue that I was ready to say goodnight. "I said we'll talk about it tomorrow, okay?"

Quite unexpectedly, he grasped me by the arm, pulled me toward him, and tried to kiss me. Appalled, I pushed him away.

"Oh, come on now," said the former premier's son turned wine steward, "don't carry on like you're sweet sixteen and never been kissed."

"I may be somewhat over sixteen," I said. "But that doesn't mean I *have* to be kissed by anybody who takes the notion. Now stay away from me, or I'll tell the management."

"I did mention, didn't I, who my father is?"

At long last, it dawned on me why it was that the hotel bothered to keep him around – underutilized, unobliging, and utterly unappealing. His father must exert considerable clout, either with the Australian managers or the offshore ownership, to keep his son in employment. "Okay, so nobody's going to fire you for hassling the one and only guest. What will it take to keep you from mauling me?"

"Just come to the front desk at six sharp, tomorrow evening. I'll be waiting for you, to take you out. Don't disappoint me, and I won't bother you again."

Meeting him at the desk in front of the staff and all their friends was a hideously embarrassing prospect. On the other hand, he was a huge man, and here we were, out behind the main part of the hotel with nobody around, and the flimsy door of my room no real defence, even if I were quick enough to pull my key out to unlock it, get myself inside, and then bolt it against my unwanted suitor. "All right," I said, through gritted teeth. "Six o'clock it is."

It was the next day, right around lunchtime, that I first met Clark, at a tiny little restaurant in town, while I was out investigating on my bike. He owned the restaurant, as it turned out, and was eager to tell me all about his new enterprise. He'd only recently arrived in the Cook Islands, he said. Previously, he'd been a chef on Marlon Brando's estate in Tahiti, where the actor had been living since falling in love with the South Pacific years before, while filming the remake of *Mutiny on the Bounty*.

"You didn't really work for Marlon Brando," I teased Clark. "You've just adopted the Cook Islanders' habit of making claims to fame about themselves. You know, the wine steward at The Reef says he's the son of the former premier?"

"Oh, that bastard. The son, I mean. I've met him. He's bad news."

"I'm afraid you're right." I told Clark about how I'd wound up having to promise him I'd be at the front desk at six o'clock that night. "I don't know what he'll do if I don't show."

"Leave it to me," said Clark.

At six p.m. precisely, I hurried purposefully toward the front desk at The Reef, where the wine steward was already waiting, spruced up in a sports jacket, car keys jingling impatiently in his hand, and a group of the staff gathered around him. As his sullen face broke into something resembling a smile of agreeable surprise, I rushed right past him, out the front door, and into the passenger seat of Clark's car, waiting in the parking lot, exactly as he'd said it would be.

We drove off into the evening, and into the beginning of a really delightful week together. As much as I could, I gave The

Reef a wide berth, for fear of running into the man I'd so publicly snubbed. However, a day or two later, as I was riding around the island on my bicycle, a car came rushing up behind me, and very nearly ran me off the road as it sped past. I was fairly certain I recognized the vehicle.

"Oh, he was pretty crazy mad with you, all right," agreed a waitress from The Reef who came into Clark's restaurant one day while I was there. "He was telling everybody all day long you and him was going out. And then – whoosh! You come, and you gone!"

"You tell him from me," Clark said to her, "he should back off and stay the hell away from her. I'm an American, you tell him, and we all pack guns and get pretty crazy mad too, when we take the notion. Tell him I don't give a fuck who his father is."

Clark was the last person in the world I could imagine with a gun. He was energetic, ambitious, and enormously proud of his abilities in the kitchen, but he lacked entirely a chef's traditionally hot temperament. The Polynesian girls were all wild about him, because of his dark, exotic skin. But unlike most of the men who washed up in places like the Cook Islands, he wasn't about to take advantage of them – either as employees or as easy sexual pickings. I couldn't believe my good luck in finding a guy like that at the ends of the earth, someone who went far beyond merely presenting a palatable alternative to the former premier's sullen son.

Not long before, the first local radio station on the island had begun broadcasting, and in the mornings I'd wake up in Clark's bed, turn on the radio – and hear Clark's voice telling the local morning host what he was heading to his restaurant to prepare for the lunch crowd. He made a point of dropping into the station every morning on his way from the market, where he'd been shopping for the day's supplies. "That's something I learned watching how weighed down Marlon Brando always seemed by fame. There *is* such a thing as bad publicity. The trick is to stay on the right side of it, and the light side of it."

In the evenings I'd go for dinner at the restaurant, then stay around as he closed the place up, share some drinks with his buddies who hung around too, and head back with him to his place near the beach for a swim. It was damn near perfect.

"So why don't you just stay?" Clark asked, the night before I was to leave on the once-a-week flight to New Zealand and beyond.

We were on the beach as usual, and in the sand he was sketching out his plan to build a house on some property nearby he said he could get a deal on. He had a lot of other plans besides – to expand the restaurant, get himself a regular gig as the host of a cooking program on the new local radio station, and throw in his lot long-term with the Islands, which he believed had a fantastic future as a resort far beyond its current, somewhat scruffy, scale.

"See," he said, indicating with the stick. "There's the upstairs room looking out to the sea, where you could write. I mean, you said that's what you do, right?"

"Right. I write." And I could write, in that upstairs room in a yet-to-be built house, overlooking a scene taken right off the label of that bygone bottle of South Seas Blue ink from which I'd filled my first fountain pen, back in grade school.

But the scene belonged on the ink-bottle label. It had nothing to do with Clark's plans for a five-star restaurant, in an erstwhile backwater that he hoped to help convert into a top-flight tourist destination. "And I *will* write," I added. "Just as soon as I get back home, I'll be in touch. Who knows? By the time I come back, you might have my room all ready for me."

But I never did go back – partly for fear Clark might have made too much headway in his plans to upgrade the island. Even by the time our brief correspondence dwindled off, a month or two later, he'd written that he was well on his way to clinching the deal for the land on which to build his house.

Over the years, I've kept my ears open for the names of other South Pacific islands that sounded unfamiliar, unheralded, unchanging, unambitious. The kind of places to which I like to hope that I can always go, to find sunburned soldiers of fortune still living like kings, on whatever remote reach they'd washed up on, underneath the stars that comprise the Southern Cross.

TOUGH GUYS

HERE ARE A FEW things we should all keep in mind about tough guys:

1) Every Guy in the World Worries about Encountering a Guy Tougher Than Himself.

It was walking down the street – any street – with a boyfriend of mine that first called my attention to that fact. Whether we were on one of the meaner streets of Vancouver's East Side, or on bustling Banff Avenue in the touristic heart of the Rockies, or Toronto's businesslike Bay Street, or la rue centrale de Tadoussac in the Saguenay area of Quebec, he would invariably clench his hand around my upper arm with a grip like a blood-pressure cuff and steer me along the pavement, past unseen hazards I could barely guess at.

"For God's sake, what are you so jumpy about?" I'd demand, rubbing the reddened area of my arm. "What do you expect to happen out here?"

"You never know," he would reply darkly. "You never know when some goof is going to come along with something to prove."

No doubt, I thought, his background as a druggie and a sometime crook had made him particularly wary of his fellow men. Certainly, it was some of his more harrowing experiences on the street that informed both his work as a writer, and, as I later learned, his drastic dream life.

One summer, well into our turbulent relationship, we spent all of a breathlessly hot August together in a secluded area of Vancouver Island, living like savages in an old, permanently docked Airstream trailer with no electricity or running water. Our meals were cooked from cans on an open fire. Our water came from a well we'd successfully dredged – to our mutual astonishment – despite our complete lack of pioneer savvy.

During the endless summer days, we wandered our other Eden wearing little but our suntans, like Adam and Eve in the early going. At nightfall, however, life took a less lyrical turn, when the arrival of myriad mosquitoes required us to spray the inside of the trailer with insecticide. Then we'd bunk down to spend the entire night inhaling Raid and listening to tree branches cracking and crashing to earth in the hot, dry darkness. Inevitably, the combination of those elements – the heat, the chemical spray, the ominous nature of the night itself – was bound to affect the quality of a person's sleep, particularly a person with a perilous and almost paranoid history.

"Put on the light! Put on the light!"

From the midst of a deep sleep, I'd awaken with a gasp, feeling his hot, anguished grip on my arm. I'd shake off the remnants of my unconsciousness and fumble for matches to light the kerosene lamp, my hand trembling as I removed the glass chimney and ignited the wick.

"What's the matter?" I'd ask, knowing the answer in advance.

"God, I dreamed . . . Leave on the light, will you, and hand me my smokes? Christ, the most godawful dream . . ."

"What was it?" I'd ask, knowing the answer to that too, but aware that, like the Ancient Mariner, it was essential for him to tell the tale in hopes of discharging its horror.

Out it would come: Some tough in a back street, coming at him with a homemade shank. Or him being forced to shank some tough in the same back street, plunging the crude blade between the ribs to feel the firm resistance of bone and gristle, as if trying to pierce a sack of gravel . . .

How much of this ghastliness was real-life recollection, and how much was fuelled by the sound of branches falling in the woods and the disorienting mist of mosquito spray we inhaled all night, I had no idea. Still, it seemed reasonable to me to suppose that other, less troubled, men would harbour far less anxiety, waking or sleeping, about sudden assaults out there on the street.

"Not true," my boyfriend insisted flatly, when I brought this up in the comforting light of day. "There isn't a guy in the world who doesn't feel as jumpy as I do. And you want to know why? It's because most men are afraid of other men. What's worse, we know women are afraid of men, too. And what we worry about most is having to protect some woman who's scared to death from some tough guy *we're* as scared to death of as they are."

In the years that have passed since he told me that, I've asked countless other men – most of them very, very different from him in temperament, background, and life experience – what they think of such a theory. And do you know something? To a man, they've agreed with him.

2) Every Guy in the World Wishes Every Woman in the World Understood How Tough It Is to Be a Guy.

Not how tough it is to be a tough guy, you understand – just a guy. Period. Women should bear in mind, however, that the complaints of guys about how tough it is merely to be a guy often have their origin in that pervasive problem we've already discussed – i.e., most men's fear of other men.

"What took you so long?"

That, as most women will readily recognize, is the sound a man makes when his female companion finally emerges from the washroom at any movie theatre you care to name.

The usual reply to this is "What do you mean, what took me so long? Look at the lineup. Now, who do you see lined up at the door marked 'Men'? Nobody, right? Is it my fault women take twice as long as guys to perform the very same function and yet aren't issued twice the number of locations to perform it in?"

To say she's lying about the lineup would be an exaggeration. Equally, it would be an exaggeration to contend that she's telling the entire truth. More than halfway home in the car, she might eventually elect to thaw the chilly silence that has ensued ever since she emerged from the movie-theatre washroom to proffer her half-baked excuse to a man who clearly knows that a lot more went on in that washroom than she's so far divulged.

"I didn't think Gwyneth Paltrow and Jennifer Lopez made particularly convincing sisters, did you?"

"Oh, I don't know . . ." Also eager to forget the restroom rift, her male companion is quick to grapple with a quibble about casting which, in reality, he cares little about. "Could be you're just more critical about those kinds of things than most people."

"No, I'm not. *Nobody* bought them as sisters, as a matter of fact."

"Nobody? What nobody are you talking about?"

"The women in the washroom. We all agreed their sister act was entirely bogus."

With a wince of pain, he turns his glance away from her to focus fixedly on the road. "Ah. The women in the washroom. I might have known."

Indeed he might have. As a man who's been around the block more than once – and could, in fact, have circled that block far more than once while waiting for any of the succession of women he has dated to finish doing whatever it is women do while in the washroom – he is far from unfamiliar with this female-only phenomenon of movie post-mortems at the sink in the cinema.

What's more, as a man condemned to conduct his bathroom business as speedily as possible in full view of other men doing the selfsame thing, then washing his hands and getting out with a minimum of eye contact, he openly envies the easy camaraderie enjoyed by his female counterpart with other women met in front of the mirror. Not only – as he understands it – are these total strangers in the habit of rehashing their reactions to the movie, scene by scene, they also offer spontaneous statements of support to each other on a whole host of unrelated topics.

"Oh, God, look at this awful hair of mine!"

"Nonsense, honey, it looks terrific. Say, does anybody here happen to know a nice, inexpensive place to eat in this neighbourhood?"

"Does anybody know a nice, inexpensive place to eat in this *town?*"

"Does anybody know a nice, inexpensive place to eat in this *world* where the food is entirely non-caloric?"

"You? Worried about your weight? Honest to God, you're a rake!"

With that kind of positive infield-chatter available on demand and free of charge from utter strangers, is it any wonder women linger endlessly to bask in the glow of those good Ladies' Room vibes?

"You guys don't talk to each other at *all?*" a man's female companion might inquire sympathetically, and incredulously, after the movie. "What is it – you're worried about somebody getting the wrong idea if you tell him his hair looks nice?"

"Of course I am! Besides, why should I tell a complete stranger his hair looks nice? Why should I even notice? Why would I care?"

"Ah!" With infuriating feminine omniscience, his companion nods sagely and rolls her eyes. "Well, of course, if you even have to *ask* . . ."

Still, in spite of the futility of expecting females to understand how tough it is to be a guy, forced to pee in total silence with people he doesn't even care about, a man can be consoled after the movies by one small compensation. He can come swaggering out of the Men's Room past that line of increasingly desperate dames, snaking all the way from the door labelled "Women" to the lobbyful of impatient boyfriends and husbands, all waiting and wondering what the heck takes women so long.

3) Every Guy in the World Feels Required by Every Woman in the World, Whether She Realizes It or Not, to Play the Part of a Tough Guy.

And who can blame him? As a woman who has lived both alone and (sequentially) with a number of men, I am compelled to blush whenever I force myself to face the difference between my level of capability on my own and my level of dependency if there's a man around to hide behind.

In the dying stages of my marriage, for instance, one of the key considerations that kept me hanging on long past the point at which we should both have bailed was my fear of bugs and electrical storms. "What would I do all by myself if a real big moth got in? Right in the middle of a giant zap of forked lightning and a huge volley of thunder?"

The truth – once I'd worked up the courage to decamp – turned out to be that, like most people, I can cope with insects when I have to. Once, by myself in Bermuda, I succeeded in clubbing to death with my tennis racquet a cockroach the size of a cocker spaniel, then shovelling its not inconsiderable remains down the bathtub drain with all the steely sang-froid of Tony Perkins swaddling the corpse of Janet Leigh in that shower curtain and dragging her bloody body out the door.

On another occasion, on a little island called Tanna in the South Pacific, I managed to ignore, on my bedroom wall, a brigade of spiders the size of lawn sprinklers, impatiently drumming their long beefy forelegs as they waited for me to fall asleep. And when I lived in a small rural house in the Berkshires, largely on my own, I once had to precede the (male) pest-control expert into the cellar, because he'd seen a snake down there and needed me to clear it out before he would venture to look for evidence of carpenter ants. All that being said, why is it, to this day, in the tameness of cottage country north of Toronto, I have to call on my (male) partner, or my (male) cat to take care of some poor stag beetle who's bumbled indoors and is now lying up-ended on the living-room floor, legs flailing in some form of frantic semaphore?

As for thunderstorms, or any other sort of noise in the night, well, needless to say, I've dealt with my normal allotment of those too – up to and including the sound of my neighbours' horses, mysteriously loose one night, running around and around my house as I desperately tried and failed to shove two large and terrified dogs from my lap, so that I could creep over to the window to figure out what was the source of those demonic snuffling noises and continual series of thumps out there in the dark. But put a man in bed beside me, and I'm beside myself, at the first rumble of thunder, or bump of unknown origin.

"Honey? Honey!" In the darkness, I dig his rib with my elbow, in the best tradition of Blondie urging Dagwood out of blissful unconsciousness. "Did you hear that?"

In defence of my inconsistency in these matters, I can only point to my family, where, typically enough of those times, all matters of household security were immediately referred to my father. Of course, when he wasn't around, my mother managed just fine on her own. Yet, somehow or other, that failed to signify the second my father was back on the bridge.

"Car doors locked?" he'd interrogate her. "Did you turn off the headlights? Plug in the block heater? Put the garage key back on the hook?"

It wasn't that my father denigrated female intelligence. It was simply that the weight of being the one in charge made him compulsively suspicious of everyone else's competence – especially my mother's.

For her part, my mother seemed unable to avoid playing to her own perceived weaknesses. The day my dad took her out to teach her to drive she steered the family Studebaker into a ditch full of water – yet went on to be a far more orthodox driver than he, once she was licensed and out on her own.

Noises in the night, strangers at the door, bad boys out in the back alley, those she duly left to my father to investigate, even though it was that same mother, out on the golf course in a foursome of ladies, who dared to march over to an enormous off-duty Mountie in an abutting pasture to berate him for abusing a horse.

"For God's sake," my father growled, when she told him the story. "Why didn't you just phone the police on him?"

"Pete, he *was* the police," she replied patiently. "Besides, once I shook my five-iron at him, he seemed to get the point just fine."

4) Every Guy in the World Feels Pressured to Turn His Son into a Tough Guy.

My father was not the sort of man who ever laid any claim to being a macho man. A chronically bad back had kept him out of service in the Second World War, and for that he never pretended to be anything but grateful. He didn't mind admitting that, as a kid, he'd been an indifferent athlete – too slight, too tentative, too reluctant to risk life and limb. As an adult, the upmarket men's clothing store he worked in was the most white-collar of worlds. He knew fine cloth; he believed that good clothes made the man; he took pride in wearing his own suits well.

While he was a young man, reed-slender, sensitive-looking, and attractive in an intellectual way, my dad played clarinet in a swing band with other young men whose names became famous only to my brother and me, in Dad's dinnertime stories about the dances they'd played back in the fabled Thirties. Although no natural musician, as he modestly insisted, he'd made painstaking efforts to overcome his lack of innate skill by memorizing sheets and sheets of songs and making crib notes for stealthy onstage reference.

Still, he'd had more musical longings than we ever imagined. After his death, among a handful of his personal papers, my brother and I came across a certificate from his primary school back in the 1920s, signed by a nun, proclaiming his successful completion of the class's piano program.

Despite the refined nature of his own aspirations and accomplishments, my dad for some reason seemed to feel compelled to treat my brother more or less like a raw recruit to the military. "Don't be such a pansy!" was a familiar reproof – and possibly an updated variant on some similar admonishment from his own father. Similarly, the "lickings" he dealt out with a long-handled hairbrush were, no doubt, what our Grandpa – deceptively mild-mannered in his old age – had handed out to his own boys, including my father, with youthful vigour.

What made my father's treatment of my brother seem all the more significant to me was the fact it was reserved exclusively for the only boy and appeared aimed at eradicating something in him that infuriated my father, simply on principle. Or perhaps the objective was to instill something, the lack of which was the unknown source of our father's frequent displeasure with his son, and the world at large.

My brother was a good-looking kid, with beautiful rich black hair. For years, however, he was forced by our father to betake himself to the barber for a brush cut – a shearing with electric clippers that produced a short, stiff, bristling pelt, instead of the longish, gleaming locks he'd spent hours perfecting in the bathroom.

Ridiculed for his vanity, denounced for the time he wasted with his primping, and excoriated for his wilfulness, my brother had no choice but to get his head razored regularly, or face a licking. But it was terrible to see him come shrinking home from the barbershop, freshly shorn, his shame burning bright circles into his cheeks and tears of anger in his eyes as he hurried past my mother and me to barricade himself, sobbing, in the bathroom – for even longer hours than he'd formerly spent combing down his cowlick and smoothing his long sideburns, just so, in front of the mirror.

What rite of manhood was our dad attempting to observe? What brand of life lesson did he set out to impart each time he ordered my brother to undergo the humiliation of coming home to show his shaven head?

"Did you ever figure it out?" I asked my brother, long after we were both into adulthood. "Have you ever understood why Dad made you get that goddamn brush cut?"

"I don't know," my brother shrugged, still tight-lipped with anger, even after so many years. "I guess because he *could*."

Or, perhaps because he had to, for reasons equally as mysterious as why he'd chosen to keep a piano certificate he'd earned when he was eight years old.

5) Every Man in the World Worries Whether He's Tough Enough
to Kill Something He Cares About.

Oscar Wilde may have defined the fear with his observation "Each
man kills the thing he loves." But concern on that score was likely
already rampant long centuries before – even by the time Abraham
was instructed by God to eliminate his beloved son. In Abraham
and Isaac's case, it turned out that God was only putting the pro-
posal out there as a talking point. Nevertheless, it must have struck
both father and son that Isaac's mother, Sarah, had received no
such divine demand. And in fact it's not easy to find instances, then
or now, of women required to stand up to a similar test.

In the children's classic *Old Yeller*, for instance, it's Travis the son
who's required to dispatch his dog. The mother of the family
offers to do the awful deed, but Travis insists on killing his own
dog himself.

For a generation of children – and for their children and even
grandchildren by now, made familiar with the movie through
video – the death of Old Yeller easily rivals the demise of Bambi's
mother for sheer seismic effect in the cinema. The dog, who has
contracted rabies from fighting off a wolf that threatened the
family, has quite literally laid down his life for the family he loves.
Now that this same life has become a menace, it's up to the one
who loves him most to take it away. As young Travis closes one
eye, takes aim, cocks the hammer, then shoots his dog, it may be
little girls (and big girls) who cry the most overtly, but it's the boys
in the audience who are left to wonder, Could I do that?

Another American classic, *The Yearling*, puts a boy in the same
situation. This time, it's a pet deer who must die, but again it's the
boy in the family, who loves it, who's required to pull the trigger.
And once more, in the death of the beloved animal, the boy dies a
little too, for the sake of the man in the making.

How do the boys in such stories bear the burden of what they must do? How do the boys who read the novel or watch the film bear the burden of their own inheritance as dealers of death, even in the best of causes? Most perplexing of all, Would it be a blow for female equality if Old Testament mothers had been instructed by God to carry out the slaughter of their sons? Or if little girls in classic stories of childhood were obliged to shoot their horses or strangle their cats?

6) Every Guy in the World Resents Those Few Fortunate Guys Who Get Girls and Whatever Else They Want Without Having to Be Tough for a Single Minute.

I think it may be fair to say that, in the annals of American celebrity, there is no living man who inspires such radically different reactions from men and women than former U.S. president Bill Clinton. Men resent the heck out of someone they regard as a moral weakling, and women concede he's a weakling and worse, but can't help liking him all the same.

In fact, it may well be that Bill Clinton's baffling attractiveness to women is the keenest source of other men's resentment toward him. I know that if I were a man, Clinton's bland ability to succeed, no matter what, would really piss me off. I also know that, as a woman, I can't help quietly congratulating the guy for being so off-pissing to men in a way that's utterly understandable but amusing nonetheless.

Not long ago, I had a dream about Bill Clinton that clarified for me his sleazy appeal. I dreamed that, with the longueurs of post-presidency hanging heavy on his roaming hands, Clinton came to work where I did, at CBC Radio, as my personal intern.

Despite the comparative meniality of the assignment – not to mention the inevitable intern jokes – Bill didn't seem to mind a

bit. He sat smiling that Clarabelle-the-Clown smile of his, at a
rather cramped desk not far from mine, wearing a clean white
shirt and decent work slacks, but casually barefoot, as he collated
documents with the best will in the world and happily awaited the
next assignment I might send his way.

Eventually, though, his true nature could not help but emerge,
and he leaned over to me with a lascivious wink. "How be we
head out and git some dinner after work, you and me? Say . . .
round about ten-thirty tonight?"

In my dream, it was exactly the voice I've heard on television a
hundred times: slightly hoarse, slightly Southern, slightly insinu-
ating – a cross between Elvis and Andy Devine.

"Ten-thirty?" I said in response. "Isn't that a little late for dinner,
Bill?"

"Yes'm." And he winked again. "Maybe we could call it early
breakfast, then?"

I awoke laughing at his insolence, and at the absolute accuracy
of what my unconscious had captured. That *was* Bill Clinton to
the life – likeable, louche, sybaritic, and self-mocking. Not one
apparent muscle of conscience in his overindulged body. The
antithesis of the tough guy, but a guy for all that – barefoot, incapable of embarrassment, happy and unashamed as a clam.

How to excuse the attractiveness of someone so unworthy, to
men who've striven much harder but achieved much less? Or to
men who've taken much less and parlayed it into something so
much greater? More important, how to explain why, in a world
where most men worry in some way or other about being tough
enough, there are other men who don't seem to give it a single
thought – and get farther by feeling others' pain than by concealing their own?

"Hey, that's easy," Bill Clinton might say with the inevitable wink. "Rules are made to be broken, hadn't you heard? Even rules about tough guys."

Which is, perhaps, just one more thing we should all keep in mind about tough guys as we add items to our list.

Underdogs

DOGS ARE A LOT like men, although somewhat more complicated. That, however, is no reason to disregard their potential as
loyal lifelong partners. True, we're talking the dog's lifetime,
rather than yours. But try to look at the relationship like this: A
dog may not live a long time, but while he's on the planet, you'll
have his full attention – which is more than can be said for some
of the two-legged alternatives.

The bond between a woman and her dog can be a special one.
Not to suggest for a moment that men don't sincerely love their
dogs, too. Any of us who's ever been bored to tears by some guy
of our acquaintance, running and rerunning that obedience-class
graduation video of Mad Max or Big Blue at the drop of a hat,
can readily attest to the continued pertinence of the phrase
"man's best friend."

But that's just it. For the male owner, his dog's role is as a
buddy – neckerchief knotted around his ruff, salivating cheerfully in the back of a pickup, or tongue lolling as he sits tied to a
fence, while his leather-jacket-clad owner lingers over a latte in
an oversized bowl and makes high-decibel calls of low priority
on his cellphone.

Basically, when it comes to guys and dogs, it all goes back to
caveman days – the image of two bold adventurers out hunting

together. (Gathering, it appears, does not play a part in the fantasy. Not when you consider the number of male dog-owners who will gladly waste hours helping Buddy ambush a squirrel in the park but won't spend a second bending down with a plastic bag to scoop up what Buddy's behind left behind on the grass.)

Yessir, you put a couple of guys and their dogs together for a weekend up at the cottage, say, and you've got an interspecies experience in the making – at least, to hear the human half of the team tell it, come Monday morning. You can almost picture the pack of them, drumming down by the beach, or all sitting around their improvised sweat lodge, getting in touch with their Inner Male Animal. Then, emerging at last to clasp hands in paws and vow never again to let the lure of female kind get in the way of their brotherly bond.

Now, put some women together with these same dogs in the same cottage setting, and I can guarantee that something quite different is bound to occur. At some point, some dog is going to get his toenails painted, just for fun. Or be posed for photos wearing an old rubber bathing cap. Instead of barely seared steaks over an outdoor flame, the menu will run to marshmallows toasted while loafing beside the fireplace, and batches of brownies whipped up on impulse in the middle of the night, while crying copiously (this includes dogs) over an old video of *Greyfriars Bobby*.

But just because that special bond exists between some women and certain dogs, does it necessarily follow that any dog is right for every woman in search of a life companion? Of course not. No more than we can safely say that every woman's life is better for having a man – any man – as her mate.

Still, there are some general rules a woman can apply when searching out the species that best meets her needs. There are basic questions she can ask herself before deciding whether it's worse to risk sharing her bed with a slimy chew-toy, or with someone who calls out to Belinda Stronach in his sleep. Here are some essential concepts to consider:

Intelligence – What exactly do we mean by "consciousness," and to what extent can such a term be applied to subhuman creatures? For that matter, can a man sprawled in front of the TV set watching sports on a Saturday afternoon truly be said to be "conscious"? By contrast, assessing the intellect of a dog is child's play, especially when you take into account the comparatively well-developed communication skills of the average canine. When he wants out, a dog will, at least, bark – as opposed to cleaning out your purse and leaving a note scrawled in lipstick on your bathroom mirror.

Inner Life – Further to the whole question of canine consciousness, is it possible to postulate complex motivations, moral values, or a code of social conduct in dogs? Here again, a quick comparison with the human realm may be helpful. When a man disguises his voice on the phone because he suspects it's his mother calling, how complex could his motives be said to seem? By the same token, how do we assess the "moral values" of a four-legged species unacquainted with the concepts of insider trading, wet-T-shirt contests, and fly-by-night liposuction clinics? As for a code of social conduct, have you ever been to an Atom hockey game at which a father in the stands is unhappy with a call against his son by the referee? Or on the sidewalk at closing time outside a bar that's just concluded their popular "Chug-One-Keg-of-Beer-All-By-Yourself-and-the-Second-One's-Free Event"? And if so, do you think the presence of a dog might have raised or lowered the tone of the occasion? I rest my case.

As for the question of what a dog thinks about his role in your life, assume that your own expectations will play a part in shaping his understanding of his duties. As an escort, he is certainly capable of being as hairy-chested and as protective out there on the street as any man who ever asked to see you home, and – very likely – twice as silent.

At night, you'll appreciate that lack of loquaciousness when he curls up with you to watch TV without hogging the remote or making overly appreciative comments about big-breasted blondes who appear on the screen. So what if he tends to dribble when he drinks? Or is inclined to relieve an itch by rubbing his rear end on the rug? Come on now, you've dated men with less endearing habits, and you know it.

Humour – Whether it comes to his willingness to wear fake antlers at Christmastime, pretend to smoke a pipe, or howl along obligingly with your harmonica, a dog never seems to mind looking foolish. Of course, the same could be said for that guy in your office who likes to wear a fez and ride a kiddy-car in all the local parades. The dog, however, appears aware of the fact that he's handing you a cheap laugh.

Compulsions – A man who indulges in compulsive tail-chasing is often described as "a real ladies' man." A dog who does the same thing is often described as neurotic. As for getting him to stop, a sharp tap on the nose with a rolled-up newspaper can work wonders. The dog's problem, on the other hand, may require the expertise of a trained behaviourist.

Conditioning – Speaking of behaviour, positive reinforcement is your very best training tool. The sound of a bell associated with food will cause a dog to salivate, just as it will prompt a man to inquire, "Hey, you got any change on you? I just heard the coffee-cart arriving on the elevator." Be aware as well of how keenly a dog enjoys learning. Start with simple tricks, like fetching the leash every time he whines to go out. Soon, you'll graduate to more complex tasks, like feeding him whenever he rings the bell – and, no wait a minute. Who's conditioning who here? What? No, damn it. For the last time, I do *not* have any change for the coffee-cart. Besides, whoever heard of a dog who drinks coffee?

Identifying the Alpha Male – Like the Delta Kappa Epsilon male, or the Sigma Chi male, the Alpha can easily be distinguished by the women's panties festooning the trees outside his frat house, his fondness for the secret handshake, and the little Greek letters on his lapel-pin. As for Alpha male *dogs*, I'm afraid I haven't the faintest idea how to pick them out, except to suggest that if you have to ask his permission when you want to vacuum under his special chair, you've either got a dominant dog on your hands or else very compelling grounds for divorce.

Feeding – Do not expect a dog to be consistent about what he eats, nor even what he's prepared to include in the realm of food. As with real estate, it all comes down to three basic things: loca-tion, location, location. The rubber bands, bits of chalk, daubs of bird-doo, birthday candles, broken fan belts, and rain-soaked pizza crusts that your pet might like to snack on al fresco are not necessarily what he'll accept indoors in a dish. Food eaten out of doors just tastes better, that's all. If you don't believe me, ask your boyfriend how on earth, when he's at a football game, he can eat a paper tray of nachos with what looks and smells like a yellow polyvinyl chloride raincoat melted all over it, yet turn up his nose at your sister's special pot roast every time she invites you two kids over for a good homecooked meal with her husband, her husband's mother, the mother's caregiver, their four hyperactive kids, and that cockatiel that won't shut up, all wedged around the table in the dining nook in their overheated condo.

Separation Anxiety – Such a major form of neurosis that it deserves its own heading. Almost every dog has to deal with the fact that his owner is going to leave the house to go to work. How much of a problem that can constitute is, of course, up to *you*. Will worry, loneliness, boredom, and resentment lead to destructive activities while you're at the office? Or will you cope maturely with the fact that you're stuck there, hour after hour, expected to produce reports, chair meetings, and take clients for lunch while your dog gets to loll around on the sofa watching soap operas all day long?

Try telling yourself that he can't be expected to fill his days productively or contribute to household expenses. If that doesn't work, try reminding yourself that the last three guys you lived with didn't have remunerative employment either, and at least it isn't X-rated videos the dog is watching while you're at work. And so what if he's a little destructive? What are a few up-ended plants compared to that regulation-size pool table one of your boyfriends installed in your study the week you were away? Or some toothmarks on the second-floor banister, alongside – Actually, come to think of it, those toothmarks on the second-floor banister *are* alongside much worse ones made by another boyfriend, who really could not handle being left alone by himself, even though he was thirty-seven years old. The dog, at least, stands a chance of growing out of it.

Speaking of separation, I'm afraid I'm out of advice, and out of here. But there you have it: some of the pros and cons of what could well be the beginning of a beautiful friendship. Now that you've had an opportunity to consider some of what's involved in involving yourself with a dog, you'll be better able to decide whether man's best friend is your best bet.

But no matter what you choose for yourself, there's no question that, for many women, dogs are here to stay. Even if very few of them can be successfully induced to stay on command. It is perhaps in that respect, above all others, that they are the most like men.

Varmints

I

Now that I stop to think about it, I guess it all began – as major adventures so often do – with one too many drinks, down at the Manhunters' Club. I should back up a bit and explain that the Manhunters' isn't really a "club" in any formal sense – you know, with those green-shaded table lamps, potted ferns, and some liveried servant named Higgenby hovering in attendance with a cut-glass decanter of tawny old port and a copy of the *Sunday Times*.

No, we Manhunters are somewhat rougher and readier than that, or so we pride ourselves. All we're out for, whenever we get together, is a little light-hearted bragging, some serious drinking, and the opportunity to talk about what we all love best: good hunting.

If you know manhunters at all, you'll already be aware that talking about big game – especially the game that got away – is almost as much fun for us as stalking our prey, drawing a bead, and closing in for the kill. Which, of course, is where the bragging and drinking come in, and why our regular gatherings are so riotous, as we take turns ragging each other about some of the bigger whoppers that get passed around the table as truth, as well as whistling in genuine envy whenever another member of the Manhunters' offers incontrovertible evidence of a successful score, out in the field.

On the particular evening in question, I believe it was Mindy who more or less got the ball rolling, with her tale of a recent trip she'd taken to a singles bar somewhere up in the suburbs.

"Come on! A *singles* bar?" That would be Viv, the resident skeptic. I guess every group has to have one. "Don't try to tell me singles bars exist any more, in this day and age, even in the suburbs."

"I wouldn't waste my breath trying to tell *you* anything," Mindy shot back, but in a good-natured way.

"Then show me," Viv said. "I'm from Missouri."

That's another thing you need to know about Viv. She always says she's from Missouri, but the truth of it is, she's from somewhere farther south in the States, like Louisiana or maybe even Florida. Anyway, she's got this great slow-talking drawl, which really adds an element of excitement to *her* hunting stories. Why, one time I remember her holding an entire table spellbound for over an hour as she described, in spine-tingling detail, how she lay perfectly motionless by a pool, slathered in sunscreen, waiting for this cute but extremely shy attendant to venture down to her end and skim off the few dead leaves she'd strategically placed on the water to lure him.

"Sure, Viv," said Mindy. "I'll be glad to show you." From her purse, she fished a folder of freshly developed snapshots, and slid them across the table to Viv. "Luckily, one of the girls from my office was celebrating her birthday there, so we all had our cameras handy."

"A *birthday?*" Viv scoffed with a laugh. "What kind of singles bar worthy of the name caters to the birthday crowd? Next, you'll be telling us all about Karaoke Night."

"Hey," Jennifer piped up. "Don't knock it. Did I ever tell you about that great big beautiful investment banker I nearly bagged at a Karaoke Night on that cruise I took in March? Wow. His billfold must have been *that* thick with credit cards, if it was an inch."

"Yeah, yeah, whatever." Viv had turned her attention back to Mindy's snapshots, and was thumbing through them appraisingly. "Hmm, well maybe *this* one'd be worth wasting a bullet on." She singled out one of the snaps and handed it back to Mindy. "You must have been at pretty close range to get a shot like this."

"Yes, I was." As the photo was passed around, to murmurs of appreciation from the group at large, Mindy sighed, drank deeply from her goblet of white wine, and launched into an explanation of how she'd come so close, yet also come up short.

It seems that the good-looking guy in the photo had latched on to her right away, and was soon plying her with drinks, his card, and all kinds of proposals for future encounters. "But then, just when it looked as though I pretty much had his head over my mantelpiece . . . Brring! Off goes his cellphone. He answers it, and the next thing I know he's out the door in a single bound."

"Except not so single, the rat," Elizabeth offered. "Boy, that is so exactly like what happened to me that time, when I was out clubbing, and I really thought I'd nailed this guy – wham! – right between the eyes. Only, guess who the bartender turned out to be?"

"His wife?"

"Worse. His husband. Cripes! I'm all for opening up marriage to anybody who cares to come in, but if they want weddings like everybody else, the least they can do is wear a *ring* like everybody else."

"You're not kidding, like everybody else!" That was Lenora, who's never heard a near-miss story she doesn't think she can top. "Did I ever tell you about being involved with this married guy – until I found out the ring the weasel wore on his third finger was off a *curtain* rod, for crissake, and the whole married-man persona had been a fabrication to keep me from feeling trapped in the relationship?"

"That skunk!" Elizabeth said sympathetically. "I mean, what a plagiarist! You know, I'm the person who practically invented the entire idea of attracting dates by pretending to be married to somebody else."

"Oh, men are clever mimics, all right," I agreed. "That's how they survive in nature, you know, by being copycats, who –"

"Sweet suffering succotash! Would you listen to yourselves?" That, of course, was Viv, now one stiff drink over her limit, and ready to pooh-pooh the pack of us. "Rats! Weasels! Skunks! Polecats!"

"*Copy*cat," I tried to correct her. "I said men mimic the –"

"Oh, shut up. I get your point already – and yours, and yours. And, may I say, never have I heard such a pathetic pile of excuses for failing to bring home the bacon and nail its hide to the barn door. Some bacon! Some hide! Fellow Manhunters, we're a disgrace to the noble name of Nimrod, if this is what passes for pelts worthy of our pursuit! Varmints, nothing but no-account varmints!"

Viv, it's worth noting, had been drinking vodka martinis, and the combined effect of the alcohol and her rising sense of outrage on her Southern accent was to make her sound more and more like a sharecropper holding off a revenue agent with a shotgun.

"Oh, for goodness' sake, Viv," said Lenora crossly. "What are you on about? We hunt what's out there. That's how it's always been, and always will be, and there's no point in downrating the quality of the quarry, just because it happened to get away."

"Is there any point in pretending that if we do catch them, we're any better off?" replied Viv. "Stuffed and mounted, a polecat is still a polecat, my friends. A weasel is a weasel is a weasel, and a varmint by any other name is just a varmint."

By now, we were all used to Viv's sweeping skepticism. But this latest statement struck us all as different – angry somehow, even a tad despairing.

"What do you want us to do?" I asked her. "Lenora's right: For better or worse, manhunting is our cultural tradition. Can we help it if civilization has encroached on their former habitat, and interfered with the ways of nature?"

"Civilization? In a pig's eye." With that, Viv spat on the floor, actually spat. Elizabeth went "Ew!" and a couple of the others flinched with distaste, but some of us, I think, were taken by Viv's sincerity, and the depth of her disillusionment. "You call it 'civilization' to have to go out stalking game in cramped singles bars and crowded clubs, and pretend there's anything sporting about it? Do you call it civilized to turn a once noble, independent species like men into urban scavengers, caught up in the commercial rat-race, and forced to subsist on a diet of lottery tickets, computer games, office politics, and pornographic Web sites, because there's no more nourishment left in the environment they've been reduced to?"

Silence fell over the membership of the Manhunters' Club, as each of us, in her own way, sought to absorb the impact of Viv's damning analysis.

"Even if that's so," ventured Janet at long last, in a small, subdued voice. "Even if men, as we once knew them, have more or less vanished . . . you still haven't answered the important question. What are we supposed to do about it? Besides drink, and shed a few futile tears, and then go back to the business of trying to trap those second-rate specimens we do manage to track down at the bars and clubs?"

"Well," Viv drawled, holding up her glass in a mocking toast, "I can't speak for anyone else, of course. But here's what I intend to do: Go looking farther afield, to see if, beyond the boundaries of this so-called civilization, there might not be something left of men's former glory – one or two splendid stags out there on some distant hill, perhaps, still boasting a noble spirit, and gift-wrapped in a good-looking hide. Anybody interested in signing on?"

What it all boiled down to – once Viv had sobered up enough to tone down the Tennessee Ernie Ford delivery and the corn-pone prose – was that she'd already decided to throw over her job in the city and move up to a cabin on some northern lake in hopes of getting back to the land and communing with a better class of wildlife. Frankly, it struck the rest of us as a drastic step, simply for the sake of happier hunting grounds. But we all clinked our glasses with hers in silent admiration, and then downed our drinks with the degree of solemnity appropriate to the occasion.

II

Say what you will about Viv, she's always been a woman of her word. Within a month, she'd sold her condo, packed up her Honda, and headed off to where the highway finally petered out into a gravel road, running down to the edge of a serene sylvan lake.

"It sounds like Paradise," I said, when she phoned me on a crackling line from her cabin to invite me and a few of the other Manhunters up for a visit.

"Oh, it is," she assured me. "Why, it's just as peaceful as –"

As peaceful as what, I never did learn, because at that moment, a loud buzzing noise cut right through Viv's voice on the other end of the line.

"What's that?" I demanded, raising my own voice in hopes she could still hear me. "Some sort of interference on the phone?"

"No, I reckon it's someone with a big old chainsaw a few doors down, or maybe a Jet-Ski on –"

"Chainsaw? Jet-Ski? Viv, I thought you left the rat race behind!"

"Oh, I have, I have," she yelled over the din. "The hunting up here is excellent! You'll see. None of them there scrawny excuses for varmints you gals are used to. So pack your bittiest bikinis, your cutest crop tops, and all your other ammo and let the big-game games begin!"

Maybe the mistake we Manhunters made was to let Viv invite us up on the first long weekend of the summer. Not only was the traffic bumper-to-bumper all the way up, even that gravel road running down to her lake seemed to be in a state of gridlock.

"My God," Mindy remarked, as we inched our way toward Viv's place, past wood-burned signs with names like "Loonacy" and "Tequila Sunset" to indicate the numerous cottages hidden amongst the trees. "Could this be that distant hill with those noble stags Viv left the city in search of?"

"Not on your nelly," said Elizabeth, squinting unhappily at two skinny men in sagging wetsuits walking along the roadside toting a big case of beer between them. "What on earth could Viv have been thinking?"

"Okay, so in summertime things up here are a little less . . . pastoral," Viv greeted us defensively when we finally made it to her door.

The rustic cabin we'd all envisioned wasn't quite as advertised, either. It was, in fact, an ugly A-frame on a thirty-foot lot that offered, instead of an uninterrupted view of the lake, a view of another cottage that looked upon yet another, which in turn may well have looked upon the lake, for all we could tell. I wondered whether, before our arrival, it had ever occurred to Viv how far this reality was from the rural refuge of her dreams. Now, forced to see these surroundings through other eyes, she seemed suddenly struck, like the rest of us, with its overwhelming awfulness.

"Never mind," I told her, hoping to salvage the situation at least somewhat. "Less pastoral means more populous, and maybe more populous spells better prospects for some first-class hunting. So tell us, Viv. Where are all those big, brawny, bronzed, single cottage guys? Because I'm thinking one of them would look good next to your fireplace . . . or, okay, in the absence of a fireplace, right there beside that rusted Kenmore gas range."

Well, perhaps it goes without saying that there were no big, brawny, single cottage guys – bronzed or otherwise – anywhere within a forty-mile radius. Having ditched, with such disdain, the club circuit, the singles bar scene, and all other urban opportunities to flush out, pursue, and possibly bring home her prey, Viv had ended up in a place where most of the men came complete with wives and kids – except for the occasional pack of rogue teenage boys, up for a weekend of unsupervised mayhem at the family cottage, and a lonely old widower who lived next door and did nothing but clear his throat and hose down his deck.

With no other way to amuse ourselves during those three endless mornings, afternoons, and evenings we spent up at Viv's, we would-be Manhunters were driven to taking turns peering out at these inhabitants of the hinterland through Viv's battered old binoculars. Eventually, our sense of humour got the better of us, and we wound up compiling a crude list of some of the more egregious male species we could spot at that distance.

Just beyond the widower, for instance, we could not help but hear as well as observe The Greater Hammerhead, whose curious nesting activities only escalated as the weekend progressed. Every waking minute, this curious creature busied himself in ceaseless toil, noisily constructing decks, submerging docks, and crafting assorted other doodads that he seemed far too busy building to enjoy. Out on the water, meanwhile, Elizabeth took particular pleasure in noting the behaviour of the many aquatic species – including the Beer-Bellied Suds Sucker, who often bombed around the lake in his boat alongside an accompanying flock of jet-skiing buzz-ards.

Not all of these holidaying human males had chosen to settle in the great outdoors. At the Blockbuster in the centre of the nearby town, many splendid specimens of the Red-eyed Videophile came and went, odder than anything in Audubon, with their apparent plan of getting away from the tensions of city life by hibernating inside the den of a darkened cottage, all weekend long, screening Steven Segal hits, or playing and replaying the best bits from the original *Dumb and Dumber*.

By the third afternoon, all of us had become somewhat slap-happy – arguably somewhat *too* slap-happy. Particularly Mindy, who was so absorbed in advertising aloud what she could see going on down by the shore, that she neglected to take note of the fact that Viv was well within earshot. "Ah yes, the distinctive high-pitched, indignant cry of the Ruffled Grouse, perched on his floating dock, and shrieking in protest as a group of female Bare-Breasted Nutbars drop the tops of their bathing suits. Meanwhile, shivering from too many hours out on his water skis, the poor Blue-Footed Booby cries out –"

"Cries out, 'That's about enough from you guys!'" Viv strode angrily into the room and snatched the binoculars out of Mindy's hands. "Okay, girls, I get it. My life here is a bad joke. Almost as bad as the jokes you all have been making since you got here."

"Oh, Viv . . ." Mindy, like the rest of us, was red-faced with guilt. "I'm so sorry. Your hospitality has been wonderful, and we have no call to –"

"Oh yes, you do," said Viv, suddenly no longer angry. "I mean it. My life here *is* a bad joke. Nothing has worked out the way I wanted it to. And after all this, I'm still asking myself, Where have all the real men gone?"

"Funny you should ask," Elizabeth said. "Because I just had a call on my cell from Lenora, back in the city. She's all excited about something called Man Alive Tours, and she's invited a representative from the company to come and speak at the Manhunters' Club – all about where the real men have gone."

III

As we all filed into the club, the representative from Man Alive Tours handed us each a colourful brochure. "Exotic Wilderness Excursions," it read. "Experience up close and in their natural habitat the majesty of a great but disappearing species!"

Before I could read the rest, the representative gave the signal to dim the lights, and the slide-and-lecture portion of the evening began. The woman at the podium greeted us all warmly, thanked us for allowing her an opportunity to address our group, then launched right in.

"As with any arduous adventure tour, the trick is to get in shape for it. We're not just talking the purchase of flattering safari skirts and monsoon-proof mascara, ladies. We're talking the kind of psychological preparations you'll have to make, in order to encounter this extraordinary species out in the wild.

"First slide, please. Ah, here we see members of a future Man Alive tour schooling themselves not to startle our quarry with any sudden move when we first meet them – such as presenting our business cards or offering to buy lunch. Real men are old-fashioned men, comfortable only when taking the initiative.

"Next slide? Thank you. Here's another group of would-be women adventurers, spending long hours in the passenger seat of a car, repeating 'You drive, honey,' over and over, as well as practising the patience required for any real man who might be in the vicinity to come around to the passenger side to open the door."

I stole a glance over at Viv, who'd come back to town expressly for this. Even in the semi-darkness, the look of rapt attention in her eyes was apparent, and a hint of a smile had begun to play around her lips.

I leaned over and whispered to her, "This sounds a bit more like it, eh?"

"I'll tell the world!" she replied, accomplishing virtually that with her hoarse stage whisper. "No varmints out there on the veldt, you can bet. I cain't hardly wait to sign myself up!"

Nor, it seemed, could any of us. No sooner was the slide projector switched off and the lights switched back on than Elizabeth, Janet, Lenora, Mindy, Viv, and I all found ourselves lining up to append our names to an already lengthy list of applicants for the next trip of a lifetime on offer from Man Alive Tours.

Not long after, we were on our way.

At the outset of our trip, I had promised myself I would keep a complete written record of every moment of the Man Alive Tour. But that was easier said than done as we jounced along in the Land Rover, hour after hour, over impossibly rutted roads. Besides, there was so much to see all around that I didn't dare risk turning my gaze from the window for even a moment.

Tracking real men, our guide, Melinda, had informed us right off the top, was a matter of keeping eyes and ears constantly open. And even at that, there was no assurance that we'd actually encounter one. Still, she added, the signs of habitation were encouraging. On our very first day, she was able to point to a crumpled Cruex box, a trail of *Popular Mechanics* subscription coupons, and a couple of old Zippo lighter flints as evidence.

"Real men," she said, "have passed this way, and not more than a few hours ago."

When it actually comes to describing First Contact with an all-but-extinct species, words fail me, even to this day. For weeks, it seemed, we women had been crawling on our bellies over terrain made even more rugged by empty Coors cans, discarded Black & Decker saw blades, and a dog-eared catalogue listing "What's New in Sailor Tattoos." Finally, however, we were rewarded by a sight none of us will ever forget.

"Look," whispered Melinda, and look we did, to the spot behind the water hole where she was pointing.

Men. As far as the eye could see, real men were approaching to drink at the watering hole, illuminated in the glow of a cinema marquee still advertising some long-gone Charles Bronson retrospective.

It was Janet who first spotted the distinctive flash of white of Ernest Hemingway's cable-stitch pullover, across the river and into the trees. Next thing we knew, Papa himself came crashing into view. Not my favourite writer by any means, but an undeniably magnificent specimen of a real man: able to drink, swear, womanize, and all the while type, in his trademark two-fisted style, some self-aggrandizing anecdote about himself.

Then "Look!" Melinda commanded again, and again we followed the direction indicated by her finger. There was Gary Cooper, walking tall beside Knute Rockne, General Norman Schwarzkopf, and Tom Clancy. With the wind in our favour, we couldn't mistake the manly aroma of bay rum and day-old sweat.

At such a moving sight, it was hard to suppress a sob. Even Viv, honorary inhabitant of the Show-Me State, seemed close to tears at the sight of so many real men, ranging so free.

"Perfect, aren't they?" I said to her in a voice trembling with emotion. "Out here, all by themselves, just as Nature intended."

"Just as Nature intended," she agreed, but something in the way she said it made me glance sharply at her face, which in the half-shadow of the surrounding bushes, had a calculating, crafty look. "On the other hand, I've got a few natural tendencies of my own."

"Viv," I cautioned, "don't do anything rash. You remember that waiver we all signed: No interfering with the wildlife. You so much as hitch up your safari skirt in their direction, and Melinda's going to make sure you're out of here on the next cargo plane."

But I should have saved my breath, and I knew it. Fresh from her failed experiment in out-of-town living, Viv had no intention of coming up empty a second time. All that was left of her savings she'd sunk into this tour, and there was no doubt in my mind that she'd left home determined to get her money's worth.

Still, when she hauled off and brought down one of the real men, her choice took even me by surprise. Not that he lacked physical appeal – with his Stewart Grainger cleft chin, and the cocky strut of Norman Mailer, yet with wistful overtones of the Wichita Lineman in the Glen Campbell classic. But he was a simple soul – primitive, practically – one of the specimens who'd taken to lurking near our campsite at dusk in hopes of catching sight of us women without our nylons. As if women wore nylons any more, especially while on safari!

I could see Viv was a goner, from the minute she made the mistake of giving him a name – Studs. Studs seemed flattered by all the attention, and quick on the uptake. Soon he'd learned how to shove his deck of unfiltered Exports up under the sleeve of the too-tight T-shirt Viv had given him, again in contravention of the tour rules, which strictly forbade not only feeding the real men, but upgrading them in any way, either by helping them with their resumés, correcting their grammar, or teaching them how to choose a tailor.

In the end, though, there was nothing any of the rest of us could do to save Viv from herself, and from Studs. By the time Melinda cottoned on to what had happened, and had marched into Viv's tent to order her to pack up and leave, there was no Viv to been seen, and her packing had already been done. Viv had gone native with a vengeance, by following Studs and all the other real men off into the bush.

IV

Without Viv, the Manhunters' Club is a quieter place, and our meetings seem to lack a certain combative flair. Not to say that fervent debate has become entirely a thing of the past. Since all of us but Viv returned from our once-in-a-lifetime trip, we still get together to toast our exploits – real and imagined – with our alcoholic beverage of choice, order a vodka martini in memory of our friend, and reminisce about the highlights of our Man Alive tour before things took such a sobering turn with Viv's departure.

We've had fun squealing over the photos Janet took of a bunch of real men caught unawares by the watering hole, butt-snapping each other with wet towels and vying for the Best Beer Burp honours. And of course, there are Lenora's absolutely eerie audio tapes of a lone real man, out there somewhere on a moonlit savannah, giving solo voice to some age-old hurtin' song, in the manner of Percy Sledge.

However, at some point in the evening, once the nostalgic memories are put away, the conversation inevitably drifts back to Viv – our funny, fiery, fucked-up friend – somewhere out there where the real men are. Happy? We can only hope so.

"I don't know," Mindy says skeptically, perhaps still smarting over some bygone slight of Viv's about suburban singles bars. "A real man Studs may be, but what kind of future would any woman face with someone so romantically retarded he thinks 'Diamond Ring' must be the name of some men's magazine about baseball and boxing?"

Elizabeth laughs, in spite of herself. "No wonder real men are an endangered species. By the time Studs figures out it's a case of 'procreate or perish,' he won't have the wherewithal to reproduce himself."

"Come on," I say. "Think of poor Viv. You know, even by the time she went walkabout with him, Studs hadn't managed to master her name, much less her phone number, birthday, or preferred perfume?"

"I know." Like me, Janet is genuinely compassionate. "The only way she could ever get his attention was by crinkling a bag of Rold Gold pretzels within his hearing or riffling the pages of a girlie calendar."

"Poor Viv," Mindy snorts. "The mightiest huntress of them all. You know, keeping a real man like Studs interested might prove to be a bit of a challenge, given his attention span. She'll have to start dabbing a little Valvoline behind her ear, or coughing like an old Corvette in need of a tune-up."

"Mindy!" chides Lenora, in a mock Southern drawl. "Are you all tryin' to tell me that a real man ain't the critter he's cracked up ta be, after all?"

"Could be, Lenny, could be. 'Cause you know what they say when it comes to huntin': One critter looks pretty much like another, when he's turn tail to run. In the end, they're all just varmints."

By this time, we're all laughing uncontrollably, and we drink to this latest bit of lore we've learned as members of the Manhunters' Club.

"Skunks, weasels, polecats, rats, super-rats, and . . . Studs. Here's to them all." We clink our glasses, and then order another round, including one more for Viv. "Here's to those varmints! And here's to Viv, wherever she is!"

WEEKEND WARRIORS

NOT LONG AGO, THERE was a headline atop an article in the *Globe and Mail* that only confirmed what many men – and the women they rant to – have suspected for years: "Tight Ties Put Vision in Danger, Study Says." The study in question, conducted by the *British Journal of Ophthalmology*, had determined that tightly knotted neckties press on the jugular vein, thus potentially injuring the optic nerve, and thus greatly increasing the risk of glaucoma in men who are, quite literally, too tightly wrapped.

Well, good for the *British Journal of Ophthalmology* for sounding the alarm. But that study on ties seems to raise, on a less physiological level, as many questions as it answers. Not the least of which is the query tie-hating men have been bellowing for the better part of the last century, usually while in front of a bedroom mirror, struggling unhappily with a Windsor knot: "Why the hell do men wear ties in the first place?"

After all, it wasn't supposed to be this way, not by the time the twenty-first century rolled around. As far back as the 1960s, fashion set out to liberate men from the tyranny of ties that bind by offering them the leisure suit and its even kookier cousin, the Nehru jacket. For some reason, neither style really caught on. Men opted to stick with the status quo. But not, surely, out of an allegiance to the humble necktie and its noose-like knot?

Well, perhaps. After all, here we are, almost half a century beyond the lapel-less leisure suit, the clerical-looking Nehru collar, and all the other efforts made by concerned *disegnatori* to offer men outfits that may have looked a little too much like formal wear on the Starship *Enterprise*, but at least let them off the leash, so to speak.

Yet here are men regardless, still in a knot, long after Pierre Trudeau clowned for the cameras by pretending to strangle himself with his tie, his eyes rolled back and tongue stuck out. And surely it wasn't too long after *that* when some crown prince of some European royal family or other created a sensation in a session of his country's legislative assembly by tearing off his necktie, throwing it on the floor in front of the mostly male parliamentarians, and likening its strictures to wearing a snake around his neck.

Women, God knows, are no strangers to what it means to be a similarly reluctant slave to fashion. But they would never let themselves be slaves to just one way of accessorizing the Adam's apple. When women choose to wear anything at all around their necks, look at the range of options: ascots, lockets, pendants, brooches, beads, pearls, chokers, turtlenecks, kerchiefs, dickies . . . and ties. Yes, you heard right. Men's ties. Long before Avril Lavigne there was Diane Keaton, and before her Lucille Ball, Judy Garland, Marlene Dietrich, and a host of other lady luminaries who co-opted men's neckties for their own purposes.

But know what? None of the women you've ever seen in a tie ever wore that tie knotted too tight. Not because they got an advance peek at the *British Journal of Ophthalmology*, but because women get the lighter side of ties in a way that men have mysteriously missed. A tie, after all, is just a length of silken ribbon, meant to pretty up the package that is the human face.

So, here we have a society of men loudly negative about their neckwear yet seemingly unable – or unwilling – to move on. Why? Having listened for decades to men's complaints while observing them continue to tie themselves up all the same, women have little choice but to conclude *that this must be what men want.* Still the question remains: Why?

Maybe for the same reason that men tie the ties they hate too tightly: Because the more constrictive their weekday dress, the more liberating it feels to rebel against it, come Friday night. Okay, you say. But even if so, so what? Nothing all that mystifying there. Rules are made for the satisfaction of breaking them. Just ask any female executive easing herself out of her painful workaday pumps after office hours.

But when it comes to some men and the form their weekend rebellion takes, it's not a case of just slipping into an old sweatshirt for a carefree jog around the block. Some men (and these may well be the same men who complain most strenuously about the restrictions of wearing a tie) are as organized, codified, and self-conscious in their recreational attire and accoutrements as any buttoned-down captain of industry, perfectly turned out for work, from the points of the hanky peeking out of his pocket to the gleam on his Florsheims.

We've all seen the kind of man whose idea of dressing down for a weekend of kicking back strongly suggests a member of some militia dressed to kick butt. U.S. President George W. Bush is a case in point. Here's a man who chose never to see action in any army, navy, or air force, but frequently chooses, as casual attire, a windbreaker modelled on those worn by members of the Joint Chiefs of Staff. On one hand, it's puzzling, like a form of play-acting the prez should surely have outgrown, along with his cowboy suit. On the other hand, it seems so serious, to doff your business suit in order to relax by donning another kind of uniform, especially one with connotations of killing.

Canadians, of course, prefer the sort of symbol of recreation embodied by prime minister Trudeau – the same Pierre Elliott

Trudeau who sent up his workday wardrobe in that unforgettable photograph of self-strangulation. An even more indelible image is Trudeau in fringed buckskin, canoeing solo in the wilderness, like some incorruptible cameo of Canadian identity. Yet a kind of weekend warrior all the same, in his animal hides, like a hunter or trapper from an earlier era. Even Trudeau, ever the individualist, seems to belong, in that buckskin jacket, to some tradition of recreation as trophy-taking, as playing the part, as wearing the carefully coordinated costume that proclaims membership in a culture of men proud to be as hard at play as they are at work. (However, PM Pierre, and even George Dubya, for that matter, had a far better handle on the right kind of he-man recreational attire than one-time Canadian Alliance leader Stockwell Day. His infamous wetsuit-and-personal-watercraft publicity shot forever branded him, among men of action, as a mere wienie, unable to aspire even to hot-dog stature.)

Back in the 1940s and 50s, it may have been magazines like *Argosy* – with its monthly depiction of some embattled man of action – that set the standard for all the weekend warriors to come. Even women who grew up in that era must remember a glimpse of the covers of such men's magazines, perhaps when taking a younger brother to the barbershop, or when up with the family at some fishing camp.

On the luridly painted cover, invariably facing down a towering grizzly, or slavering wolf, or stampeding elk, the archetypal *Argosy* guy boasted a jutting jaw firmly clenched around the stub of a cigar, several days' growth of beard, some sort of torn combat attire or remnant of camouflage gear, and a bravely brandished gun – or else, under more desperate conditions, a buck knife, a hatchet, a hacksaw, or, better still, nothing but his own brawny bare hands.

As quaintly distant as such an image of masculinity *in extremis* might strike us today, it persists more potently in our culture than we realize. Certainly among contemporary male hunter types, pursuing duck or deer over terrain that's often far more suburban than savage, commando-style costumes seem *de rigueur* – balaclavas, flak jackets, camouflage caps and pants, a far cry from the hokey red plaid shirts and Day-Glo hats we used to glimpse moving through the woods.

Cigars still seem to have a role to play, too, as a weekend warrior's essential accessory, even among health-conscious men who years ago eschewed cigarettes. What is it about smoking a cigar that makes a good old boy feel like part of something so very, very bad? There's the old-fashioned association with underworld wise guys, of course, as well as that enduring image of the Man With No Name, appearing out of no place in his poncho, a slim cigarillo protruding between his teeth. More recently, details of the dalliance between former president Bill Clinton and intern Monica Lewinsky have made it seem as if *not* smoking a cigar carries with it connotations of even higher risk.

But when it comes to the image of the warrior-cum-woodsman, the biggest development since the advent of the *Argosy* adventurer surely has to be the Sport Utility Vehicle. Even guys who've never strayed farther off-road than their own driveway appear to dream of themselves coursing across the veldt with Denis Finch-Hatton, or crashing over a wooded mountain range in pursuit of a big-horned ram, or purring through the Everglades, up to their axles in alligators.

Perhaps not surprisingly, for the serious SUV aspirant, such images of adventure out in the wild seem to morph effortlessly into motifs that are more militaristic – judging from the popularity of Hummers among the hunting set, along with a host of other hulking assemblages of mean-looking metal that might previously have been seen on CNN, racing across the Iraqi desert toward Baghdad, with an embedded journalist or two on board reporting gleefully into his own reflection in the side-mirror. It's not exactly that the men who make enough money to afford these artillery-style automobiles and the gas to power them regret missing out on military action themselves, or regret the demise of the old-time draft. Frankly, they've been just as happy to give Vietnam, Desert Storm, the Balkans, Mozambique, and the occupation of Iraq a miss. But when the automotive equipment is as cool as it is in the wars on TV, who wouldn't want to wade into the Motor Pool to acquire it?

Besides, there's a kind of discipline, organization, and uniformity about the entire idea of the military that's irresistible when you need to get the most out of the weekend's adventure – whether your destination is the duck-blind, or an ATV rally, or your favourite . . . golf course. *Golf* course? No, seriously. Previously regarded as a sedate activity for those not up to the rigours of croquet, golf, in recent years, has undergone a macho makeover at the meaty hands of the kind of guys who put together their Sunday foursome with all the I-search-for-adventure edge of D'Artagnan hooking up with the Three Musketeers.

The fact that professional athletes from such rough-and-ready realms as the NHL and the NBA now seemingly do nothing but golf in the off-season has, undoubtedly, added some necessary he-man cachet to the quaint Scottish sport. In a possibly related development, the clothes and other accoutrements of golf have also begun to move with the masculine demand of the times we live in.

Once upon a time, if you will recall, golf was a game frequently derided for the fact that the equipment appeared better dressed than the players. Those cute little club-covers of tartan or smoothly stitched leather struck many outside observers as far classier than the pom-pommed tams or Tilley-style toadstool hats, or strange straw snap-brim numbers modelled by male players making their way around the course. Such headgear accessorized all sorts of equally cornball costumes, ranging from Palm Beach shirts, to plus-fours, to lime-green polyester slacks secured by a wide white belt buckled well below a belly made even more bulgy by riding a golf cart the few yards – or even feet – between shots.

These days men are attiring themselves in rugged, good-looking clothes and approaching the entire enterprise with a new serious-ness suggested by something menacing in the essence of this seem-ingly sissified sport. After all, isn't there a hint of the compellingly cold-blooded in a pastime played with equipment called "clubs" – some of which, like the "mashie" and "wedge," carry connotations of a highly specialized form of death-dealing? Nowadays, each weapon in this arsenal is forged in high-test materials for its own specific fell purpose, ready to be carted around the course in a handsomely tooled bag, which when mounted on wheels, resem-bles nothing so much as a battlefield cannon.

Women, as we know, also play golf – often wearing outfits and lugging around equipment not much different from what their husbands, brothers, and bosses are sporting. But somehow, how-ever serious women are about what is simply supposed to be a game, they fail to bring to their weekly or bi-weekly round that sense of primal urgency embodied by successive groups of men, moving over the fairways, exploring every square centimetre of high grass in earnest quest of balls they fear may be forever lost.

Like hunting and other activities that men seem uniquely able to transform into military campaigns in miniature, golf is a game whose air of efficient organization has been greatly assisted by advances in electronics. Not only can the expedition be mounted, manned, mobilized, and micromanaged in its planning stages by digital organizer, e-mail, and cellphone, every important detail can be further confirmed, reconfirmed, refined, and – when nec-essary – revamped, in a subsequent series of negotiations. Even once out on the course, the members of the group can continue to use their phones to communicate from fairway to bunker, to green, to rough, much as point men in the military keep current with each other in the field by means of walkie-talkies.

Looking at such a precisely programmed foursome out on the links, or observing a squadron of flak-jacketed sportsmen moving along the highway in their SUVs with a sense of mission, it is hard to understand how they can count themselves happy when their recreation seems so regimented. Yet, we must imagine them happy – these brave weekend warriors – just as we used to assume that he-man figure on the cover of men's adventure magazines was happy too, going mano-a-mano with Nature's nastiest. After all, much worse awaits, come Monday morning, for those forced to doff their combat camouflage, stub the cigar, shave off that stubble – and then tighten the noose of a necktie around their own throats.

X-Men

I GOT MARRIED AT the start of September – a time when county fairs and fall exhibitions are in full swing. In fact, once my husband and I moved to Toronto, late in our marriage, we made a habit of attending what's known there as "the Ex" to celebrate our anniversary. The habit stuck. Even after we separated and then divorced, we continued to enjoy the Canadian National Exhibition together every September 1. "Going to the Ex with your ex," we dubbed it, to our own amusement and that of our friends.

The jauntiness of the phrase, and indeed the generally good-natured way we dealt with each other after our breakup, somewhat belied the inevitable sense of sorrow, regret, and even bitterness that accompanied the loss of an important relationship. Maybe it was our joint relief in not also having lost each other that prompted him and me to be cute and quippy about the demise of an involvement that had begun, of course, with such high hopes. Okay, so as a married couple we'd proven a total bust. At least we could succeed as fun-loving *former* spouses, right?

No doubt our union was doomed right from the outset. He, the good-looking and somewhat arrogant offspring of an upstate New York family who virtually owned the small, depressed factory town that housed their small, depressing factory. I, the extremely insecure daughter of a family of no consequence from Saskatchewan, utterly in awe of the East, particularly the many products of U.S. prep schools who made up a portion of the McGill student body.

By the time we got married, his father – who would never have allowed an alliance with a nobody like me – had died, leaving the family business in a legal and financial limbo. The stock dividends that had so regularly and reliably bankrolled my boyfriend's purchases and pastimes for years were put on hold almost at the same instant he became my husband.

While he worked on his graduate courses at McGill, I worked at a secretarial job on campus, and lay awake nights in the tiny, banana-shaped apartment we'd rented above a dress shop, trying and failing to reconcile my pitiful pay cheque with my husband's inability to reconcile his new impecuniousness with a lifetime of buying whatever he wanted. On top of everything else, he'd recently received and rejected his draft notice, which meant no more trips to the States to find out what had become of the family fortune for fear of arrest at the American border as a draft dodger.

In between rows about money and other emotional excesses of life in one's early twenties, we still managed to have many happy, even hilarious times. No matter what, we found each other endlessly entertaining, and that, amazingly, was the aspect of us that somehow survived so many other losses. Even after our alliance was effectively over, we still could and would stay up all night together talking, and laughing like carefree little kids.

It was also that quality that kept us trying to get back together, long after it made no sense on any other level. By the time we'd formally agreed to part, cheating on each other had become a way of life. My husband was facing and yet not daring to face up to the fact that he was homosexual; I was facing and not daring to face up to the fact that not only had he lied to me about it, which was terrible, he'd also accused me of being crazy after I'd guessed the truth, which was worse. Yet even once this ghastly period of Sturm und Drang had come and gone, we would still find ourselves, over a companionable drink or dinner, discussing, with ludicrous logicality, the possibility of moving away somewhere else to start our marriage afresh, in a place where nobody knew the bizarre truth about us, and where my husband would somehow revert to the straight self I'd met and married.

Mercifully, we attempted no such thing, and the annual observance of "going to the Ex with your ex" proved to be the extent of our actual allegiance to the memory of our now-defunct union. Otherwise, in the gradual way that can happen – even to the astonishment of both parties involved – our recollection of each other as lovers and spouses gave over entirely to an appreciation of each other as friends.

The fact that my former husband was now unequivocally gay undoubtedly helped to facilitate the transformation. No second wife would have tolerated my continued role in his life the way his succession of male partners did. No straight ex-husband could have made himself so available to come over to my apartment in the middle of the night to talk me down from the ledge of yet another ruptured romance with some other man – who in his view was almost invariably not worth my tears.

The impulse to stay in each other's lives in some secondary capacity was actually abetted by the comparative unorthodoxy of our situation: no competitive current spouses; no kids to complicate the pristine, and somewhat juvenile, nature of our continued involvement; no joint property or issues of custody, apart from our two cats, to sully the atmosphere between us.

Lucky us. Even at the time of our breakup, I knew that. I knew as well that I would need to hold on to my ex-husband somehow – in spite of past hurts – as a way of holding on to myself. That, of course, is the bedrock of an ongoing bond with one's ex. Once the relationship is over, the past you shared can only survive if you manage to find a way in the present to continue to share it. I needed him to remind me of who I had been when he fell for me – that neurasthenic nineteen-year-old who'd been cast opposite him in a college production of *As You Like It*. He needed me as a frame of reference for the cute and somewhat conventional frat boy I'd met back then, long since absorbed by an adult self still ambivalent about his gayness and in constant conflict about his career.

Shortly after I moved out and into an apartment of my own, he phoned to tell me he was in hospital for the removal of a tumour on his lung neither of us had known he had. I was shaken by the suddenness of this diagnosis, by the imminence of the operation, and – most of all – by the idea that there could be anything physically wrong with the broad-shouldered, well-muscled young man I'd never known to have so much as a head cold.

When I went to see him, shortly before his surgery, I found him in a typically squalid four-person ward, devoid of serenity, privacy, or even basic dignity. In one corner, behind an inadequate cloth partition, an entire family wept and wailed over a man they presumably were there to reassure prior to some minor operation. Behind another curtain, an invisible and solitary sufferer groaned. In yet another part of the room, a woman recited the Rosary aloud to her slumbering husband. In the midst of all this chaotically choreographed misery, there lay my own husband – an island of tranquility in a sea of noisy despond, calmly reading Dante's *Inferno*, oblivious both to his surroundings and to the irony of his choice of reading material.

Many years later, when he was diagnosed as HIV positive, and later developed full-blown AIDS, he handled it all with similar stoicism and unfailing courage. I, on the other hand, tried but utterly failed to prepare myself for the awful extent of what I would lose. No more movie and dinner dates with my favourite fellow film

critic and bluntest Dutch uncle – who still called me by the nickname he'd given me at nineteen and used it to soften the sting of
some of his assessments. ("Elf, the reason you can't seem to hang
on to a romantic relationship . . .")

No more affectionate excursions into the past, when all relationship woes had been with each other. ("Remember the
summer before your father died," I might remind him, "and you
were working in the plating room at the factory, where it was
about a hundred degrees, and you tried to organize the workers to
protest their conditions? I was so afraid your dad would find out,
and blame it on *me*, the Saskatchewan socialist who was trying to
steal his son!") And, maybe cruellest of all, no more memories of
myself as reflected in the myopic mirror of that long-departed
bloom of first love. ("You're beautiful. You ought to realize that,
but you don't. Not pretty like a lot of those girls you say you envy,
but beautiful in a way that's really extraordinary.")

By then, of course, the boy who'd once said those things was
no longer anywhere evident in the dying man lying in his hospital
bed as lightly as a·pile of dry sticks, his once-wavy locks sparse and
tufted like chicken down, his eyes round and protuberant in a
shrunken skull. Just as the cute college kid I'd first met had been
supplanted gradually by the chunky gay guy who'd become my
ex, so now was my ex slipping away in the spectral shape of
someone I no longer recognized, and who now seldom seemed to
recognize me. But at least, I consoled myself, we had death to
blame, not each other. For as long as it had been humanly possible,
we had continued to reinvent our relationship over the years,
according to the requirements of its constantly changing nature.

It had also been in September, over a year before I met the man I
would eventually marry, that I had had that most Canadian of all

love affairs – on a cross-country train – with the first of those men as with my husband who would continue to keep a hold on my heart, years after our brief involvement had become a thing of the past. And, I have come to realize that my long allegiance to his memory was as much about maintaining a connection with my own past self as it was about him.

Somewhere, I still have a creased old black-and-white Kodak snapshot of myself, taken minutes before departing with my parents for the CPR station in Regina, whence the two-days-and-two-nights rail trek back to McGill would commence. I'm eighteen, with the requisite black eyeliner and white lipstick of the times, and a Sassoon-style haircut, featuring a heavy flange of dark hair falling over my forehead and into my face. In fact, one eye is utterly obliterated, and whenever adults twitted me, as they sometimes did, about what had become of my right eye, I liked to reply that I didn't have one, purely for the pleasure of watching them blanch, then blush, then walk wordlessly away.

In the snapshot, the wide white smile on my face says it all. I am overjoyed to be leaving my dead-end summer job in Regina to return to my second year of university in Montreal. No longer the frightened little freshman of the previous September, I have a fund of friends I can't wait to reconnect with, high hopes for a decent role in a drama production on campus, and a corduroy skirt and hooded corduroy jacket bought and paid for through tedious toil at the aforementioned dead-end summer job. If there is one image of myself that captures a state of pure anticipatory pleasure, it is that crumpled old snapshot, in which, about to take flight from the armchair in my parents' living room, I have paused only long enough for that final photo with my hand on the head of my much-adored dog, my suitcase at my feet, and my mind already miles and miles down the train track.

No wonder, poised at such an auspicious point, I would meet a boy almost as soon as I stepped onto a train crowded with college-bound kids. This particular boy was harder to miss than most. He had shaggy blond hair, a navy-blue beret, a fringed buckskin jacket, a guitar, and a cute, droopy-eyed Paul McCartney kind of face. As well, he was sitting in my seat, surrounded by a group of hippi-esque male friends.

At least, I could only assume they were Hippies. So new was the phenomenon at the time that I hesitated to make a definite identification. Certainly the long hair was a good indication of Mod morphed into something new, although that beret on the guy sitting in my seat seemed more like a fashion statement left over from the Beatnik era. As for the fringed leather jacket . . . well, the train had originated on the West Coast, which could explain a lot – including the obvious mix-up in seating.

Even so, I was reluctant to make an issue of the fact that I owned that seat. Already, I felt uptight and old school, in my corduroy coordinates and smartly shaped haircut, next to the flowered shirts and flowing, raffish scarves of this gypsy-like band. My startling one-eyed look with its accentuating ring of eyeliner, which had stood me in such cool stead all summer long, now seemed stilted, more emblematic of a Carnaby Street wannabe than haute Haight-Ashbury.

"Hi," I essayed meekly. "Mind if I join you?"

"Sure." The blond guy in buckskin and beret kicked his boot at the shin of the guy opposite him. "Get up, will you? Lady wants to join us. Jesus, where are your manners?"

"Where are *yours*?" countered his friend. "Whyn't you give her your seat, instead?"

"Because it isn't mine to give." He looked up at me from under his thatch of blond hair, with an engaging droopy-eyed grin.

"Actually, I'm all the way back in coach, but this is closer to the bar car. I have no idea whose seat it is."

"Oh, well," I said. "I'm sure they won't mind."

Later, much later, when he and I were sitting alone together up in the darkened dome car, staring at stars made unsteady by the rhythmical rocking of the train, he confessed that he'd realized right away the seat he'd occupied was mine and had liked me right away for not making a big deal of it. "I mean, I should have leaped up immediately and apologized, right? But it was more fun watching you figure out whether I was going to turn out to be an asshole about it or not."

"And what do you think I finally decided?"

"About whether I'm an asshole? I think that's still somewhat under debate."

It wasn't, though. At least, not as far as I was concerned. By that point, I'd already decided that this blond boy, with his Beatnik beret and odd ideas of character assessment, was one of the most engaging, unusual, and contradictory men I'd met. On the one hand, he was smiling, gentle, almost sweet. On the other, he clearly controlled the brave little band who'd shipped out from various points in B.C. and Alberta to accompany him in the adventure of heading east to university.

He smoked dope, which I had not, to date. He'd done other drugs of which I hadn't even heard. But he loved books as well – everything from the hearty helpings of Tolkien that had recently become required reading among sensitive students everywhere, to the essays of Lord Macaulay (a distant relative of his, he said), to Romantic poetry, washed down with copious quantities of Bob Dylan, the Beatles, and Alan Ginsberg.

When it came to women, he seemed to view us all with a benignity unusual in a teenage boy. I couldn't tell if he'd had lots of experience, a moderate amount, or, like me, virtually none, beyond some heavy petting fuelled by alcohol and a spirit of scientific investigation. I also found it impossible to tell if he was as infatuated with me as I was with him.

Fortunately, here we were on a train, with miles and miles to go before he and his buddies got off in Ottawa. Even more fortunately, I'd earned enough at my odious summer job to afford a berth – a lower berth, at that – with a window looking out onto the night speeding past, punctuated periodically by the rushing forms of passing freight trains and the lights of what Scott Fitzgerald had termed the "little, lost towns" scattered out beyond the tracks.

By the time we left the dome, the sleeper car was quiet and dim, only the illuminated call buttons offering enough light for the porters to patrol the curtained corridors and for passengers to find their way to the lavatory. Everything swayed, as is the case with trains, both back and forth and side to side, the constant clatter of the wheels beneath like a soundtrack providing a sense of urgent expectation. Once in a while, the long, haunted sound of the train whistle way up front came echoing back toward us along the tracks, like the very essence of aloneness in the loneliest of landscapes.

With no other encroachment of humanity apart from the occasional snore of a passenger in another curtained-off cell, or some light laughter among the porters playing cards at the end of the car, we seemed to have all the time in the world to communicate in whispers the relevant facts of our lives to date, to kiss each other in an experimental way, and, eventually, to share as much as we dared in a darkened berth on a very populated train, hurtling its way across the broad face of the Canadian Shield, somewhere west of Sudbury.

It was, all things considered, a fair amount of sharing. And – despite the clumsy constraints and my own virginal nerves – strangely romantic. If only for appearance' sake, my partner insisted on slipping back into his clothes and stealing out of my berth and along the series of cars that led back to his buddies in coach. As for myself, I couldn't have cared less about how any of this looked. I had had an Experience, and on the Canadian Pacific Railway, no less.

All too soon, the train arrived in Ottawa. But before the band of hippies disembarked, addresses were exchanged and plans made for me to visit as soon as the contingent of Westerners found suitable digs for themselves near the university. There wasn't much point in my offering any hospitality in Montreal. I still lived in residence, where visits by men were strictly verboten.

The trip to Ottawa, which I made in October was – perhaps predictably – something of a disaster. The house was overrun with dopers and tokers of every description; my erstwhile open and affectionate friend from the train seemed tense and distant; worst of all, I thought I knew why. There was a girl hanging around the house who seemed to pertain particularly to him.

We barely had a moment alone together, he and I, and I felt he was somehow content with that – might even have contrived it. In the end, I didn't even stay the night. Impulsively, I got back on the bus to Montreal, my precious weekend leave sadly squandered and my heart broken by my lover's indifference.

In the months that followed, he wrote me rambling letters that seemed, somewhat cryptically, to attempt to address the hurtful alteration in his affections. I couldn't be sure what he was trying to say. Many drugs had been done in that hippie house in Ottawa. That, if nothing else, was clear. When the letters stopped altogether, I was saddened, but not surprised.

By the time he wrote to me again, months had passed. He'd dropped out of Carleton University after dropping acid thirty-nine days in a row, losing the ability to talk, and ending up in speech therapy. The wastefulness, the stupidity, infuriated me. And yet for some reason I treasured the letters themselves, sifting and resifting through them for some evidence that he had his reasons for staying in touch with me, that somewhere behind the chemical haze he remembered how he'd fallen in love on a cross-country train ride.

I knew, of course, that my infatuation was a Sixties cliché, which had ended, properly, where it had begun – on that train headed east. Even so, I wrapped myself in a mantle of conspicuous devotion that made it easy not to meet other guys as well as bearable to break up with the few I did meet, and comprehensible to myself to be alone.

The following fall, almost a year to the day since we'd met, I was no sooner back in Montreal at the end of the summer than I got a phone call – from the booth just outside the apartment into which I'd moved with a group of other girls. He was passing through town, with some of his old hippie cadre in tow. They had all booked tickets to London on a plane from Dorval later that day. Would I spend some of his last hours on Canadian soil with him?

"I guess your speech therapy was a success," I said. "You're making it perfectly clear that you're just passing through." But I agreed to meet him.

As I recall, we spent a couple of those few hours seeing *Blow Up*. I'd already seen the Antonioni film and thought it would be perfect preparation for a quixotic guy en route to London. After the movie, we walked, we talked, we may even have necked a little in my apartment, when the roommates weren't looking. In spite of everything, I couldn't help caring about him, and we made an elaborate pact to meet the following Canada Day in Trafalgar Square, when I'd already planned to be in England myself.

But the Canada Day reunion never came off. Well before that date, sometime in early spring, the phone rang in my apartment just as I was heading out the door to a rehearsal of a play my new boyfriend and I had written with several other friends.

"Hi," said a familiar voice in the receiver. "I'm at Central Station. We all got deported from England. I'm on my way back to Alberta, and I wondered if you have time to meet me down here for a coffee before my train?"

Before I could answer, my boyfriend called down the hallway, "Come on! We're supposed to be there by now!"

"Ah," said the voice on the other end of the phone, "sounds like you *don't* have time."

"N–not right now. Look, when's your train? Because maybe later –"

"It's okay. It's perfectly okay. I just wanted to make sure you knew not to expect to meet me on July first in Trafalgar Square."

That was the last I heard from him, and in the years that followed I somehow formed the impression that he must be dead. For no good reason; it just seemed fitting for someone so troubled, living in an era when so many interesting people died young. I made no serious attempt to find out. Except that, whenever I went to Banff, the town of his birth, I made a point of checking headstones in the cemetery for his name, and was both surprised and relieved not to find it there.

Still, so strong was my instinctive belief that he was gone that, in the late 1980s, I wrote a piece for the *Toronto Star* all about my first big romance on the train, more than twenty years earlier. Shortly after that column appeared, I received a postcard, in care of the *Star*, written in a familiar script. "Hi. I still remember the

CPR fondly, too. If you're ever in the vicinity of Calgary, I could come into the city to meet you. Of course, I doubt you're ever out West any more."

As it happened, I was about to host a banquet in Calgary. Given his offhandedness about this kind of thing, I knew the coincidence would not seem nearly as astounding to him as it did to me. I also knew I wanted to get together with him, and I wrote him back to make the arrangements.

As a meeting place, Trafalgar Square was, of course, out of the question. We agreed that he'd come up to my hotel room in Calgary once I was finished at the banquet below. The event was in honour of Women of Distinction, and the tone of the all-female gathering was high-spirited, irreverent, and ignited by alcohol.

Somehow or other, up there at the podium, it occurred to me a good idea would be to confide to the several hundred souls assembled that, as soon as my mistress-of-ceremonial duties were concluded, I was going up several floors in the elevator and back twenty-some years to reencounter my partner in a railroad romance I'd recently written up for Canada's largest newspaper. The women in the audience squealed with predictable delight, and encouraged me to divulge a few more details. I did so, with a quality of heavy double entendre that made the train-going-into-the-tunnel sequence in *North by Northwest* seem subtle by comparison.

Feeling vaguely guilty about the breach of confidence and the possible lapse in good taste, I made my way off the stage to hoots and applause, and up I went to my hotel room to order yet more wine from Room Service and await the arrival of a man I'd spent the past twenty-two years somewhat in love with – and the past twenty-two minutes turning into a slightly tipsy stand-up routine.

When he did appear at the door, he seemed startlingly the same. No beret, but the flap of blond hair across his brow very much as I remembered. Older, saner, much more in control of his life, but still very sweet. Of the two of us, I felt I'd changed far more in the intervening decades. Not just my hairstyle, my makeup, or my ability to slip into a skimpy little corduroy skirt. That big white innocent smile from the snapshot, that look of ready-for-anything as I sat perched on the edge of the chair in my parents' living room, already half out the door and on my way to another life . . . that, I knew, was nowhere to be seen. Although he claimed to like the person who had succeeded the girl with the severely cut Sassoon hair, I could tell he missed her all the same – almost as much as I did.

Still, the conversation we had was warm, comfortable, well worth having, at long last, as a way of revisiting what had stayed unspoken so long before.

"What I wrote about us in the *Star* – that night on the train. Is that the way you remember it?"

"Absolutely. I thought it was great. Both at the time, of course, and also reading your story. They reprinted it in the Calgary paper, in case you were wondering."

That was far from the only thing I'd been wondering about. "If it was such a great time, such a connection . . . what happened? I mean, way back when. Because by the time I came to see you in Ottawa –"

"Right. That time you came to see me in Ottawa. That was completely awful. Man, I felt terrible, but I didn't know what to say. The house we rented was a haven for couch-surfers. Less than a month into the term, and I was already cutting most of my classes. After all that crap I'd given you on the train about my high academic ambitions, I felt like a complete asshole when you arrived."

"Yes? Funnily enough, so did I."

He shot me a look that I also remembered from a long time ago – at once amused, evaluative, and shrewd. "Ah yes. The girl hanging around our house."

"Hanging around *you*, you mean."

"I knew that's what you thought. I knew it, but I didn't know what to say about that, either. I guess I kind of hoped we'd sort it out, somewhere down the line, you and I. But we never did."

He never did, not in any of those rambling, manic letters, not in the face-to-face encounter we'd had the following year. And not now, either, when none of it mattered, more than two decades later, and too far down the line to bother straightening out misunderstandings that dated from late adolescence. "No, we never did sort it out, you and I. Even so, here we both are. I never thought this would happen. Any time I was in Banff, I used to glance through the graveyard, expecting to find your name."

"Jesus!" I couldn't tell whether he was flattered or offended. "Did I seem as desperate a character as all that?"

"Yes, you did." Looking at him now, it seemed impossible that this benign, blond middle-aged man in the plaid shirt and jeans of a mountain dweller could have been the boy who dropped acid every day for more than a month and got himself deported from Britain. Now, he told me, he lived in a cabin outside Banff, worked as the pilot of a water bomber for the forestry service, still doodled on the guitar, and professed to be happy with his solitary, mostly contemplative life.

"As a matter of fact," he said, once we'd finished the wine I'd ordered and the conversation had gone about as far into the past as it was likely to go, "if you ever need some place to come and just unwind or whatever from big city life, my door is open."

"Thanks. Actually, I'm living in the country myself. Well, the Northeast's version of country. I'm mostly in the Berkshires these days."

"Ah. All by yourself?"

"No. With a man and a dog."

"Ah. Well, the offer still stands, if you're ever out this way again."

"And you?" I asked. "All by yourself?"

His smile crinkled the corners of those down-turned eyes, just as I remembered from the train. Come to think of it, he still looked a bit like a blond Paul McCartney. "Not when big city folks take up the offer to come and unwind."

When I walked him to the elevator, and hugged him in the big empty hotel corridor, his arms and shoulders felt more solidly muscular than the body of the young man I'd embraced in my berth on the cross-Canada train. Even so, the feeling of holding him was a familiar one – as familiar as the act of bidding him goodbye.

Throughout the two or so hours we'd spent deep in conversation in my room, the possibility that he might stay over had not once been broached by either of us. Whether either of us had considered the idea beforehand, then discarded it at some point within those two hours, was another question. For my own part, I may have hoped – or even feared – that some inexorable fate had brought us back together for this purpose. But if that had been my hope or fear, I most certainly was not up to admitting it, not even to myself, as I watched him step into the elevator car and disappear from my life once more.

This time, some sense of quiet completion made it seem perfectly all right to see him go. This time, it seemed perfectly possible that I would look him up again, my next visit West.

That sense of quiet completion suffered something of a blow a week or two later, when his letter showed up in my post office box in the Berkshires. His words were warm, amused, and affectionate as he wrote about how great it had been to see me, what a relief it was to find that we still had some sort of rapport, how happy he was to think of me living out in the country too – albeit in a far more genteel mountain range, in a far more genteel part of the North American continent.

It was only toward the end of the letter that the tone turned somewhat harsh. "Of course, I would have been even more nervous than I was about coming to your room in the hotel if I'd known you'd just come from cracking up an entire banquet hall full of women with the story of how we'd met, what we'd done on the train, and how you were feeling about encountering me again after so many years.

"You're entitled to say whatever you want, onstage or any place else, and as I told you, I got a kick out of what you wrote in the paper. But I gotta say, it somewhat took the edge off my memory of our evening – both in your berth on the CPR so long ago, and more recently in your hotel room – to turn on the Access Alberta channel on cable TV the other day and see you making jokes about it. Did you not have any idea that the event you were emcee-ing was being taped?"

No, I had not. Even so, ignorance was no excuse for what I'd done. I wrote him that, immediately, with apologies. I did not receive any reply. Nor did I attempt to get in touch with him the next time I found myself in southern Alberta. But I guess I'm still somewhat hoping we'll sort it out, somewhere down the line, he and I – however many miles of track that turns out to be.

I no longer live mostly in the Berkshires with a man and a dog. But my relationship with my ex-partner is such that I revisit that countryside I still love whenever I can, inveigle him up to Toronto whenever he's willing, and reminisce with him about the dear departed dog (and the dog that followed) whenever the opportunity arises in our frequent phone conversations.

As with my ex-husband, the path to friendship with this former partner has been carefully constructed from flagstones of highly selected memories, and assiduously cleared of any such obstructing

thorns and brambles as bitterness, anger, reproach, or recrimina-
tion. What's to be bitter? The fact that we simply weren't meant to
live together is amply demonstrated not only by the number of
times we attempted that feat with each other and failed, but also by
the existence of numerous other "exes" on both sides with whom
we've each successfully established ongoing friendships. Perhaps
one of the most persuasive arguments of all is that it was one of his
exes who introduced us in the first place, in a long-distance phone
call, while I was languishing at her place in the Laurentians still
heartbroken over a previous relationship gone wrong.

One long-distance conversation led to another, and soon he and
I were working out the logistics of meeting, either on his turf or
mine. In the end, I picked his – on the grounds that it was easier to
fly to New York than ready my messy apartment for the arrival of a
stranger. It took only one weekend together for us to realize that
the phone bills and plane fares would continue to mount up.

In the course of that very first weekend, he did something I
regarded at the time as extremely odd. He brought out albums of
photographs of many of the women – and they *were* many – with
whom he'd been involved. Paging through the pretty faces, I
made nervous jokes about "My Last Duchess," while trying to
understand the meaning of this tour through his gallery of ruptured romances.

Now, more than fifteen years later, it occurs to me that most of
us, in our varying ways, keep count of whom we've loved and
lost. Not, we hope, as an index of past failures, but as an optimistic
nod in the direction of future success, somewhere along the way,
in keeping "current" from continually turning into "ex."

Since the last of our many split-ups, my ex-partner and I have
both done better for ourselves in new involvements. Invariably,
however, we end our phone calls or begin our e-mails with "I miss

you," and mean no contradiction to our declarations of the happiness we've found apart from each other.

Of course, it's not every ex who continues to matter that much in the present. It's not every involvement that admits of the possibility of successful transformation from what was breathless, breathtaking, and full of promise into what is calm, caring, and full of forgiveness.

YOUNGER MEN

HI! YOU DON'T MIND if I sit here, do you? Don't worry, sonny. It's not a come-on. I'm not the slightest bit interested in younger men. No, really. I'm not.

That surprises you, right? Sure, I know what you've been reading in the magazines and seeing on television: how it's now considered perfectly okay for a woman like me to admit she's into younger guys – to brag about it, even. The way older men have always bragged about being able to bag younger women. But guess what, sonny? You can't believe everything you read in magazines or see on TV.

What? Oh "sonny" bothers you? Sorry. Just a habit of mine. I call all younger men "sonny." It eliminates the problem of learning names I'm only going to forget. Nothing personal, you understand. Just a matter of medical fact. The old memory bank, see? Not the solvent institution it used to be.

Try what? Oh, that Gingko Balboa, or whatever it's called . . . Yeah, I've heard that's supposed to help. Even cashed in an RRSP one time and bought myself a bottle from the health food store. Damned if I can remember where I put it, though . . . .

Let's see. What was it we were talking about? Oh, right. Old broads who can't recollect what they were just talking about, and the vogue in younger men. Personally, I just don't get it. I mean, even if you young bloods actually *are* advanced enough these days to pretend to be turned on by old crocks like us, why the hell would *we* want to be seen with *you*? For vanity? I don't think so.

I mean, look at poor old Demi Moore down in Hollywood and all that fuss they made about her dating that Ashley Krusher guy, in his twenties. All the tabloids could talk about was the five personal trainers she had to have to keep looking buff, the constant dieting, and the cosmetic regime required for a forty-something woman to hold up alongside a guy two decades her junior. Do I need that?

Now, you put me beside some balding geezer, with liver spots like poker chips and more chins than the Hong Kong phone book . . . and I tell you what, on the worst day of the week, I'm gonna look some luscious. So, why would I want to make it hard for myself, just to prove I've got what it takes to turn the crank of somebody so young he needs to show ID to get served at Chuck E. Cheese?

What? Oh, right. The sex. Sure, I absolutely cannot argue with you there. You know the best thing about younger men? They want to do it all the time. You know the *worst* thing about younger men? They want to do it *all the time*. No question, strictly on the issue of performance, you young guys have it all over honeymooning at Viagra Falls with any of the boys of autumn.

Nevertheless. . . . So you kids can come ten times in a single night. So what? It's always over so quickly. Like getting ten episodes of *Leave It to Beaver*, right in a row.

On the other hand, there's the old guys. A session with your average older man is like a screening of *The Sorrow and the Pity*. Only longer, and sadder. The woman nods off two or three times; she wakes up, and he's *still* at it. "I almost came that time," he says.

Eventually, she has to try to outfox him. "Oh, you came!" she tells him. "You definitely came. It's just that it's been so long, you've forgotten what it's like. But *that* was it. Trust me."

Oh sure, sonny, go ahead and laugh at the old guys' expense. You know what? You'll be there soon enough yourself. And what's more, you *do* know that, as well as I do. Yes, you do. Come on, kid, you can't kid me. There is no such thing as a guy so young he's not already terrified of what's up ahead. Or what's *not* up, as the case may be.

What? Of course women are also afraid of growing old. I'm not denying that. But you want to know something else? Women fear aging because it inevitably leads to wrinkles. Whereas men fear aging because it inevitably leads to death.

Don't ask me why the difference, but it's true. Even at your age, you're way more obsessed with dying than I am. Myself, I'm kind of looking forward. Somebody professional to do my makeup; lots of flowers, just for me; finally, an opportunity to wear that dress I spent a goddamn mint on . . . I don't know, maybe it all stems from missing out on my prom. What do you think?

How do you know I'm kidding? I'm barely sure myself. Look, sonny, I'm not trying to give you a hard time here. Honestly, I'm not. I mean, why would I? You younger guys are just terrific. Hey, you want to know the best thing about younger men, from where I sit? The fact that there are more and more of you for me to choose from all the time. It's the men *older* than me who are disappearing.

I mean, think about it: Basically, when you're a woman, life is a process whereby it gets harder and harder to find men your own age who aren't already married or dead – or indistinguishably both. And as if *that* wasn't sobering enough, one by one every authority figure eventually becomes young enough to be your son. It starts with the bicycle couriers, the movie ushers, the kids at the car wash. Next you notice the cop on the beat, the fire-fighters whizzing by, that guy from Fedex . . . why, they're *children*, all of a sudden.

Pretty soon, the school principal looks like a third-grader, along with several of the country's premiers, the president of the United States – and the Pope. No, really. One minute, you realize you're now older than the mayor of your town. Next minute, you're older than the town itself.

Oh, okay, but you get my point, don't you, sonny? You do? I'm glad. Now, remind me what it *was*.

Down on myself? Get out of here. No way I'm down on myself, young man. Whatever point I've been making, I'm pretty sure it wasn't that. You see, it's not *me* who's down on older women – it's older men. I'm serious.

You don't believe me? Then go ask your dad how he'd feel about dating a woman his own age, as compared to the average twenty-two-year-old bodacious babe. You know what he'd say, don't you? At least, out of your mother's hearing? And even when those older guys lie in their teeth, and offer some faint praise of women their own age, it's always utterly patronizing. "Older women are so goddamn *grateful*," they smile smugly. "They're comforting; they understand; they're happy just to cuddle." Hey, right, and if you put a zipper in our tummies, we could store your pajamas for you too. Thanks for nothing. And no thanks.

Which isn't to say it feels any better to be called a chicken hawk for checking out you younger men. Jesus, how predatory! Even the older women who like to shop in the Boys' Department for dates refer to themselves as cougars, and that's just as bad. I mean, where did this carnivorous imagery come from anyway? Was it Blanche DuBois, romancing the paperboy in *Streetcar Named Desire*? Or Patricia Neal in *Breakfast at Tiffany's*, with her Cruella de Vil turban and long cigarette holder, picking out suits for young George Peppard?

Uh-oh. I've lost you, haven't I, sonny? You have no idea what I'm talking about. Which is, incidentally, only another reason you young guys are so wrong for women like me. You think Lenin was one of the Beatles, that the Rolling Stones stole their name from a rock magazine, that Margaret Laurence wrote *Sons and Lovers*, that the War Measures Act was about metric conversion, that drinking straws have always been plastic, that Pierce Brosnan is the first James Bond . . . .

Patronizing? Give me a break. I'm only stating the cold, hard facts. Now, if I were to tell you the problem with going out to dinner with a younger man is that the waiter has to bring him the Child's Menu to order from and a phone book to sit on, *that* would be patronizing. You see the difference?

It's all about difference, isn't it, sonny? Difference in values, difference in perspective, difference in upbringing, difference in age. See, back when I was a little girl – shortly after Hannibal crossed the Alps by elephant – much more was made of this age differential than what you've grown up with. I remember how my parents and their friends would laugh about a couple who golfed at their club. The wife, it seems, was twelve years older than her husband. Twelve years! It might as well have been twelve hundred. It might as well have been that old battle-axe, Gloria Swanson in *Sunset Boulevard*, preying on the tender flesh of poor William Holden, who –

Whoops! Sorry. Forget that analogy, sonny. For all you know, she's the person who invented TV dinners, and he's the guy in *The Catcher in the Rye*.

Point is, according to adults back in my childhood, there was something embarrassing, laughable, even shameful about a woman marrying a man twelve years her junior. Even though their golf club was probably shot through with men whose wives were more their junior than that. That's my point, sonny, and you want to know something? It's sharp enough to stick. The kind of thing that gets stuck into you as a kid, and try as you might, all your life long, to shake it loose . . . .

What? How much older than you? I have no idea. How old do *you* think I am? Go ahead, take a shot. And for God's sake, don't you dare try to flatter me. Because, believe me, in my bifocals I can see right through that kind of bushwah at fifty yards – excuse me, fifty *metres*. I've confused you with more than enough archaic terminology for one afternoon. So, come on. How old am I, compared to you? Let's –

What??? Oh now, look here, sonny. I warned you, none of the snake-oil stuff. I told you, right off the top, I was just looking for some place to park my butt, is all, and I've got no more interest in you than you have in –

Me? Oh, Christ, well, sure. I suppose I like baseball. I mean, who doesn't, for God's –? Well, yeah, I guess you're right about that. Some things aren't entirely age-specific. Mind you, back when Abner Doubleday and I were refining the game, I did happen to –

Knock it off? Knock *what* off, sonny? God, you still can't tell when I'm kidding, can you? This bodes ill, let me tell you, for any future relationship. But what the heck? At my age, who looks at the future? For one thing, it's too damn *close* to see, even with bifocals.

Okay, okay, I promise. No more age jokes. Not at your expense, not at mine. After all, what's the differential in years, by your estimate? Right. Negligible, practically. Sure, whatever you say. Of course, could be your math skills aren't what they might be. Given the fact that you probably never learned to add or subtract without a pocket calculator, right?

Never mind, sonny. I'm from the old school. I can keep score entirely in my head. So, by all means, let's drink up and be off to the ball game. The *old* ball game. After all, what's the worst that can happen? Somebody strikes out.

ZEALOTS

MEN CAN BE AT their most endearing when caught up in their enthusiasms. What woman's heart doesn't melt at the sight of her spouse eagerly shopping for snacks at the supermarket in anticipation of the guys coming over for Poker Night? Who doesn't like to see her significant other happily absorbed by sports on TV, or tinkering under the hood of the car in the garage, or carefully polishing a particularly rare piece of feldspar for inclusion in his rock collection?

In fact, so generally adorable are men when observed in full pursuit of their passions that I hesitate to inject any element of negativity into such a pretty picture by suggesting there are times when they stray too far into the realm of fanaticism. One minute, there he is, cheerfully engaged in downloading music from his computer. The next, he's sat you down forcibly at his side so he can show how you, too, can create your own MP3 files, whatever they might be.

Nor is it enough merely to beam at him indulgently from the doorway as he hunkers over a duffle-bag-sized sack of chips in front of the Super Bowl. Before you know it, he's launched into that explanation of the fourth down again – the explanation that always begins with "Look, there's nothing complicated about this ..." and ends with "Look, maybe this is too complicated to explain. Why don't you just come and watch til you get the hang of it?"

It's not that women are unimaginative, or more impervious to excitement, or less capable of caring about things. It's simply that men are more susceptible to taking an outwardly harmless hobby – be it spectator sports, technology in the home, organized religion, electoral politics, stamp collecting, or aspirations to world domination – and turning it into an article of immutable faith, to be pursued with unflagging zeal.

Why is this? What is it in the male psyche that makes men the most obnoxious soccer hooligans, the most passionate ideologues, the most violent bigots, the most incandescent patriots? Even that word "patriot" – with its implied salute to the fatherland – bespeaks a world from which women are by definition barred: a boys-only club, unsuitable to be wielded by female hands; an organization open only to those directly descended through the male line, all the way back to the Founding Fathers. Or, perhaps even farther back, to the Founding Father of us all, who – when he chose to be represented here below – inevitably elected not a daughter but a son to go about his terrestrial business.

When I was a child, one of the most alienating aspects of religion was the apparent maleness of God. Even the Mystery of the Blessed Trinity – including the Holy Ghost, who seemed to be more of a pet of God's, like some budgie, than any part of a functioning deity – was easy to understand compared with the concept of God the Father, irascible in his long, white nightgown and long, white beard, looking somewhat like a Santa Claus not at all happy to be roused out of season by a midnight knock on the door of his North Pole den.

Though Jesus always struck me as a pleasant enough person, his father was much harder to warm up to. How, I wondered, was I expected to welcome him into my heart when I was more terrified of his arrival than I was even of my own father's whenever he came home from work to find our bicycles strewn on the front lawn or ink marks on the living-room rug?

Well into adulthood – even well past my own father's demise – I worried obsessively about my deep dislike of the idea of God as a grouchy paterfamilias, and on bad days I liked to torture myself with the prospect of his showing up at my apartment door, not so much seeking welcome into my heart as into my very home.

It was, of course, an unlikely eventuality. Sure, God moved in mysterious ways, but that was absolutely no reason to conclude that he might, for some mysterious purpose of his own, decide to move in with *me*.

Nevertheless, I frequently fussed to myself, What if he did? I'd be utterly defenceless. Should God decide to enter my life, I couldn't conceive of his even bothering to phone first. I pictured him just showing up at the door – suitcase in hand, an unprepossessing, paunchy old man, with the waistband of his polyester pants riding too high and the bagged-out knees riding too low.

"Behold thy God. I have come to dwell amongst thee."

"But . . . but there's no room. Look, I'd be glad to recommend a nice hotel. God knows – I mean *you* know – you can afford it."

But God wouldn't wish to dwell in a nice hotel. "Haste thee and prepare all things to receive thy Lord."

Ulp. "I'm serious, God. This really is a small apartment. With only one bathroom."

"That's okay," God would reassure me. "The bathroom's all yours. I never use it."

At this point in my self-tormenting fantasy, God would barge purposefully down the hall with his suitcase. Naturally, he would not stop to ask directions to the spare bedroom. Just like my own dad.

In fact, the resemblance to my father was remarkable. No sooner would God be comfortably installed in my apartment than he'd begin to exhibit all the familiar traits that used to drive me crazy whenever my dad came to visit. The obdurate old deity would also be likely to push his peas with his knife, swear loudly whenever he dropped his cane, and turn up the television set way too loud.

When watching sports, I knew he'd curse the referees' bad calls, just like my father. Unlike my dad, however, God would have the power to alter the outcome to his liking. Bad table manners, bad attitude, and a bad sport in the bargain. Behold thy God, indeed.

It was not only the imperiousness of God the Father that always made my fantasies about him so utterly enraging. Just as in real life with my own father, I had with God an impossibly difficult time in subjugating my own opinion, my own aspirations, and my own will to the demands of any such overbearing patriarch. It was the very impossibility of that struggle that had driven me away from the Church – as well as my father's secular authority – as far back as high school.

Even so, I did actually find myself at one point, many years later, going through a brief episode of nostalgia for Catholicism, and all the dark, smoky dominance I'd left behind. I was by this time in my late twenties, in Toronto, just beginning the business of sorting out the jumble of my adolescent past. I came upon a terse little advertisement in a weekend newspaper for a Catholic Mass to be conducted in Latin.

Latin! The language of magic mumbo-jumbo that had been officially dropped more than a decade before by the Roman Catholic Church – something I'd always regarded as an enormous public relations error. Like the thick, choking incense, like the glittering gold vessels in the sacristy, like the medieval pomp of purple robes and tall mitred hats, the Latin liturgy, to my mind, had been pure razzmatazz, the sort of lavish show business that Catholicism, for all its other shortcomings, did so well.

The day they'd lost Latin, they'd lost the likes of me. Now, thanks to this small ad in the Saturday *Star*, I was being offered an opportunity to return to the Church's better bygone days.

When I arrived on that Sunday morning in the basement meeting room of the old Lord Simcoe Hotel (since demolished, perhaps directly by God's Own Hand), I discovered a coven of renegade Catholics setting up rows of metal stacking chairs in preparation for a service conducted by some beyond-the-pale priest according to the old discredited Latin rite. The first thing that happened, however, was that one of the women standing guard at the door handed me a scarf with which to cover my head, as she had already covered hers.

Of course! The symbol of female subordination in church. I'd forgotten all about the hated ritual of the hat, dropped from official Catholic observance in the same era of radical reform that had forever swept Latin under the ecclesiastical carpet. Latin, I had desperately missed. But not the symbol of my subjugation to men.

With gritted teeth, I tied on the scarf and stayed for the service. Needless to say, I never returned – not to a place where what had seemed good about the past came back to me concurrently with what had been so insupportably bad.

Years later, and decades beyond even that brief yearning for the old hidebound rites, I still find my teeth clenching whenever I ride on the subway with Muslim women in their *hijabs*, mutely advertising their deference to men. It's their own business, not mine. Nevertheless, I feel enraged – I simply can't help it – at the mere sight of scarves which, similar to the female headgear of my own Catholic era, speak to me not of religious observance but to political oppression of the women who wear them, in the name of the mythic man who founded their faith, and at the behest of the modern men who control their lives.

I'm afraid I find it an easy step, all too easily taken, from the image of women, any women, bound up in headscarves, to other, more incendiary images – now all too familiar – of the Islamic Middle East: crowds of angry bearded men in the foreground of the front-page photo or TV footage, holding guns aloft and firing them off, brandishing religious objects, shaking their fists, or beating their chests. And in the background, when they are visible at all, women as mere onlookers on these world events, swathed top to toe in layers of gauzy cloth, like caryatids anonymously holding up some ancient edifice. A series of easy steps, all too easily taken, from patriotic expression to patriarchal power, to a terrifying tide of zealotry, in which men bear arms and women bear witness by covering first their heads, then their faces, and finally their eyes.

If zealotry, particularly of the religious kind, is now typically a manly pursuit, how did it get to be that way? Was there, I wonder, ever a time in the ancient past when women might have practised their own brand of rabid patriotism, subscribed to their own system of sexual discrimination, and even held in thrall fully one half of the population – the male half – by virtue of their superior power?

Probably not. Not unless you believe in the ancient culture of Amazon warriors, whose matriarchal civilization on the borders of the Black Sea was allegedly wiped out by a succession of jittery male generals from equally ancient Athens, bent on spreading the good word about patriarchy around the globe.

If you do subscribe to any of the anecdotal evidence about the existence of the Amazons, you will already know that these single-breasted archers were reputed to keep men in cages for procreative purposes only, before killing them, black-widowlike, after each successful mating. Male offspring, by those same accounts, were similarly dispatched in infancy, or else allowed to mature for later use as breeding stock before their inevitable execution.

How long such an egregiously anti-male culture – if such a culture ever existed – would have been allowed to flourish even in ancient times, nobody knows. Nor, even supposing that women once had such power, can we be certain how they came to hand it over to men. Was it simply a case of yielding to superior strength? Is it possible that women of that ancient world traded away all future access to equal employment, wage parity, proportional political representation, and corporate clout, in exchange for men's guaranteed assistance, forever more, in unscrewing too-tight lids from jars?

Of course, if you believe in Amazons, you're more likely to subscribe to the belief that the first real assault on their empire occurred when the half-divine Hercules came to the court of the Amazonian queen, Hippolyta, to ask for her girdle as one of his list of Twelve Labours.

Sadly, what may have started out as a mere fraternity stunt of sorts seems to have turned serious when the goddess Hera intervened and persuaded some of the Amazons that it was Queen Hippolyta herself whom Hercules intended to carry off, not just her belt. Would that have been Hercules's true intention? Nobody knows. Certainly, where articles of clothing are concerned, women are notoriously inclined to hold a grudge. On the other hand, it may well have been Hera's jealousy of Hercules (an illegitimate offspring of her husband, Zeus, and a mortal mother) that would prompt her to whip up the Amazons against any male insurgency and urge them to attack Hercules before he attacked them.

In the end, a foolhardy invasion of Athens itself by the Amazonian forces seems to have led to the complete subjugation of all members of the matriarchy by the Greeks. Why any of this happened could be the subject of scholarly speculation to the end of time. But if it did in fact happen, would it be remotely possible that the Amazons were simply set up? That with the help of that unhappy goddess they were lured into a battle they could never hope to win, against patriarchal forces determined to wipe out any vestige of a culture controlled by women to the detriment of men? "Never again" may well have been the battle cry of those ancient male Athenians, incensed by stories of men murdered after enforced mating with Amazons and their male progeny left to die as offspring of far less value than girls.

As I say, it's impossible to know if or why any of this ever happened, and equally difficult to divine whether our world would be a different place had the Amazonian society survived. Possibly not. After all, the might of ancient Greece gave way to the next big thing, and, indeed, the capitulation of successive cultures seems to occur irrespective of the temporary prowess of any given empire at any particular moment in time, give or take the capricious intervention of any particular member of any prevailing deity of the day.

What we do know for sure is that the polytheistic religion practised by the Greeks, and then by the Romans – with the jealous caprices of Juno, the amatory adventures of Jupiter, and the countless quarrels among the rest of the divines – was swept aside in favour of a far more sober-sided system. Monotheism involved a stern but level-headed male deity, different from culture to culture in name only, who was usually long on facial hair but short on the sort of humorous highjinks that had made ancient Olympus such a charmingly chaotic place to the Romans and Greeks.

With men only on the throne, religion got serious, and women continued to get the chewed end of the pencil. This proved especially so in religions that cleaved as firmly to the desirability of many wives as they did to the idea of a single deity. Polygamy in monotheistic religions does seem like a bit of a conundrum, given that the concept is almost always attended by the corollary notion of women as unworthy and unclean. If females really are all that inferior, why would a devout man want so many of them contaminating his life and cluttering up his bedroom?

On the other hand, it may be that, when you're a true zealot, that kind of doublethink more or less comes with the territory. Basically, it requires merely that you develop the ability to take two contradictory ideas, hold on to them simultaneously, and somehow make it seem as if embracing them both is testimony of the breadth of your spiritual vision as opposed to evidence of your moral inconsistency.

Sadly, the two solitudes that are men and women at their worst seem to grow more and more apart, in direct proportion to the pre-eminence of single-minded, male-based, monotheistic zealotry. Yet on the purely individual level, men and women seem able to grow very close. After all, it's not as if every man a woman meets is intolerably fanatical or glaringly chauvinistic. It's more as if men as a group act like some big, brawling, bossy, self-involved country, on which it is women's particular fate to border. As individuals, the natives of the nation of men are almost impossible not to like. Yet as our nearest neighbours, and taken as a whole, this bullying superpower can often be impossible to stomach.

In our Western culture, even more than religious zeal, the kind of passion men can pour into professional sport seems threatening to women and inimical to mutual understanding. There is a vicarious sense of accomplishment that many men derive from a Stanley Cup triumph or a Super Bowl win that baffles women. How could a distant athletic event compensate men for personal shortcomings or the limitations of their individual lives?

Most women have no equivalent experience of feeling vindicated by that kind of abstract victory on the grass, the gridiron, or the ice rink. Nor are we readily able to understand why some men who fanatically follow sports need to mark either the despair of defeat or the sweetness of success by beating up on their wives or girlfriends, before kicking in a few store windows.

But just as such men mystify women — and indeed many of their fellow men — with that particular species of zealotry, so do women confound men, and perhaps each other, by being smug about ourselves in ways that no male will ever understand. "What do women want?" was Sigmund Freud's famous query about the second sex. Many men I know would ask it another way: "Why don't women want it?"

What women don't seem to want, of course, is to be men. And I doubt there's a man alive who can fathom why that should be. Given that women's social status is still so often unequal, that our physical strength is and ever will be less than men's, that our ambitions for ourselves are thwarted so much more often, that so many of our bodies are bruised and our hearts broken by men, every day. . . . Why is it that there is not a woman in the world who would choose to change places even with the most exalted male?

Perhaps for the simple reason that women believe they are better than men. Shocking as that sounds, I believe it is true. The misery of our monthly periods notwithstanding, the panic of unsought pregnancies aside, the pain of childbirth apart, the spectre of sexual assault excepted, women remain by and large convinced of the superiority of their sex. When she spoke for herself, socialite Nancy Astor may have spoken for an entire gender: "I married beneath me; of course, all women do."

Whenever men perceive this unshakeable sense of superiority in us, it bewilders them. It maddens them. Why don't women want to be men? In a frustrated effort at revenge, men have historically closed their clubs to women, barred females from their boardrooms, rejiggered their religions so that their gods resembled men, and tried to keep women out of the priesthood, the parliament, and the praesidium.

Even so, women have somehow persisted in wishing to remain themselves, despite the disadvantages. If that is not exactly evidence of zealotry it is, at least, a sort of quiet moral conviction. The men who love us value that low-key species of female self-satisfaction, just as we appreciate in the men we love the kind of innocent enthusiasms we can observe warmly, without truly comprehending them.

But when men turn doctrinaire, women deplore them. We are afraid of their fanaticism, critical of their crusades, understandably apprehensive of the sort of sacred missions men have so often undertaken at our expense. Those of us with the longest memories and the greatest regard for the power of mythology begin to think of taking up archery, or start to wonder whether keeping men in cages for breeding purposes wouldn't solve more social problems than it might arguably present.

At its best, this species of mutual tension is what keeps men and women interesting to each other, and our shared sense of humour intact. At its worst, it's what keeps our two solitudes not only separate but endlessly unequal. Currently in human history, we seem to be both at the best of times, and at the very worst. In other words, business as usual on the battlefield of the sexes.

ACKNOWLEDGEMENTS

All the pieces in this book are original to me and were written specifically for *The Great Big Book of Guys*. However, in some cases, themes and ideas had their genesis in earlier works of mine, albeit in very different forms. For instance: "Bad Boys" shares some elements with a short story of mine published in *The Fiddlehead*; aspects of "Jude the Obscure" were touched on in my book *Urban Scrawl*, published by Macmillan of Canada, and in my essay "I Only Laugh When It Hurts," published in the anthology *Our Own Agendas* by McGill-Queens University Press; some of "Listmakers" appeared in a short humour piece of mine in *Chatelaine*; phrases in "Quipsters" originated in that same essay in *Our Own Agendas* and in my stage play *Automatic Pilot*, published by Playwrights Canada Press; one of the incidents described in "Soldiers of Fortune" first appeared in another form in *En Route* magazine; points made in "Underdogs" are echoed in one of my "Unmuzzled" columns in *Dogs in Canada* magazine and in my novel *The Hidden Life of Humans*, published by Key Porter Books; occasional phrases in "Younger Men" were first heard in *Automatic Pilot*; and a sentence or two in "Zealots" appeared in a very different context in "Damage Control in the Ancient World," from my collection of essays *Ritter in Residence*, published by McClelland & Stewart.

I'd like to thank all the above-mentioned publishers for their previous support and encouragement, as well as McClelland & Stewart for support and encouragement with this book; my editor Alex Schultz for intelligent, caring, and humane handling of all aspects of this undertaking; Jenny Bradshaw for her sensitive and astute copy editing; Hilary McMahon, Amy Tompkins, and Bruce Westwood, of Westwood Creative Artists, for representing me so ably; the Canada Council for assistance in the past that has helped me take time necessary to complete this book; CBC Radio for the flexibility to allow me to take time off when I needed it to complete this book; my CBC listeners who let me know they were looking forward to this book; my friends, who bucked me up when I worried about ever finishing this book; and, of course, all the men – real and imagined, loved and loathed, human and animal, famous and infamous, named and anonymous – without whom this book would never have got past "A," much less to "Z." And, by no means least, Gene Allen for reasons from "A" to "Z" and beyond.